International Business: Cases and Exercises

Charles A. Rarick

Bloomington, IN Milton Keynes, UK

authorHOUSE

AuthorHouse™
1663 Liberty Drive, Suite 200
Bloomington, IN 47403
www.authorhouse.com
Phone: 1-800-839-8640

AuthorHouse™ UK Ltd.
500 Avebury Boulevard
Central Milton Keynes, MK9 2BE
www.authorhouse.co.uk
Phone: 08001974150

First published by AuthorHouse 5/9/2006

ISBN: 1-4259-3573-7 (sc)

Printed in the United States of America
Bloomington, Indiana

This book is printed on acid-free paper.

PREFACE

This book acts as a supplement to the traditional text in international business and is considered appropriate for both an undergraduate and a graduate audience. The cases and exercises can be utilized as in-class activities or assigned as homework; whichever is deemed most appropriate by the instructor. Case length and time required for analysis varies in order to utilize the book in a variety of ways.

The casebook provides a more application-oriented approach to the teaching of international business. Students apply what they have read in the textbook or in class to problems relevant to global business activities.

The cases ask students to solve a problem related to various aspects of international business, and the discussion questions are provided as a guide to this analysis. The experiential exercises provide for either individual or group learning, and some of the exercises can be completed outside of class. The Web-based exercises are especially good assignments for individual, outside-of-class work. Many of the cases can be effectively conducted during class time in a small group setting. Most of the cases have been written so as not to require too much class time. The longer cases can be used for group projects and/or presentations.

Cases and exercises are grouped into basic themes regarding international business; however, many of the cases can be used to teach a variety of topics, and users should feel free to assign them in the course where they seem most appropriate. Problems in international business do not always fit into just one topical area, and cross-fertilization of ideas can be a useful to the learning experience. **A previous edition of this book was published by Prentice Hall in 2003.**

ABOUT THE AUTHOR

Charles A. Rarick is the Director of International Business and Professor of Management in the Andreas School of Business, Barry University in Miami Shores, Florida. He has also taught at Transylvania University, University of Kentucky, Xavier University, Northwest Missouri State University, and Brescia University, and lectured at Instituto Tecnologico y Estudios Superiores de Monterrey ITESM in Mexico, Romanian-American University in Bucharest, EAFIT in Colombia, and the Yangon Institute of Economics where he served as a Fulbright Senior Specialist to Myanmar in 2005, providing Burmese business leaders with advice on strategic international management. Dr. Rarick received his Ph.D. from Saint Louis University and he is certified as a Senior Professional in Human Resource Management. He is a member of the Academy of International Business, International Case Studies Academy, and the Society for the Advancement of Management, and has published numerous articles in academic journals including: *The Journal of Management Research*, *Advanced Management Journal*, *Journal of Business Perspective*, *Mid-American Journal of Business*, *International Journal of Business Disciplines*, *International Journal of Value-Based Management*, *Journal of International Case Studies*, *Central Business Review*, *Journal of Educational Leadership*, *Journal of Business Education*, and the *Journal of Business Strategy*. Dr. Rarick is on the editorial review board *Advanced Management Journal* and is Associate Editor of the *International Case Journal*. In addition to this book, he is the author of *Cases and Exercises in International Management*, *The Wisdom of Chinese Management*, and *The Confucian Advantage*. Dr. Rarick has made professional presentations in India, Taiwan, Ireland, Mexico, Myanmar, Jamaica, Puerto Rico, Romania, Bermuda, Austria, Greece, Slovakia, Colombia, Australia, Venezuela, Costa Rica, Egypt, and throughout the United States and Canada.

CONTRIBUTORS

Birute Clottey, Ph.D. (Oklahoma State University) is Professor of Marketing in the Andreas School of Business, Barry University.

Martine Duchatelet, Ph.D. (Stanford University) is an Associate Dean and Professor of Economics and Finance in the Andreas School of Business, Barry University.

Anne Fiedler, Ph.D. (Florida International University) is Professor of Management in the Andreas School of Business, Barry University.

Charles Hill, Ph.D. (University of Manchester Institute of Science and Technology) is the Hughes M. Blake Professor of International Business at the University of Washington.

Lawrence Hudack, Ph.D., C.P.A. (University of North Texas) is Professor and Director of Accounting in the Andreas School of Business, Barry University.

Jack Kleban, MBA (University of Toledo) is a lecturer in the Andreas School of Business, Barry University and Florida International University, in addition to being an entrepreneur.

Suzanne Lowensohn, Ph.D., C.P.A. (University of Miami) is Assistant Professor of Accounting at Colorado State University.

Luz Marie Luna, MBA. (ITESM) is a lecturer at ITESM in Monterrey, Mexico.

Stephen O. Morrell, Ph.D. (Virginia Polytechnic Institute) is Professor of Economics in the Andreas School of Business, Barry University and an international financial consultant.

Inge Nickerson, DBA (Louisiana Tech University) is Professor of Management in the Andreas School of Business, Barry University.

Charles A. Rarick, Ph.D. (Saint Louis University) is the Director of International Business in the Andreas School of Business, Barry University.

Michael Wilcox, MBA (Barry University) is a retired manager and local entrepreneur.

Greg Winter, Ph.D. (University of Illinois) is Assistant Professor of Management and International Business in the Andreas School of Business, Barry University.

CONTENTS

PART FOUR: International Strategy and Alliances

PART FIVE: International Marketing

PART SIX: Import/Export, location Decisions, Global Manufacturing

PART SEVEN: International HUMAN RESOURCE MANAGEMENT and Culture

PART EIGHT: International Finance, Accounting, and Taxation

PART NINE: Social Responsibility in International Business

Part One

THE ENVIRONMENT OF INTERNATIONAL BUSINESS

Cases:

Is Coke Still "It" in the Global Marketplace?
McDonald's Sells Hamburgers in India
A Canadian Mystery
Bahamas Rum Cake Factory
Mecca Cola
Ted and Harry's Ice Cream Adventure – Russia
Monterrey Sultanes and Major League Baseball
The Rise of International Healthcare Tourism

Exercise:

Multinational Corporations

CASE 1

Is Coke Still "It" in the Global Marketplace?

It is believed that the world's most favored brand, Coca-Cola, was invented in 1886 by accident. As the story goes, a druggist in Atlanta who was mixing a headache remedy for a customer accidentally mixed syrup with soda water instead of plain water. The customer commented on how good the drink tasted and a new product was born. Coke became a quick success in America and in 1906 was being exported to Canada, Cuba, and Panama. By the 1920s the product was being sold in Europe.

Coke's major international expansion began at the end of World War II. During the war, Coke's president, Robert Woodruff, provided American G.I.'s with the product in each area in which they fought. He shipped bottling equipment all over the world so that every American soldier could buy a Coke for a nickel. At the end of the war, Coke had in place a global bottling network.

Coca-Cola developed a first-class brand at home and abroad, eventually rising to the top of the global consumer's most recognized brand name list. More world consumers recognize the brand name "Coke" than any other. Because of its marketing and production savvy, Coca-Cola became a world icon and a very successful international company. Operational indicators continued to show improvement over the years in terms of sales, profits, and economic value added (EVA). Coke shareholders and managers were rewarded with an impressive appreciation in the company's share price.

As Coke reached the new millennium, it faced several significant problems. Global volume growth began to slow, operating profits were dropping, and market share was beginning to shrink. Although Coke remained the favorite soft drink brand among teenagers in many countries, adult consumers began to shift preferences to other beverages.

Coke began to lose ground to bottled water, sports drinks, fruit juices, and tea. In addition, private-label bottlers such as Cott, which produces soft drinks like Sam's Choice for Wal-Mart, began to increase market share. Private brands are usually a less expensive option for consumers, and their increasing popularity was putting pricing pressures on both Coke and Pepsi. A backlash against "American Imperialism" also resulted in the creation of a competitor called Mecca Cola, sold in the Middle East and targeted towards political young consumers.

In 1999, Coke experienced problems with some of its European production facilities and received negative publicity as a result of these product quality problems. The troubles began in Belgium, when Coke received reports of foul-tasting products. The company pulled 2.5 million bottles off the market in Belgium and reported that the problem (a bad batch of carbon dioxide gas) had been fixed. Shortly thereafter, however, additional reports of problems in Belgium emerged. Consumers were reporting feeling ill after consuming Coke products and the Belgian government ordered the removal of all Coke products from the country.

Although the Belgian market is small (less than 1% of sales), news of the problem with Coke spread around the world. Similar reported problems were occurring in Italy, France, Spain, and in Netherlands. Some observers felt that Coke was slow to react to the initial problem and, as a result, experienced a much larger PR problem than the actual incident warranted. Coke was also facing additional problems with declining sales due to the Asian economic crisis, a federal racial discrimination lawsuit in the United States, and an antitrust investigation in Europe. Some observers began to wonder if Coke still had "it."

Later in 1999, Coca-Cola announced the appointment of a new CEO. Douglas Daft, an Australian who had worked for the company for 30 years would replace Douglas Ivester who was retiring after a very short tenure as CEO of only two years. For the first time in its history, Coca-Cola had selected someone who had begun his career in Coke's international division to head the company. Most of Daft's experience with Coca-Cola was in operations outside the United States. Taking over the top position at Coke, Daft told reporters of his strategic intent: "The Coke formula represents the wisdom of the past. We have to look forward." Some analysts interpreted his remarks to indicate that significant changes in beverage offerings and marketing position were to follow. After five years on the job, Coke continued to suffer in terms of market share, profitability, and stock price. Another new CEO was named, Neville Isdell, a native of Ireland with extensive international experience with Coca-Cola's worldwide operations. Faced with many of the same problems as before, Isdell has to try and solve product contamination problems in India, a rising outcry against the unhealthy image of sugar-based drinks, and an antitrust judgment against the company in Mexico for its use of exclusive retail contracts. In an effort to build sales, Mr. Isdell has called for a new approach to advertising; one in which all Coca-Cola brands (fizzy drinks, water, juices) will be promoted under one umbrella promotional campaign, linking all products to the Coca-Cola brand.

Discussion Questions:

1. What approach to international business does Coca-Cola follow in your opinion: ethnocentric, polycentric, or geocentric?

2. What are the most significant problems facing Coca-Cola in the next five years?

3. In your opinion, what can Coca-Cola do to correct its recent problems and position itself for continued growth and profitability?

Sources: "International Survey Shows that Coca-Cola and McDonald's are Teenager's Favorite Brands." Business Wire, February 7, 1999; "A Bitter Aftertaste: Coke Tries to Wash Down a European PR Nightmare." The Washington Post, June 24, 1999; J. Pilcher, "New Coke Chief's Experience Touted: Global Outlook Key for Firm that has Struggled Outside US." The Dallas Morning News, December 8, 1999; "Debunking Coke." The Economist, February 12, 2000; "Coke's US Market Share Dips but Still No. 1." Reuters Business Reports, February 18, 2000; "Now Coke, is No Longer It." Business Week, February 28, 2000; A. Adiga, "When Will Coke Be it Again?" Money, September 1, 2001; S. Leith, "Coke Again Drops its Sales Forecast." Atlanta Constitution, September 26, 2001; "Coca-Cola, Bottlers are Fined in Mexico by Antitrust Agency." The Wall Street Journal, August 17, 2005; N. Clark, "Brand Coca-Cola's Big Gamble." Marketing, August 3, 2005.

Case prepared by Charles A. Rarick.

CASE 2

McDONALD'S SELLS HAMBURGERS IN INDIA

In 1954, a milkshake mixer salesman named Ray Kroc traveled to San Bernardino, California, to see why one restaurant had ordered so many of his Multimixers. The McDonald brothers had invented a new concept in the restaurant business and Kroc wanted to see for himself why the business was so popular. Dick and Mac McDonald had pioneered fast food based on high volume, low prices, limited menu, and quick service. The restaurant was a success, and Ray Kroc wanted it. He negotiated an agreement with the McDonald brothers in which he would become the exclusive franchiser of the McDonald name.

In 1955, the first McDonald's franchise opened in Des Plaines, Illinois. The McDonald's empire would be based on four core values providing customers with *quality, service, cleanliness,* and *value* (QSCV). Kroc believed that consistency in these core values would allow McDonald's to build a strong brand image throughout the United States. He was right. The concept was a success, and by 1963 McDonald's was selling 1 million hamburgers a day.

The first international McDonald's opened in Canada in 1967. McDonald's continued its international expansion into Japan, Germany, Australia, France, and England in the 1970s. Additional outlets were established in Latin America, the Middle East, Central and Eastern Europe, Russia, and China. The motive for McDonald's international expansion was the realization that most potential sales existed outside the United States. As Kroc had said in 1954, when he witnessed the McDonald brothers' original restaurant concept, "This idea can sell anywhere." Based on the need for additional sales growth and the belief that the concept could be exported, McDonald's embarked on an aggressive international expansion effort beginning in the 1970s. Today, McDonald's has restaurants in over 100 countries and derives approximately 60% of its profits from sales overseas. On average, the company opens a new restaurant somewhere in the world every five hours, and McDonald's can be found on every continent, except Antarctica.

Prior to 1996, McDonald's did not have a restaurant anywhere on the Indian subcontinent. With a population of over 1 billion, India is viewed by many as a market with enormous potential. India's population is second only to that of China, and, with differing birth rates, India will become the most populated country in the world by 2020, according to some estimates.

India represented a big challenge to McDonald's because most Indians could not eat the main menu item: the beef hamburger. Over 80% of the Indian population is Hindu and this religion prohibits the consumption of cow products. Also, approximately 40% of Indians are strict vegetarians and eat no meat of any kind. A significant percentage of the Indian population is Muslim, which also prohibits the consumption of pork products.

India is a federal republic, which gained its independence from Great Britain in 1947. After many years of British rule, Mahatma Gandhi led a mass movement for independence. Since that time, India has been as its constitution states, a "sovereign, socialist, secular, democratic republic." The economic self-reliance or "swadeshi" begun under Gandhi influenced public policy in India for over 40 years. India finally began to liberalize economic policy after experiencing a severe foreign currency crisis. In 1991, major changes occurred that made foreign investment easier, including reduced tariffs, removal of non-tariff barriers to trade, and loosened foreign investment restrictions and currency controls.

India still remains a poor country and a difficult market for Western companies. Per capita GDP is $420 and at least 350 million Indians live on less than a dollar a day. The government recognizes eighteen languages, with Hindi being the most widely spoken. English is also spoken, especially in urban areas and among the better-educated component of the population. Violent religious clashes occur between Hindus and Christians and between Hindus and Muslims, and there is a current movement to establish an all-

Hindu India. The religious and social class tolerances advocated by Gandhi do not seem to be as well accepted by many in India today. India is a country divided by languages, religion, and caste.

In 1996, McDonald's opened its first restaurant in India. The first McDonald's in India was located in Delhi and was the only McDonald's outlet worldwide not to offer beef on its menu. Due to dietary restrictions imposed by religion, McDonald's had to be creative in its product offerings. Without the possibility of serving beef or pork, McDonald's offered the lamb patty and a veggie burger. The Big Mac was named the Maharaja Mac and substituted ground lamb for beef. After opening its second restaurant in India, this one in Mumbai (Bombay), McDonald's had invested $14 million, yet the company was not completely sure of the potential of the Indian market. Although business was brisk at both locations, some concerns were raised.

Some consumers complained about the bland taste of the food. Accustomed to the spicy traditional Indian food, McDonald's meals seemed too plain for some consumers. There was also a concern about the political stability of the country and long-term acceptance of McDonald's in India. The Indian government did not support the entry of McDonald's into the country and some Indians protested the arrival of the American multinational. Previous American franchises have been the target of vandalism in India in the past. KFC, Dominos Pizza, and Pizza Hut all have several locations in India, and some of the restaurants have experienced difficulties with political mobs. McDonald's is perhaps in an even more vulnerable position because its primary product worldwide (beef) is viewed by many Hindus as not appropriate for consumption. As one protestor remarked "They are the chief killers of the cow." Other protestors see McDonald's as a symbol of the exploitation of the world's poor by rich American multinationals. In 2005, McDonald's settled a $10 million lawsuit brought by vegetarians in the United States who had charged McDonald's with misleading advertising. McDonald's had been using a beef flavoring for its French fries without telling consumers. The news of this culinary process caused protest in India and some store vandalism, however, McDonald's had been careful not to use the beef flavoring in India.

Faced with the difficulties of product acceptance, low purchasing power among consumers, and the ever-present potential of political conflict, McDonald's must decide if further expansion in India is a good investment.

Discussion Questions:

1. In your opinion, is India a good market for McDonald's? Explain.

2. Has McDonald's responded to the advice often given transnational companies to "think globally and act locally"?

3. Do you think McDonald's will be a success in India? Explain.

Sources: McDonald's corporate web site (www.mcdonalds.com); S. Mohanty, "India's Maharaja Mac Has No Beef" Reuters Business Report, October 11, 1996; S. Mohanty "Where's the Beef: India's McDonald's Eschews Chuck" Reuters, October 11, 1996; "McDonald's Goes to India Without Beef" Dallas Morning News, October 12, 1996; K. Cooper, "Where's the Beef: McDonald's Menu in India Culturally Correct, But Company's Presence Cooks up Controversy" Dallas Morning News, November 10, 1996; "Big in Bombay: The Maharaja Mac is One Hot Item" The Philadelphia Inquirer, April 22, 1998; "Background Notes: India" U.S. Department of State, March 2000; S. Dutta, "Domino Theory" Business India, May 1, 2000; L. Kadaba, D. Gardner, "India's Elusive Reforms" Financial Times, August 4, 2000; C. Raghatta, "McDonald's Pays Up Hindu Veggie Group in US" The New Times of India, July 12, 2005.

Case prepared by Charles A. Rarick.

CASE 3

A CANDIAN MYSTERY

Bonnie, an account executive at MICS, had just returned from a trip to CDC, one of her major customers in Toronto, Canada. This was her third visit in the past six months and she was extremely frustrated. The orders from her long- time customer had been steadily falling off and were now only 25 percent of what she had expected to meet in her sales forecast.

During all of her visits, she believed that she had done the right things. Her contacts with CDC were friendly and they smiled, as they always had. In their meetings with Bonnie, they assured her that everything was alright, telling her that "things wee just a little slow now." Bonnie had heard this repeatedly, yet things didn't add up. Her intuition was telling her that something was wrong; there had to be something going on that her contacts wouldn't divulge. She knew that CDC needed a lot more product than they were buying from her in order to satisfy their requirements. No matter how hard she tried to determine what was happening, she got no good answers.

Bonnie was a highly experienced and successful account executive. She tried every trick in the book. She asked others for help in trying to solve the problem. Kennedy, Inc., a Los Angeles company, manufactured the specific product that CDC was purchasing. Bonnie was in contact with Nikki, her supplier, and arranged for Nikki to meet her in Toronto so that they both could visit CDC. Bonnie reasoned that maybe the two of them could figure out the problem. After their meeting, and on the way to the airport, they discussed what they had observed. Neither one had any insight into the problem.

A few weeks later Bonnie heard from Nikki. Nikki, upon her return to Los Angeles did some investigating and had discovered that CDC was indeed purchasing just as many items as before.

CDC was purchasing more for a competitor, a Canadian company located in Missasagua, a short distance from Toronto. Nikki had also discovered that the Canadian distributor was charging 20% more for the identical product.

Bonnie was puzzled as to why her good customer of so many years would be paying so much for the same product, and why they were being so secretive about it. Further investigation revealed that MCS's total quality commitment to its customers was highly valued and appreciated by CDC. As time went on Bonnie was able to learn from her inside sources at CDC that the company was purchasing from the Canadian supplier and that this supplier didn't offer the total quality services offered by MCS. Bonnie was confused – why would CDC pay more for less?

Discussion Questions:

1. Why do you think a company would pay more for an identical product?

2. Could Bonnie have done anything to keep CDC's business?

3. What should Bonnie do now?

Case prepared by Jack Kleban.

CASE 4

BAHAMAS RUM CAKE FACTORY

The Commonwealth of the Bahamas is an independent country comprised of over 700 islands off the southeastern coast of the United States. Well known as a tourist destination, the Bahamas provides visitors with sand, sun, and snorkeling among other attractions. When Columbus first arrived in the New World he landed on a small island that he named San Salvador, an island in present day Bahamas. He claimed the island for Spain and eventually the rest of the islands came under Spanish control. When pirates such as Black Beard and Calico Jack began using the Bahamian islands to raid British trading vessels, the British appointed a governor to rid the Bahamas of pirates and to claim the territory for England. When the British lost the American War of Independence, a number of British colonists immigrated to the Bahamas along with their slaves. Spain finally ceded the Bahamas to Great Britain in 1783. Prohibition in the United States provided an economic boom to the Bahamas as the islands became a source of illegal alcohol. World War II also helped with the economic development of the islands as the British built up the infrastructure of the country to use as pilot training and a strategic base for anti-submarine warfare. This infrastructure helped the Bahamas develop its successful tourism industry. Although the Bahamas gained its independence from Great Britain in 1973, the British monarchy is still recognized as its head of state. With a thriving tourism industry, and as a center for offshore business and banking, the Bahamas has managed to develop its economy well beyond that typically found in the other island states of the region.

TOURISM IN THE BAHAMAS

Although not technically located in the Caribbean, the Bahamas is viewed as a Caribbean tourist destination. The islands of the

Bahamas are located in the Atlantic Ocean, close to the Florida coast and within easy reach either by sea or air. With a population of just 266,000, the Bahamas benefits greatly from tourism. Over 4 million visitors per year, the vast majority from the United States, are attracted to the islands for shopping, beaches, water sports, and the attractions offered by the luxurious hotels such as Atlantis in Nassau. The Bahamas offers visitors parasailing, diving, snorkeling, historical tours, Caribbean dining, and much sunshine. Most tourists visit the capital, Nassau, or the other major city, Freeport. The tourism industry employs over 40% of the Bahamian workforce and tourism is expected to increase in the coming years as resorts such as Atlantis expand and offer even greater recreational opportunities. Many tourists arrive in the Bahamas by cruise ship and disembark at the port of Nassau near the busy shopping area of Bay Street. Here tourists can find designer named-goods, tee shirts, conch shells, and other Caribbean souvenirs such as bottles of rum and rum cakes.

THE HISTORY OF RUM AND THE RUM CAKE

Rum production can be traced to ancient India and Egypt. Both countries had developed a sugar-based alcoholic beverage many years before the New World was discovered. On his second voyage to the New World Christopher Columbus brought sugarcane from the Canary Islands. The crop flourished in the hot, humid environment of the Caribbean. The crop became a major export for the various colonies of the Caribbean. When it was discovered that a by-product of sugarcane, molasses, could be fermented and distilled, a new alcoholic drink was born. The new drink called rumbullion, or sometimes "kill devil" was a favorite of sailors who noticed that the drink held up better during long voyages than beer or water. In fact, the drink got even better with age. Eventually, the drink became known as rum and was widely produced throughout the Caribbean. Rum production developed in the Caribbean with the establishment of the sugar plantations and most well-know brands come from the Caribbean, including the world's most popular brand, Bacardi of Puerto Rico. Other well known brands include Captain Morgan and Castillo, also of Puerto Rico, Appleton of Jamaica, Malibu and Mount Gay of Barbados, Barbancourt of Haiti, Flor de Caña of

Nicaragua, and Don Lorenzo of the Bahamas.

While the history of rum is well documented, the history of the rum cake includes two different stories. Some propose that the rum cake is an invention of African slaves who prepared meals for early British settlers in the Caribbean. The colonial masters brought Christmas pudding to the Caribbean and slave cooks added their own ingredients and baking techniques to make the first rum cakes. Another account gives credit for the invention of the rum cake to Polish Prince Leczinski, who, while living in France, made it his practice to pour rum onto what he considered very dry French cake. The practice spread throughout France and was called Baba au rhum. Modern day rum cakes can be traced to the most successful rum cake company, the Tortuga Rum Cakes Company of the Cayman Islands. Begun by a husband and wife team who began baking the cakes in their kitchen, Tortuga has become the leading supplier of rum cakes to cruise ships and retailers in the Caribbean. Tortuga has made the rum cake the top-selling souvenir among tourists in the Caribbean.

THE BAHAMAS RUM CAKE FACTORY

Located on the main tourist strip of Nassau (although about a mile from the center of the main shopping area) is the Bahamas Rum Cake Factory. If tourists continue to wander along East Bay Street they may come upon the smell of freshly baked rum cakes. Once inside the store they find a small shop with a bakery next door. In the Bahamas Rum Cake Factory customers can find many Bahamian products including rum, candies, jams and sauces, Bahamian cigars, and, of course, rum cakes.

The Company was established as a partnership by two Bahamians named George Bates and Simon Smith. George had worked for Bacardi in Nassau and his entrepreneurial desires led him to bake rum cakes for tourists. George sold the cakes he produced to local tourist's shops. One of those retailers, Simon Smith, decided that the two men could join forces and specialize in rum cakes to be baked on the premises and sold to tourists. In 2000, the Bahamas Rum Cake Factory was born.

Tourist and locals can purchase three varieties of rum cakes in differing sizes in the shop along with the local Don Lorenzo rum. Consumers can select from three flavors of rum cake including chocolate, piña colada, and original. The cakes are sold in either 6 ounce ($4.99) or 20-ounce sizes ($14.99). The cakes are packaged in attractive tin containers and contain a jig of rum that can be poured on top of the cakes when ready to be eaten. Rum cakes have a long shelf life and can be expected to remain fresh for six to twelve months when left unopened in their containers. The company maintains an attractive website through GourmetFoodMall.Com.

The Bahamas Rum Cake Factory sells about 500,000 rum cakes a year, eighty percent of those are sold in the Bahamas. The Bahamas Rum Cake Factory exports approximately twenty percent of its products. Bahamas Rum Cake Factory cakes are sold in eleven retail outlets in Florida, Texas, New York, New Jersey, and Pennsylvania. The cakes can also be purchased online at GourmetFoodMall.com. The Company sells about 60,000 rum cakes a week online. The Company sells no rum cakes to cruise lines at this time, however, the Company would like very much to penetrate this growing market.

COMPETITORS

The Bahamas Rum Cake Factory faces a number of strong competitors. The biggest and best known of its competitors is the Tortuga Rum Cakes Company of the Cayman Islands. Tortuga sells its cakes on over 140 cruise ships, through the company Internet site, and through a network of retailers in the United States and the Caribbean. Tortuga rum cakes are also sold on Amazon.com and through Yahoo Shopping. Tortuga rum cakes sold through Amazon.com are priced at $25.95 for a 33-ounce cake, $15.50 for a 16-ounce cake, and $8.00 for a small 4-ounce cake. Tourist visiting the Caribbean can find Tortuga rum cakes in most tourist shops and find them a tasty and interesting gift to bring back home to friends.

Many other competitors exist in this market. Many Caribbean countries have a local rum cake producer and they sell their cakes in local tourist shops. The rum cake has become associated with island life, even if beyond the Caribbean. In Bermuda for example, Horton's sells its black rum cake locally and through the Internet. Horton's large Bermuda Blake Rum Cakes are sold online and Bermuda retail shops for $26.50. Bacardi, another large competitor, sells its 20-

ounce cake for $14.95 and its 4-ounce for $4.95 throughout the Caribbean and beyond. Jamaica's Buccaneer Rum Cake can be purchased through Caricon.com, and a number of entrepreneurs sell their own homemade rum cakes on ebay. Rum cakes are fairly simple and easy to make and recipes can be found on the Internet. To make a rum cake all that is needed is yellow cake mix, vanilla pudding, eggs, walnuts, oil, water, and rum. After the cake is baked, it is topped with a rum glaze consisting of sugar, butter, and rum. Tourists who purchase a rum cake while on vacation can continue to enjoy the desert at home by making their own cakes for about 50% or less the retail cost of the cakes.

Discussion Questions:

1. What are the strengths, weaknesses, opportunities, and threats of the Bahamas Rum Cake Factory?

2. Can a product that can easily be made by consumers sustain a large retail premium price?

3. What would you recommend to George Bates and Simon Smith as they struggle to compete with larger and more-well known brands?

Sources: Barlas, R. (2000). Bahamas. New York: Marshall Cavendish; Brownlie, A. (2003). The Changing Face of the Caribbean. New York: Raintree Steck-Vaughn; Coulombe, C. (2004). Rum: The Epic Story of the Drink that Conquered the World. New York: Citadel Press Books; Gorin, E. (2004). Rum Cakes Recipe for Success. Miami Herald. August 8; Henderson, J. (2003). The Caribbean and Bahamas. London: Cadogan; Personal interview of George Bates conducted by Cassandra Newton on August 26, 2004; www.bahamasrumcakefactory.com; www.countrywatch.com/bahamas.

Case prepared by Charles A. Rarick, with the help of Cassandra Newton.

CASE 5

MECCA COLA

In November 2002 French political activist, Tawfik Mathlouthi began selling a new brand of cola in France. Mathouthi called his cola Mecca, after the city in Saudi Arabia when Muhammad was born. While some religious leaders question the use of Islam's holiest city for a brand name, not many people are questioning the brand's success. Mecca, the site of the Great Mosque and the yearly hajj, or pilgrimage, holds a very significant meaning to followers of Islam. Mathlouthi hopes the name can have an equally significant meaning for consumers of soft drinks.

Mathlouthi is capitalizing on the rising tide of anti-Americanism in the Arab world and beyond. He has fashioned his product on Zamzam Cola, an Iranian Coca-Cola substitute sold in Iran, Saudi Arabia, and Bahrain. Mecca Cola sponsored a large peace rally in London to promote opposition to America's war in Iraq and the Mecca brand. The company gave out 36,000 bottles of Mecca Cola, and 10,000 shirts with the Mecca logo and the words "Stop the War" and "Not in my Name." The product uses phrases such as "No more drinking stupid" and "Drink with commitment" to sell the brand and makes no apologies for its political position. Mathouthi, who was born in Tunisia and moved to Paris in 1997 to start a radio station admits that his product is political in nature. He states that it is an attempt to fight "American imperialism and Zionism by providing a substitute for American goods and increasing the blockade of countries boycotting American goods."

A particularly strong appeal of the product for some consumers appears to be the fact that twenty percent of the company's net profit goes to charities, including ten percent to Palestinian charities. One consumer in Paris, Youssef, age 26 states "The product is very good too. It has a taste somewhat between Coke's and Pepsi's." In certain markets it appears that Mecca Cola has begun eating into Coca-Cola's popularity. A storeowner in a Muslim part of Paris states, "Since I started selling Mecca Cola, consumption of Coca-Cola has fallen 80%. People are attracted to the idea of supporting the Palestinians." Mathlouthi defends the charge that the company may be funding terrorism by claiming that money is not given directly to the Palestinians, but rather, the company provides the Palestinians with food, clothing, and the construction of buildings. Mecca Cola also uses proceeds from its sales to support some European non-government organizations (NGOs).

Mecca Cola (the packaging which looks much like the product it is attempting to replace) is now sold in over 28 countries, including a number of Western European countries. At first the product was only sold in small ethnic shops in Muslim areas, however, the product can now be found in large grocery stores in the Arab world and in France, Britain, Italy, Spain, Belgium, and Germany. Mathlouthi purports to be filling orders for two million bottles a month in England alone. Mecca Cola plans on a rapid expansion of Europe and even into the United States market.

As the popularity of Mecca Cola increases, Mathlouthi has set his sights on other products. He plans on introducing Halal Fried Chicken (HFC) and Mecca Coffee soon.

Discussion Questions:

1. If you saw Mecca Cola on a store shelf would you consider purchasing it? Why or why not?

2. What should be the response of Coca-Cola to the Mecca brand?

3. Will Mecca Cola and the other protest products do long-term harm to American brands?

Sources: Anonymous. (2002). Mecca Cola to Finance Palestinian Charity Work. *Arabic News. October 5; Anonymous. (2003);* Mecca Cola Gaining Ground. *Monday Morning. www.mmorning.com. Accessed March 31, 2003; Britt, B. (2003);* Coca-Cola Mimics Coke. *AdAge. February 24; Hood, J. (2003);* US Companies Need to be Locally Minded Overseas. *PRWeek. February 24; Murphy, V. (2003);* Mecca Cola Challenges US Rival. *BBC News. January 8.*

Case prepared by Charles A. Rarick

CASE 6

TED & HARRY'S ICE CREAM ADVENTURE: THE RUSSIAN EXPERIENCE

In 1975 Ted Cooper and Harry Greenberg began selling ice cream in a converted church in Little Rock, Arkansas. The two young men, who had recently completed a correspondence course in ice cream making, seemed an unlikely pair to eventually lead a multimillion-dollar enterprise, which would challenge corporate America's sense of social responsibility. The company began to manufacture, and sell on the retail level, a premium ice cream with unusual sounding names such as Silly Strawberry Surprise and Harry's Very Berries. The pair sold their product through retail shops, which they called Ted & Harry's Ice Cream Factory, and consumers could order ice cream by the scoop, or in packaged form for home consumption.

By 1985 Ted & Harry's was a publicly traded company with over 50 retail operations in the United States. Gross sales were in excess of $35 million and the company had taken a very proactive stance in the area of social responsibility. The company employed disadvantaged members of society and donated 15% of its pretax profit to various charities. Ted and Harry were also actively involved in a worldwide peace movement and openly supported the bilateral disarming of the United States and the Soviet Union.

In 1989 Ted Cooper visited Russia and decided that international peace could be promoted through cooperative business ventures. Since domestic sales growth was still very strong, Ted & Harry's had not branched out into any foreign markets. In 1992 it was decided that Ted & Harry's would establish foreign direct investment in Russia. Although promotion of peace was a main objective, it was intended that the Russian venture would make a profit and provide a return on invested capital. It was hoped that profit from the operation would allow for further campaigns for peace and generate an entrepreneurial spirit in the Russian people. Ted & Harry's developed a manufacturing and distribution capacity in Russia that included six ice cream shops.

Ted & Harry's Russia sold its regular products, such as Whitewater Crunch and Kookie Chocolate, along with products unique to Russia, such as a vodka-laced ice cream, called Russian Holiday. Most of the products sold in Russia were identical to the products sold in the United States, including identical product packaging. Although Russian labels were placed over some of the packaging, the product was essentially the same product sold in the United States. The product was unique to Russian consumers, who were used to smooth ice cream as opposed to the "chunky" variety sold by Ted & Harry's.

Originally Ted and Harry planned on hiring a bilingual American to head the Russian operation. An external recruiting effort was undertaken, and recent business school graduates were interviewed from some of America's best business schools. Ted and Harry had hoped that a bright M.B.A. who spoke Russian, possessed significant business experience, and shared the vision of the company in terms of social responsibility could be hired. It was felt that someone with good business training and a strong sense of social accountability could spark an entrepreneurial spirit in the Russian people and be a good role model for others. When no suitable candidate could be found, the search shifted to internal recruiting.

The internal search resulted in the selection of Billy Bob Whitson. Billy Bob had been with Ted & Harry's for nine years, moving up from factory worker to production manager. Billy Bob did not speak Russian, and he had not received any business training other than on-the-job training at Ted & Harry's. He had never lived outside Arkansas; however, he did have a strong interest in Russia, and his enthusiasm impressed the selection team. He was appointed general manager of Ted & Harry's Russia, and the selection team was confident that he could handle the responsibility. There was a general belief that experience with product quality and acceptance of corporate values were more important than experience with Russian culture. Billy Bob was technically well qualified to supervise the making of ice cream and he possessed the character Ted sought for the position.

The Russian operation was established as a joint venture between Ted & Harry's and three Russian partners. Although the local partners had originally presented themselves as active members of the Russian business community, they were in fact very inexperienced and lacked connections. The three men impressed Ted Cooper with their intelligence, friendliness, and entrepreneurial spirit. Ted also found them appealing in that they represented the average Russian citizen.

The arrangement established an equal partnership between the two parties, with Billy Bob Whitson acting as general manager. It was agreed, however, that decisions would be made jointly between Billy Bob and the Russian partners. Ted & Harry's provided almost all of the capital required to establish the venture, and the Russian partners agreed to provide the necessary experience and effort required to establish the new business.

The Russian partners flew to Arkansas to learn how to make ice cream and Billy Bob moved his family to Russia to begin building the business. While the Russian partners learned the science of ice cream making, Billy Bob was learning how to conduct business in Russia. From the start Billy Bob experienced numerous problems with permits, construction crews, supplier agreements, and employee recruitment. The Russian business environment was more difficult than expected, and it appeared at times that it would be impossible to ever establish Ted & Harry's Russia. Billy Bob discovered that it was quite common for bribes to be paid to Russian officials to expedite the needed permits, and that the Russian mafia was deeply involved in the transportation and construction industries.

Since it was against Ted & Harry's corporate culture (and illegal under the Foreign Corrupt Practices Act) to pay bribes or engage in other questionable business practices, Billy Bob felt very frustrated with his inability to quickly get the business up and running. With the help of a Russian attorney and much patience, Ted & Harry's Russia finally began operation in 1996. Although it had taken much longer than anticipated, Billy Bob was content in the knowledge that the business had been established without the use of bribes or other forms of payoff.

Ted & Harry's entered the Russian market at a very difficult time. As the political and economic environment rapidly changed, the firm constantly experienced difficulties. Supplier relationships were unreliable, product quality was inconsistent, transportation was a nightmare, and it was often unclear who was really in charge of many government functions. Russia was also becoming a dangerous place to do business, and it was not uncommon for foreign expatriates to hire bodyguards for personal protection.

Product sales were lower, and costs were higher, than expected. Additional capital had to be supplied by Ted & Harry's in order to keep the operation functioning. The relationship between Ted & Harry's and the Russian partners was becoming strained as the local partners pushed for more growth. The Russian partners had envisioned becoming wealthy in a short period of time, and were becoming dissatisfied with the progress of Billy Bob and the management team back in Arkansas. Lacking any signs of near-term profitability, Ted & Harry were not inclined to entertain any suggestions of a growth strategy. Billy Bob felt that he could not manage any further expansion at this time, and he began to question the integrity of the local partners.

By 1998 the business had lost so much money, and the relationship between the joint venture partners had deteriorated to such an extent that it was decided to end the partnership. Ted & Harry's would pull out of Russia, leaving the investment and equity interest to the local partners. Ted Cooper stated in a press release that the decision was made jointly, and that a mutual agreement had been reached to end the Russian venture. Both parties had "parted on good terms and the experiment had been a success." Cooper stated that the objective of the joint venture was to bring entrepreneurship to Russia, and that by turning over the operations to the Russians "that objective had been accomplished." The business would continue with Russian ownership and the name of Ted & Harry's would not be used by the local partners. While admitting that some unexpected problems had occurred, Ted continued to defend the operation as an experiment and proclaim it a success.

Discussion Questions:

1. Do you think Ted & Harry's Russia was a success? Explain.

2. Do you think that Ted & Harry's made any mistakes in either country, partner, or management selection?

3. What, if anything, could Ted & Harry's have done more effectively?

Note: This case is fictional; however, it is based on an actual situation. It is not an actual account of this real case and no representation is implied.

Sources: Berdrow and Lane, "Iceverks," University of Western Ontario Cases, 1993; Kurtis, "World Full of Trouble: Fraud Comes in Many Flavors," International Business, 1997; Liesman, "Ben & Jerry's Reaches a Fork in its Rocky Russian Road", The New York Times, 1994.

Case prepared by Charles A. Rarick.

CASE 7

MONTERREY SULTANES AND MAJOR LEAGUE BASEBALL

In March 2004, the World Series Florida Marlins played the Houston Astros in a preseason goodwill game in Mexico City. The game ended in a 2-2 tie and many of the 11,000 fans in attendance pelted the field with debris as the game came to an undecided end. While professional basketball and American football have begun to see significant increases in international interest, baseball's interest globally has remained flat. With the failure of the Montreal Expos franchise, Major League Baseball (MLB) had to find a new city for the team, and one serious contender was a city in Mexico.

HISTORY OF BASEBALL

Baseball, as played in the United States, dates back to the mid-1700s and evolved from a very similar British game called rounders. Rounders, or "base" as it was sometimes called was played on a diamond-shaped field and had many of the characteristics of modern day baseball. Credit for the invention of baseball often goes to Abner Doubleday, a general in the U.S. Civil War. Historians now doubt Doubleday's invention of the sport and generally believe that the legend was created by A.G. Spalding in an attempt to make baseball "America's Pastime" and to sell more baseball equipment. Having a Civil War hero as the invention of an American game was good for his business.

It can be argued that American baseball was really created by Alexander Cartwright in 1845 when he created the rules of the modern game. In 1846 the first game as played between two amateur teams in Hoboken, New Jersey. It was amateurs who enjoyed the sport enough to play without compensation who first played baseball in America. As amateur teams multiplied in the U.S., travel and other expenses increased which required the charging of an admission fee to view a game. In 1869 Harry and George Wright organized the first team of paid players, the Cincinnati Red Stockings. The brothers were able to recruit the best players and won many games. The era of professional baseball had arrived.

In 1875 the National League was formed to set standards for ticket prices and to regulate player contracts. In 1901 a rival league was formed called the American League. Over time the two leagues learned to work together and to successfully defend against new entrants. In 1922 the United States Supreme Court decided in their favor and ruled that baseball was exempt from anti-trust legislation. The National and American Leagues no longer had to worry about competition. The game grew in popularity in the U.S. and was played on a limited basis in other countries as well. Mexico was quick to follow the U.S. in appreciating the sport.

BASEBALL IN MEXICO

The origins of baseball in Mexico are somewhat unclear, however, it is generally believed that the game arrived sometime between 1870 and 1890. Many areas of Mexico claim to have been the birthplace of baseball in the country, including Mazatlan, Veracruz, and Nuevo Leon. Monterrey, Mexico in the Mexican state of Nuevo Leon developed a strong interest in baseball in the early years, and has maintained that interest up to the present. Monterrey today boasts a popular team called the Sultanes, is home to the Baseball Hall of Fame for Mexico, and is proud of the fact that its Little League team was the first non-United States team to win the Little League World Series. In 1957 Jose "Pepe" Maiz Garcia was the star player for the Monterrey Little Giants which won the World Series. Maiz is still actively involved in Mexican baseball.

The relationship between Mexico and the United States in terms of baseball goes back even earlier than the Little League World Series. In the 1940s eighteen Major League players accepted higher salaries to play for Mexican teams. Liquor dealer Jorge Pasqual offered many Major League players salaries that were often as high as five times their normal salary if they would play for Mexican teams. A number of players from the Negro Leagues accepted Pasqual's offer, as did some players from the Major Leagues. Baseball Commissioner, A.B. "Happy" Chandler did not like Major League players defecting to Mexico and threatened to ban any players who made the move. The few players who did play in Mexico found conditions to be difficult, including one playing field that consisted of a railroad track running through the outfield. Most of the players soon returned to the U.S. and attempted to get their jobs back. All the players were blacklisted and not allowed to play until they challenged the League in court and the League rescinded its ban.

By 1955 the Mexican League was struggling for survival and Anuar Canavati, president of the Monterrey Sultanes created a plan to begin working with the Major Leagues. The Mexican Leagues prospered and grew to twenty teams. Today the Mexican League consists of 16 summer teams and 8 winter teams. Roughly half of the Major League teams have working relationships with Mexican teams. In addition, a number of Mexican players have gone on to the Major Leagues.

Mexican baseball teams do not draw the same attendance figures as the Major Leagues and are closer to the Minor Leagues in revenues. Attendance for the 16 summer teams can be seen below.

Mexican League Average Attendance
2003

Saltillo Sarape Makers	11,387
Monterrey Sultanes	9,301
Yucatan Lions	4,424
Monclova Stealers	4,053
Luguna Cowboys	3,559
Puebla Parrots	3,024
Angelopolis Tigers	2,732
Cancun Lobstermen	2,604
Oaxaca Warriors	2,430
Cordoba Coffeegrowers	2,044
Reynosa Broncos	1,643
Mexico City Red Devils	1,559

Tabasco Carrlemen	1,540
Veracruz Reds	1,475
Two Laredo Owls	1,351
Campeche Pirates	1,225

MONTREAL TO MONTERREY?

In 2002 the Montreal Expos were purchased by the other 29 Major League teams due to the team's inability to attract a sizable fan base in Montreal. The decision was made to relocate the team to a city that would be more supportive of a Major League team. A number of cities had expressed an interest in being the new home of the Expos including Washington, D.C, Portland, San Antonio, Las Vegas, and San Juan Puerto Rico. Monterrey, Mexico was also a strong contender for selection. Monterrey is located in Northern Mexico which puts the city within a few hours by air of many U.S. cities. The city is relatively clean, economically viable, and safe. With 3.5 million inhabitants, Monterrey exceeds the population of some U.S. cities with successful baseball programs. Monterrey has a desert climate, making it a good choice for outdoor sports. Currently the city has a 27,000-seat stadium which is considered by many to be the best in Latin America. The stadium has an impressive view of the Cerro de la Silla Mountains and residents are excited about the prospects of Major League baseball coming to Monterrey. The MLB relocation committee visited Monterrey and declared that the stadium was suitable for Major League play. Some modifications would have to be made including the addition of 3,000 more seats. The Commissioner of baseball, Bud Selig stated, however, that the city chosen for the Expos would have to be willing to build a new stadium within five years.

Monterrey has a very supportive ownership group headed by wealthy financier Carlos Bremer and Jose Maiz of World Little League fame and the owner of the Monterrey Sultanes. MLB has been eyeing the international market since 1999, playing 60 games in Mexico, Cuba, Venezuela, Japan, Puerto Rico, and the Dominican Republic. MLB plans to start playing some games in Europe next season. The Mexican League is a member of the National Association of Professional Baseball Leagues which regulates the Minor Leagues in the United States. Mexican baseball is at present considered the equivalent of America's Triple A League. Attendance at Mexican League games increased by 4.2% in 2003. Some observers worried that moving a team to Mexico would lead to many difficulties due to language barriers and the volatility of the Mexican peso. Others felt that since over 40% of players under MLB contract are from Latin America, that it is perhaps time for a Mexican team. As Jose Maiz states: "If we had the team here (Monterrey), 104 million Mexicans could follow the team, plus 25 million Mexicans working in the States."

WASHINGTON OVER MONTERREY

While some had predicted that Monterrey would be selected as the new home of the Expos, on September 29, 2004 it was announced that Washington, D.C. had won the bid to host the team. The mayor of Washington, Anthony Williams made the announcement by stating: "After 30 years of waiting, and waiting, and waiting, and a lot of hard work and more than a few prayers, there will be baseball in Washington in 2005." The team will play its first three seasons in R.F.K. Stadium until a new $400 million stadium is built. Baseball Commissioner Bud Selig released a statement justifying the selection of Washington by stating "There has been tremendous growth in the Washington, D.C. area over the last 33 years and we in Major League Baseball believe that baseball will be welcomed there and will be a great success." Selig praised the city of Washington, D.C. for its tenacity and dedication to having baseball return to the city. Washington has been home to previous Major League teams. From 1901 to 1960 the Senators played in Washington before moving to Minnesota to become the Twins. From 1961 to 1971 Washington hosted another team called the Senators, but this team also moved, this time to Texas to become the Rangers. The Washington, D.C. area has a wealthy and growing population, however, it is only 35 miles from another Major League team, the Baltimore Orioles. Concerns have been raised about the possibility of Washington eroding the fan base of the Orioles.

As MLB eyes competing markets, the organization must not only consider the sale of pennants and hats, but also television revenue and the possible expansion into other cities and markets. While other American sports have been successfully exported to the global market, baseball has experienced limited international appeal. As MLB baseball ponders international expansion, the people of Monterrey are still hopeful that they too will soon be able to host a Major League Baseball team.

Discussion Questions:

1. Did MLB make a mistake in selecting Washington, D.C. over Monterrey, Mexico?

2. Should MLB establish a Mexican franchise?

3. How important is internationalization to the success of MLB?

Sources: Baxter, K. (2004). MLB eyes Mexico. *Miami Herald*, March 14; Baxter, K. (2004). Extra-disappointed fans litter field with debris. *Miami Herald*, March 15; Beyer, R. (2004). *The greatest stories never told*. New York: HarperCollins Publishers; Dellios, H. (2004). Monterrey makes a pitch for the Expos. *Chicago Tribune*, February 10; Lahman, S. (1996). *A brief history of baseball*. Retrieved March 14, 2004 from www.baseball.com; Sanchez, J. (2004). *History of baseball in Mexico*. Retrieved March 14, 2004 from www. mlb.com; Sandomir, R. (2004). Baseball returns to Washington as Expos move from Montreal. *The New York Times*. September 29; Tayler, L. (2004). From Montreal to Monterrey? *Cincinnati Post*, March 12 Ward, G. & K. Burns. (1994); *Baseball: An illustrated history*. New York: Alfred A. Knopf.

Case prepared by Charles A. Rarick, Inge Nickerson, and Gregory Winter.

Charles A. Rarick

CASE 8

THE RISE IN INTERNATIONAL HEALTH CARE TOURISM

Amy, a thirty-nine year-old American wanted a chin implant, eyelid surgery, and an exotic vacation. She found all three at the Half Moon Golf, Tennis, and Beach Club in Montego Bay, Jamaica. The facility's medical center is only three years old, is considered state-of-the-art, and is doing well catering to Americans and Europeans who want to combine a vacation with cosmetic surgery. While the Half Moon Resort is not a particularly inexpensive option, it does offer the advantage of more privacy for its patients and the option of combining the recovery period with a relaxing vacation.

Many international health care travelers, however, are opting for low-cost options and increasingly are choosing locations such as India, Thailand, Costa Rica, Cuba, Mexico, and South Africa. One of the better-known programs for cosmetic surgery is called Surgery and Safari which began operating in 2000 in South Africa. The medical treatment combines cosmetic and/or orthopedic surgery, and an African safari. The entire cost of the surgical procedures and vacation can be much lower than a patient would pay back home just for the surgery alone. For example, the cost of a full-body liposuction procedure in the U.S. can cost $19,000, compared to Surgery and Safari's cost of $8,500, which includes lodging and the safari.

Patients seeking low-cost care without a safari can choose a number of less adventurous options. Thailand has increasingly become the location of choice for many traveling patients. Patients first receive a video consultation before they travel to Thailand, are met at the airport by limousine, and are treated to a luxury spa and recovery facility after their surgery. The cost of most procedures is a fraction of the cost of the same procedure in the United States. For example, a hip replacement procedure in the United States can

30

cost up to $35,000, where the same procedure can be performed in Thailand for less than $8,000. The additional costs associated with travel are small compared to the savings from the medical procedures. In addition, most of the medical facilities offer longer hospital stays, and additional amenities not typically found in the U.S., such as luxury hospital rooms, massages, cafes, and adjoining rooms for family members. American patients are selecting Thailand for a variety of medical procedures including orthopedic, cosmetic, and heart operations. Many patients returning from Thailand report high levels of satisfaction with the facilities and the quality of services.

Many of the countries that are capitalizing on the increasing global market for medical care are doing so to increase foreign exchange. Cuba has leveraged its well-respected health care industry into a global enterprise and caters mainly to other Latin American consumers. Because of the legal restrictions on travel to Cuba for Americans, the Cuban medical industry has not grown as rapidly as Thailand's, but is well known for its treatment programs in certain areas such as cosmetic surgery, and treatments for vitiligo, psoriasis, and long-term care of HIV patients. Funds from international patients are channeled back into medical research on the island.

Much of the promotion of offshore medical services is conducted via the Internet and word-of-mouth advertising. Satisfied consumers can be a good source of additional patients for the clinics, and most of the clinics have Web pages promoting their services. Dentistas de Tijuana.Com, for example, provides potential dental patients with a list of Mexican dentists who provide services ranging from orthodontics and dental implants to cosmetic dentistry and root canals. Web viewers can see the qualifications of the dentists and get directions and travel trips from the Web pages.

Not all foreign medical travel is to less-developed countries. Due to a surplus of doctors in Germany, the German government has been promoting the country as an alternative medical shopping destination. With a declining general population and an increasing number of physicians, Germany has experienced an unusual unemployment situation in medical services. The primary foreign markets for German medical services include wealthy consumers in the Middle East, Africa, and Russia, and also patients tired of waiting for treatment in Scandinavian countries. German officials are now planning on establishing hospitals in China where consumers are impressed with the quality of German engineering. It is hoped that medical services can reap spillover benefits from the increasing sales of German automobiles in China.

While the advantages of international health care are primarily in cost savings and/or more luxurious care facilities, many potential international consumers have reservations about traveling abroad for medical treatment. One of the major disadvantages consumers may see in foreign medical services is the difficulty of after-surgery care and potential complications. Another disadvantage is the lack of insurance coverage. While some American insurers have paid for foreign surgery, the incentive to travel for surgery is reduced for consumers who have health insurance. The majority of the international patients either do not have health care insurance, or they are electing a procedure such as cosmetic surgery that is not covered by their policies. Still other potential consumers are concerned about the quality of care and the potential for disease. Thailand has lost some patients due to the outbreak of avian flu and the SARS virus in the region.

Regardless of the disadvantages, consumers are increasingly electing to travel abroad to receive medical treatment and to take in the sun or a safari. With rising health care costs in the United States and an increasing percent of the population becoming uninsured, it is likely that even more patients will be returning from a visit from their doctors with suntans and a photo album filled with adventure.

Discussion Questions:

1. Would you travel abroad to have a surgical procedure? Explain.

2. What do you see as the potential impact on the medical industry of developed countries to this approach to global medicine?

3. How might the medical industry of developed countries change its marketing strategies to compete against this international threat?

Sources: Author Unknown. (1997). Health Care Booms in Cuba. NACLA Report on the Americas, January–February; Author Unknown. (2002). Sun, Fun, and Plastic Surgery? Forbes Travel Feature, November 17; Balfour, F., M. Kripalani, K. Capell, L. Cohn. (2004). Sand, Sun, and Surgery. Business Week, February 16; Louis, M. (2000); Germans Lure Patients to Hospitals. Wall Street Journal, December 6.

Case prepared by Charles A. Rarick

Part Two

INTERNATIONAL TRADE ISSUES

Cases:
Sunshine Farms: Withering Since NAFTA
The Rise and Fall of IBM's PC Business
India: Employment Black Hole?
Levi Strauss: No Longer "Made in USA"
Potters for Peace

Exercises:
NAFTA
Free Trade Area of the Americas
World Trade Organization

CASE 9

SUNSHINE FARMS: WITHERING SINCE NAFTA

Sunshine Farms, Inc. is a fourth-generation family business located in South Florida. Sunshine began as a small farm devoted to citrus fruits and vegetables, and over the years the company has prospered. Sunshine Farms now grows and markets limes, lemons, mangos, snap beans, tomatoes, and other "row crops." Sunshine Farms has endured hurricanes, tropical flooding, freezes, and plant diseases; however, its most recent challenge appears to be its greatest.

Since the passage of the North American Free Trade Agreement (NAFTA), a number of Florida farms have been closed. With the reduction of tariffs on agricultural products, farmers have had difficulty competing with Mexican producers. Many Mexican farm products are imported into the United States and sold at a price that is considerably below the cost of domestic products. Row crop farmers, as compared to nurseries, have been particularly hard hit by the Mexican competition.

Domestic producers complain that lower labor costs, and fewer environmental regulations in Mexico, allow Mexican farmers to export their products into the United States at a price that will not allow American farmers to make a profit. Without tariffs on these goods, and given the inability to differentiate their products, some American farms have not been able to make a profit and stay in business.

Sunshine Farms possessed a strong competitive advantage prior to NAFTA. Florida weather allows for a growing season that is much longer than that in other parts of the United States. Florida farmers were able to grow products in December and January when much of the country was experiencing frigid temperatures. Mexican farmers were exporting agricultural products into the United States prior to NAFTA; however, the tariffs assessed on those products made Sunshine's prices competitive. With lower production costs, longer growing seasons, and the elimination of tariffs, Mexican farm products have become a significant threat to the survival of some domestic farmers.

Ben McDonald, CEO of Sunshine Farms, is worried not only about the survival of his business, but the survival of the entire Florida farming community. "In 20 years you won't have a single row crop farmer left in Florida," McDonald predicts. Since farm products are commodities, it is difficult to brand the products and extract a premium price. "Consumers are usually not aware of where their tomatoes come from, and in most cases they simply don't care. All they care about is price," says McDonald. He has stated on several occasions that "We should learn from the country's dependence on foreign oil and the disruptions in supply. Just wait until this happens in food production."

Some have recommended that Ben and others shift their focus toward the nursery business. The nurseries of South Florida have been doing very well with the construction increases in the U.S., and they seem less vulnerable to foreign imports. Others have recommended that American farmers begin to brand their products or place a "Grown in the USA" label on them in order to charge a higher price. Few row crop farmers have successfully made the shift into nurseries or seem willing to brand their products. As more farms continue to close each year, Ben wonders if Sunshine Farms can survive in a free-trade environment.

Discussion Questions:

1. Is NAFTA unfair to American farmers? Explain.

2. Could Sunshine Farms differentiate its products by placing a "Grown in the USA" label on them in order to charge a premium price?

3. What would you recommend to Ben McDonald in order to save the farm?

This case is fictional; however, it is based on actual situations as reported in "Farming on Faith." <u>Miami Herald</u>, January 1, 2001.

Case prepared by Charles A. Rarick.

CASE 10

THE RISE AND FALL OF IBM'S PERSONAL COMPUTER BUSINESS

The company that would become IBM was incorporated in 1911 as the Computing-Tabulation-Recording Company (CTR). The origins of the company can, however, be traced back to Herman Hollerith and his punch card tabulating machine. Hollerith, a Census Bureau statistican invented a card with holes that could be read by an electric current. Hollerith began the Tabulating Machine Company in 1896. It was Charles Flint who merged the Tabulating Machine Company with two other companies to create the Computing-Tabulating-Recording Company.

Flint hired an executive from NCR named Thomas Watson, Sr. as the general manager of the new company. Watson soon became president of CTR and developed his famous slogan, "THINK" for the emerging company. In 1924 the company's name was changed to International Business Machines (IBM) to reflect the company's expanded product offerings. By the 1940s IBM was moving into computing with the development of the Mark I. In 1952 the company introduced the IBM 701, the first large computer to use vacuum tubes. In the 1950s the company also developed the FORTRAN computer language. The 1960s saw the introduction of the very successful IBM 360 series computer. IBM was a very successful company during the 1950s, 1960s, and 1970s, however, as the company grew, it developed into a large bureaucratic organization.

The late 1970s saw the beginning of a radical transformation in the computer industry. Earlier in the decade Intel had developed the first microprocessor, and Altair had begun selling a kit computer for less than $400. The age of personal computing had begun. In 1976 Steve Jobs and Steve Wozniak built the first Apple computer, and later Commodore and Radio Shack began offering inexpensive personal computers. IBM saw the market changing from large systems to smaller units, and in 1980 began to plan its introduction into personal computers. Five years earlier IBM had developed the IBM 5100, the company's first personal computer, but at a price of over $8,000 it was not a big seller and quickly faded from consumer awareness.

BOCA RATON PC UNIT

IBM decided that to be successful in the personal computer industry, it would have to establish a new business unit away from IBM headquarters. John Opel, IBM's CEO at the time created a team of engineers and selected Boca Raton, Florida as the location of its new PC business. In a facility designed to withstand hurricanes, and almost any other unforeseen disaster short of a direct hit by a nuclear bomb, the Boca facility was poised to become a leading business unit for IBM. The code name for the new product was called "Acorn" and it was headed by IBMer Don Estridge. Estridge and his team created the IBM 5150 in 1981. IBM announced its entry to the PC market with great fanfare at the Waldorf Astoria in New York City. To gain widespread distribution of the unit, IBM would sell its PC through retailers such as Computerland and Sears. The model retailed for $2,880 and had 64K Ram, one 5 ¼" floppy disk drive, and used the Intel 8088 central processing unit.

With a sense of urgency to rush a product to market, the 5150 was developed using an open design and off-the-shelf parts. IBM also outsourced its operating system (OS) to a little known company called Microsoft, who at the time really had no operating system to sell IBM. Microsoft acquired rights to an OS called QDOS from Seattle Computer and resold the OS to IBM on a nonexclusive basis. The nonexclusive use of the OS and the open design of the PC would eventually lead to competitors who would offer "IBM PC clones." IBM developed other PC models such as the IBM PC Junior, but sales were disappointing. IBM was operating in an environment where entry barriers were low and competitors were quick to develop new technologies and exploit cost advantages. IBM's PC unit got of to a good start, but quickly began to struggle. Boca Raton had for a short time been the PC capital of the world, but in the 1990s IBM began moving its PC operations to Raleigh, North Carolina and Austin, Texas. Many former IBMer at the Boca facility chose to remain in Florida and started new companies such as Citrix Systems, Cybergate, and Inprimis. The business unit that was created in South Florida would eventually have a new owner, one located half a world away.

SOLD TO THE CHINESE

In the summer of 2002, IBM began to look for a buyer for its PC unit that was now losing $400 million a year. IBM sent it's chief financial officer to China to make a pitch to the Legend Group, China's leading PC manufacturer. Legend wasn't interested in purchasing the money-losing business, but eighteen months later the situation was different. IBM had cut costs by outsourcing most of its production, making the unit a most desirable acquisition. In 2004, at a press conference in Beijing it was announced that Legend, now called the Lenovo Group, was purchasing IBM's Personal Computing Division for $1.75 billion and an 18.9 percent stake in Lenevo.

It was announced that Lenovo would be the preferred supplier of PC's to IBM, and that Lenovo would be allowed to use the IBM brand name for five years. IBM would provide Lenovo with warranty service and customer leasing and financing. Lenovo would have the right to sell the IBM ThinkPad and ThinkCenter desktop computers. A new company, also called Lenovo, was created to capitalize on the PC unit acquisition. The new company would be headquartered in Purchase, New York, five miles from IBM's headquarters. Lenovo announced that its CEO would be Stephen Ward, a former head of IBM's PC operations, and its chairman would be Yang Yuanqing, CEO of the Lenovo Group.

LENOVO'S NEW DIRECTION

The Lenovo Group (Legend) was founded in Beijing in 1984 by eleven Chinese scientists in a small one-story building. By 1994 the company was trading on the Hong Kong Stock Exchange, and by 1998 it had sold its one-millionth personal computer. The company now employs over 19,000 and is China's largest PC manufacturer. The name Lenovo comes from its previous name Legend (Le), and the Latin word for new (novo). Lenovo also produces servers, handheld computers, mobile headsets, and imaging equipment. The company seeks to be a leader in what it calls the "3C Era" - meaning computers, communications, and consumer electronics.

The newly established business unit seeks to be an innovator in personal computers. While the Legend Group had not been strong in research and development, the new unit is expected to become a leader in new product development. The company describes its values by the following pronouncement:

> *We reject the status quo*
> *We reject mediocrity*
> *We choose not to follow*
> *We choose to INNOVATE*

Lenovo makes a point of emphasizing the importance of an innovative and entrepreneurial spirit for the long-term success of the new company. Lenovo is hoping to leverage the IBM acquisition and to move into a more leading edge capacity in the industry.

The merging of the Lenovo Group and the IBM Personal Computing Division gives Lenovo a stronger position in terms of market share. Dell is the world's leading PC seller with 16.4% of the global market, followed by HP with 13.9%. Lenovo will be in the third position with an estimated 7.2% of global sales. The merger will also facilitate Lenovo's drive to expand outside of China. The Lenovo Group has a proven track record in developing countries (China), and personal computer demand is expected to be greatest in developing countries such as China, India, Russia, and Brazil. Unlike Dell, Lenovo sells almost all of its computer products through retail outlets. In developing countries it is sometimes important for consumers to have hands-on experience with products before purchasing them. Many consumers in developing markets also do not have credit cards, which makes on-line purchasing more difficult. Lenovo is more familiar with the nuances of marketing in less developed countries.

DIFFERING OPINIONS

The wisdom of IBM's sale, and Lenovo's purchase, has been questioned by some observers. Some have argued that by selling its PC unit, IBM has in effect admitted defeat in an important segment of the industry. Also, past experience with mergers and acquisitions in the computer industry shows a poor track record of success. Michael Dell, chairman of Dell Computers, said when referring to the IBM-Lenovo merger: "We're not a big fan of the idea of taking companies and smashing them together. When was the last time you saw a successful acquisition or merger in the computer industry?" A noted computer industry analyst was even more direct in his assessment of the merger by saying: "This has all the earmarks of a train wreck of biblical proportions." Others feel that IBM made the correct decision to unload its PC unit and to focus on its core competency – big systems and big customers. That component of the industry is more profitable and moves IBM out of the "commodity" computer business. Lenovo feels that with its rock bottom $3 per unit labor cost, and newly acquired research competency, it will be able to challenge the efficiencies and innovation of industry leaders.

Charles A. Rarick

Discussion Questions:

1. Do you think IBM's decision to sell its PC unit was a good decision?

2. Do you think Lenovo will be able to leverage its purchase of IBM's PC unit and challenge companies like Dell and HP?

3. Does the sale of IBM's PC unit to a Chinese company represent a threat to the economy of the United States?

Sources: Cox, J. (2005). *IBM employees have a new boss.* Knight Ridder Tribune Business News, May 2; Enderle, R. (2004). *Big Blue's departure from the PC biz.* Mac News World, December 9; Kanellos, M. (2004). *IBM sells PC group to Lenovo.* C/Net News, December 8; Robets, D. and L. Lee. (2005) *East meets West, big-timeLenovo deal forIBM's PC unit led to merger of talent – and threat to Dell.* Business Week, May 9; Scott-Joynt, J. (2004). *PC pioneer leaves its history behind.* BBC News, December 8; Winter, C. (2001). *IBM alumni founded many of S. Florida's high-tech companies.* Sun-Sentinel, August 10; www.hoovers.com. Accessed on May 25, 2005; www.IBM.com. Accessed on May 25, 2005; www.lenovo.com. Accessed on May 25, 2005.

Case prepared by Charles A. Rarick.

CASE 11

INDIA: THE EMPLOYMENT
BLACK HOLE?

After independence from Great Britain in 1947, India established a socialist-oriented government that discouraged foreign investment. Major industries were state-owned and government heavily regulated private businesses. Westerners viewed India as a very poor country with little to offer the international business community. In 1991, India experienced a currency crisis and was forced to fly its remaining stock of gold to London as collateral for an IMF loan. Faced with a very difficult situation, India then began to reform its economy. Since the early 1990s the Indian economy has transformed itself into a very competitive global competitor. With an abundance of workers and very low wage levels, India is attractive to international companies for low-end manufacturing and service delivery. Of special interest is the recent outsourcing of service jobs that can be performed over satellite and fiber optics communication channels.

India produces over 3 million college graduates a year. With high unemployment, companies have no difficulty in finding young college graduates who are content to handle customer service for American and European companies, at a fraction of the cost of their American and European counterparts. Typical of this new approach is AOL which now employs 1,500 people in India to answer its calls for customer service. Even though AOL is not available in India, AOL customers in the U.S. and elsewhere call an 800 number and may never realize that they are talking with someone half way around the world. AOL reports much lower operating costs, and lower turnover in its Indian call center than it experiences in the United States. Costs are lower even though training costs are higher, and the company must provide employees with transportation to and from work.

Like AOL, other well-known American companies have beaten

a path to India to outsource their back-office services. Recently, Microsoft announced that it was moving some of its customer service jobs to India. Microsoft joins a long list of American companies already operating back-office operations in India, such as: Oracle, IBM, Intel, and HP. Lloyds TSB, the UK's fourth-largest bank, has announced the closing of its call center in England, and its movement to India. Lloyds TSB call center workers earn on average ten times the wages to be paid to their Indian substitutes. Even the World Bank has moved its accounting function from Washington to India. American businesses are realizing that almost any back-office or service job can be moved overseas.

While the call center and other lower-level service jobs which have moved to India are becoming commonplace, India is also embarking on a much more ambitious approach to job creation. India has attracted work from the United States and Europe in software development, chip design, IT consulting, financial services, and drug research. An estimated 20,000 U.S. tax returns were prepared in India last year, and the number is expected to skyrocket to 200,000 this year. The returns are prepared by Indian accountants familiar with the U.S. tax code and are signed by CPAs in the United States. Indians now process mortgage applications, do legal and medical transcription, and book travel reservations. The management consulting firm, McKinsey, now outsources to India the design of its PowerPoint presentations that it shows its clients.

The skill level of jobs being outsourced is increasing. GE has established the Jack Welch Technology Center in India and employs 1,800 engineers, many with doctoral degrees, to conduct basic research. The relatively new center has already earned 95 patents in the United States. India has an abundance of well-trained engineers and scientists, and MNCs are beginning to realize the potential of this human capital. According to the managing director of the Welch Center, it isn't about saving money on labor costs. "The game here really isn't about saving costs but to speed innovation and generate growth for the company." Nevertheless, a top of the line electrical engineer in India earns only about $10,000 USD a year, a fraction of the salary of an American or European with the same qualifications.

While GE may not be primarily concerned with cost-savings, most companies moving, or establishing operations in India are doing so because of the labor rate differential. One UK travel agency has put a different spin on the outsourcing concept. Ebookings is moving both its work, and workers to India. The London-based travel agency is not only moving the jobs of selling and booking travel, but also moving workers to India, and paying the prevailing Indian wage level. Ebookings is selling the idea of living in India as an adventure and a way to sell the world. The firm's employees in India, both European and Indian will be paid about $6,000 USD a year, resulting in a significant cost savings to the company. While most companies that have moved their back-office operations to India are American or British, India is seeking additional jobs from other English speaking countries such as Australia, and non-English speaking countries in which customer service is conducted in English.

India has the advantage of having an educated workforce that can speak English and is willing to work for a fraction of the wage level of developed country workers. India, however, does have a number of disadvantages to consider when companies decide to outsource work. India has experienced very impressive economic growth in the years since economic liberalization; however, India is still very much a less developed country. An estimated one-third of the population is illiterate and only the higher classes speak English well. The official language of India is not English but Hindi. And India still possesses a very poor infrastructure with unreliable power sourcing and frequent flooding. Government bureaucracy is still very much a factor in business activity, and presently India's fiscal deficit is running at over 10% of GDP. While India has made great strides in eliminating excessive government, much improvement needs to be made. In addition to concerns over budget deficits, political tensions are also troublesome. India has an uneasy relationship with its neighbor, Pakistan, and the tension between Muslims and Hindus produces violent conflict at times.

While educated Indians speak English, it is considered to be the "Queens English" and has a different accent from American English. Although many Indians are enrolling in accent reduction classes, some American customers have complained about the ability to communicate with Indian customer service personnel. Indians tend to speak rapidly, averaging 180 words a minute, compared to 120 for Americans and 90 for the British. Dell recently announced that it was moving its call center operations out of Bangalore, India and back to Texas because it "had issues with differing Indian accents." GE, while investing heavily in research in India, nevertheless, moved its appliance call center from India back to the United States. GE had discovered that many Indian employees could not relate well to the concerns of GE's customers because many did not own, or were not familiar with the appliances they were discussing.

At the present time, India is the lead country in attracting service outsourcing, however, other countries are now beginning to compete with India. Like India, the Philippines is an English speaking country with a low wage level. Unlike India, the Philippines, a former colony of the United States, is closer to the U.S. in language and culture. While the number of jobs outsourced to the Philippines is currently much lower, estimated to be around 30,000, the number is expected to grow rapidly. Currently, Filipinos work in the Philippines for American companies doing medical and legal transcription, answering call centers, and providing technical support. In addition to the Philippines, a number of Eastern European countries may rival India for job outsourcing. One indication is the bidding process on a web site for programmers called Rent-A-Coder. Companies, mostly small and medium sized firms from the United States and Europe, post jobs for free-lancing software developers. Indians still are able to solicit most of the programming jobs from the site, however, Romania is the second most popular country for this outsourcing. Under Soviet domination, Romania like many Eastern European countries emphasized science, math, and engineering instruction and now has an abundance of technically qualified people who are willing to work at low wage levels. Like Romania, the Czech Republic has an abundance of technically qualified workers who are available at a lower wage level. The Czech Republic also has the advantage of impeding membership in the European Union. Recently, DHL announced a 500 million euro investment that will employ Czechs to track shipments, provide customer service, and perform billing operations. The Czech republic has a strong telecommunication infrastructure, workers who are proficient in many languages, and a skilled and inexpensive labor force.

An additional factor which may slow the growth of outsourcing to India is political backlash caused by job loss in the United States and Great Britain. In the United States, the state of Indiana recently cancelled a $15 million contract with the software arm of large Indian company, Tata Group, over fears of unemployment in the United States. Protection of domestic jobs is a very strong political motive and one that will likely be raised as more and more jobs are outsourced to India. Many will argue the costs and benefits of overseas outsourcing. A study by the McKinsey Global Institute found that for every dollar invested in overseas outsourcing, $1.25 returned to the United States. Supporters of foreign outsourcing argue the benefits of free trade and comparative advantage, while critics argue that foreign workers are taking jobs and potentially destroying the country's technical competitive advantage.

Discussion Questions:

1. From the perspective of American and European companies, analyze the advantages and disadvantages of outsourcing work to India.

2. What would you recommend to Indian government officials to ensure continued job creation?

3. Is it fair to workers of developed countries when companies shift work to lower wage countries? Explain.

Sources: Andress, M. (2003). *You're Speaking to Prague.* Financial Times, November 19; Angwin, J. (2003). *AOL's Tech Center in India is Money Saver.* Wall Street Journal, August 7; Delaney, K. (2003). *Outsourcing Job and Workers to India.* Wall Street Journal, October 13; Fox, M. (2003). *Where Your Job is Going.* Fortune, November 24; Gomes, L. (2003). *Romanians Become Latest Tech Rivals for Off-Shore Jobs.* Wall Street Journal, November 17; Hagenbaugh, B. (2003). *Moving Work Abroad Tough for Some Firms.* USA Today, December 2; Kripalani, M. and P. Engardio. (2003). *The Rise of India.* Business Week, December 8; Luce, E. and K. Merchant. (2003). *Dell Cuts Back Indian Customer Service Center.*; Financial Times, November 26; Merchant, K. (2003). *India's Call Centers Drop Fake Accents.* Financial Times, December 8; Slater, J. (2001). *Back-Office Bonanza.* Far Eastern Economic Review, August 30; Teves, O. (2003). *A Faraway Wakeup Call.* Miami Herald, December 9; Vina, G. and T. Mudd. (2003). *Call Centers Migrate to India, and North of England Loses Jobs.* Wall Street Journal, November 5.

Case prepared by Charles A. Rarick.

CASE 12

LEVI STRAUSS & COMPANY:
NO LONGER "MADE IN THE USA"

Levi Strauss & Company (LS&C) of San Francisco, California has been in the clothing business for 150 years. The company developed, and set the standard for denim jeans and has been manufacturing them for over 130 years. Throughout most of LS&C's existence its clothing has been manufactured, at least in part, in the United States. The firm recently announced that it will no longer manufacturer its products in North America, shutting down its one remaining plant in the United States and two in Canada. For most of its history, the company founded by Levi Strauss proudly manufactured clothing in the United States.

Levi Strauss was born in Bavaria in 1829. He immigrated to the United States with his mother to join other family members in a dry goods business in New York. At age 24 Strauss moved to San Francisco to open a west coast branch of the family business. While the dry goods business was successful, Strauss stumbled upon a product line that would make Levi's a household name in the United States, and much of the rest of the world.

Jacob Davis, a tailor in Reno, Nevada was a customer of Levi Strauss. Davis wrote Strauss in 1872 telling him of an invention in which he might be interested. Davis had developed a new way of insuring that men did not rip the pockets of their pants. He had installed metal rivets at the corners of the pants pockets to strengthen them, and he found that customers liked the new product. Davis sought a patent on this process; however, he did not have the money required for the legal protection of his invention, so he sought the financial aid of Strauss. Realizing that riveted pants might have potential, Strauss provided the $68 needed to obtain the patent. Using denim to create work pants, the partnership of Strauss and

Davis created the "original, authentic jeans."

Today Levi Strauss & Company is privately owned by the Haas family, decedents of Levi Strauss. LS&C sells its products in over 100 countries. The firm continues to sell its traditional product under the Levi brand, and has added the successful Dockers brand of khaki-type products to its product offerings. LS&C also sells a value-oriented brand called Signature that it markets through mass merchandisers such as Wal-Mart.

While the company enjoyed enormous success throughout many years of its existence, it has suffered in recent years as competitors have significantly eroded market share. The company, once the premier supplier of clothing for America's youth has witnessed sizable decreases in sales and earnings over the past few years. A new strategy of product development is underway in an effort to recapture the loyalty of the youth market. At the same time, LS&C is attempting to reduce its costs through a change in its product sourcing.

In the past, LS&C relied on its own manufacturing capability to source its product. The company operated many manufacturing facilities in the United States. Eventually foreign manufacturing was established and production capability began to shift to lower cost countries. The company also began to contract the manufacturing of its products to independent producers. The decision in 2003 to end all North American production caused some to question the ethical orientation of a company well-known for being a socially responsible organization. The change in strategy will allow LS&C to focus on product design and marketing, and to free resources previously devoted to manufacturing.

LS&C was built on four core values: empathy, originality, integrity, and courage. The company feels that these core values have served the organization well, and they continue to be the driving forces for change at LS&C. Levi Strauss has been a pioneer not only in clothing design, but also in other areas of business as well. The firm's progressive employment policies predated the civil rights movement in the United States, and LS&C has been listed as one of "America's 50 Best Companies for Minorities" by *Fortune* magazine. LS&C has been awarded the Excellence in Ethics designation by *Business Ethics* magazine, and the company was a pioneer in establishing and supporting employee volunteers through its Community Involvement Teams. In addition, the Levi Strauss Foundation awards $15 million annually to community-based organizations. LS&C was an early supporter of ethical guidelines for contractors. In 1991 the Company created the Global Sourcing and Operating Guidelines that regulate its contractors in areas of worker health and safety, environmental standards, and general employment practices.

Critics of the company contend that LS&C is simply following other American companies in outsourcing its production to lower labor cost countries. This practice reduces the employment opportunities available in the United States and further erodes the industrial base of the country. It is felt by some that the company relies on the important U.S. market for sales, however, the company does not provide employment opportunities to support those sales. LS&C has responded to these charges by stating that outsourcing of production is necessary in order for the company to survive. As CEO Phil Marineau states, "We're in a highly competitive industry where few apparel brands own and operate manufacturing facilities in North America." The company also counters its critics with the fact that a Community Trust Fund has been established by the company to aid the communities affected by the plant closures, and that comprehensive separation packages will be offered to the terminated employees. Some critics feel that Levi, an American icon, has a greater responsibility in stopping the deindustralization of America.

Charles A. Rarick

Discussion Questions:

1. Do you feel that LS&C is acting in a responsible manner in closing its North American production operations? Explain.

2. Do American companies like LS&C that transfer production to lower wage countries hurt or help the economy of the United States?

3. Evaluate the soundness of the strategic shift away from production and towards a focus on design and marketing.

Sources: Foster, L. (2003). *Levi to End North America Production*. Financial Times. September 26; Matthews, S. (2003). *Levi to Fire 1,980, Shut Plants*. Miami Herald. September 26; www.hoovers.com. Accessed on September 29, 2003; www.levistrauss.com. Accessed on September 26, 2003.

Case prepared by Charles A. Rarick.

CASE 13

POTTERS FOR PEACE:
THROWING CLAY IN NICARAGUA
FOR PEACE AND PROFIT

In 1986 a group of a potters in Washington, DC held a benefit sale to support fellow potters from Nicaragua, and to oppose U.S. military aid to the Nicaraguan contras. One of the organizers of the event created a banner that read: "Potters for Peace," and a nonprofit organization by the same name was soon developed. Potters for Peace (PFP) was created due to the political and economic difficulties of Nicaragua in the 1980s and a desire to see change in a troubled country.

NICARAGUA

During much of its recent past, Nicaragua has been known for dictators, revolutions, earthquakes, and hurricanes. The second poorest country in the Americas has seen more than its share of difficulties. While the country is now a democracy, and has been since 1990, per capita GDP amounts to only $2,200 and unemployment remains stubbornly high. By some estimates, 50% of the Nicaraguan workforce is unemployed or underemployed. Many Nicaraguans have had to leave their homes in the rural parts of the country to seek work in the larger cities. Many of the rural citizens are experienced artists, with craft skills that have been developed from generation to generation.

Nicaragua gets its name from the Native American tribe name, Nicarao. The tribe name was combined with the Spanish word for water and the name Nicaragua was born. Spanish explorers claimed Nicaragua for Spain, but Spanish rulers had little interest in the territory due to its lack of significant gold and silver deposits.

Nicaragua gained its independence from Spain in 1881 and briefly joined the other newly freed Central America countries in a federation. Nicaragua declared its independence in 1883 and has experienced political instability during much of its early existence. American involvement in the internal affairs of the country eventually led to the Somoza family ruling the country. The Somoza's accumulated vast wealth while the people remained extremely poor. An earthquake in 1972 led to the end of Somoza rule in Nicaragua as international funds intended for relief ended up in Somoza family bank accounts. Opposition against the Somoza regime grew and the communist Sandinistas gained power in 1979. The Sandinistas nationalized many industries, and the United States suspended aid to the country in 1980. The U.S. began to fund a counter-revolutionary group, the contras, as the economy of Nicaragua remained in ruins. It was against this backdrop of economic desperation and political instability that a group of altruistic potters from the United States formed an organization to promote the pottery industry of Nicaragua.

SAN JUAN DE ORIENTE

Located about an hour's drive from Managua is the town of San Juan de Oriente, the pottery capital of Nicaragua. The town is close to another town well known for its artistry, Masaya. Visitors to San Juan de Oriente pass Masaya and a large figure of Sandino, the inspirational figure of the Sandinistas, as they make their way to the many pottery shops of the town. San Juan de Oriente is the location where Potters for Peace first began its helping operations.

The Nicaraguan potters of San Juan de Oriente have also benefited from another nonprofit group dedicated to advancing the economic welfare of the less fortunate. Pro Mujer is a women's development organization that operates in Latin America and provides micro-loans to female entrepreneurs and women who wish to start a business. Pro Mujer also provides educational activities devoted to entrepreneurial education. The organization has a branch in Nicaragua, and has provided over 13,000 micro-loans to women in Nicaragua. Typical is Elsa del Carmen Mercado Nicoya, a mother of five who used a micro-loan to purchase a potter's wheel and begin her pottery business in San Juan de Oriente.

Another typical potter, Dina Gutierrez owns a pottery store in San Juan de Oriente where she and her mother sell the pottery made by the family at home. Dina has an outdoor oven, a room for pottery painting, and several rooms filled with inventory. Not only does Dina sell the family's pottery in her store, but she has also developed an exporting component to her business. Potters for Peace has helped Dina and other women of San Juan de Oriente develop a business that employs the entire family. With few employment opportunities in the area, the family businesses allow a measure of financial independence. Unlike some of its neighbors, Nicaragua does not have a thriving tourism industry. Without a tourist infrastructure in place, Nicaragua is bypassed as other Central American countries such as Costa Rica and Belize attract wealthy visitors from Europe, Asia, and the United States. Many Nicaraguans are forced to work in the country's many free zones, earning a meager living in the many forms of light manufacturing found in those zones.

The women of San Juan de Oriente make pottery basically the same way previously generations before them made their pottery. Clay arrives, sometimes via oxcart to the pottery area from nearby farms and it placed in water to make it more plyable. Sand is added to the clay and the clay is worked to remove any air bubbles. The clay is then shaped into the desired form, and a black liquid form of clay is painted on the object. After drying, the piece is painted again, this time with a white oxide and then dried again. The object is then decorated and placed in a wood-fired kiln and baked. The piece is removed from the kiln and polished, and is then ready for sale. Nicaraguan pottery has increased in popularity in recent years, however, the production process lacks efficiency and is not always considered healthy. The United Nations Industrial Development Organization warns that smoke from the rudimentary ovens of such home-based businesses generate an unhealthy home environment, and that chemicals used, such as oxides, produce an additional hazard to the potters' families. The pottery designs are a mixture of Native American and Spanish influences. San Juan de Oriente pottery is now sold in local retail outlet, to wholesalers in the United States and Central America, through the Internet, and promoted by Potters for Peace.

Charles A. Rarick

POTTERS FOR PEACE

Headquartered in Bisbee, Arizona, Potters for Peace seeks to fulfill its dual mission of promoting peace and advancing the economic well being of Nicaraguan pottery makers and other less fortunate artists. The organization's mission statement follows:

POTTERS FOR PEACE MISSION

We seek to build an independent, nonprofit, international network of potters concerned with peace and justice issues. We will maintain this concern principally through interchanges involving potters of the (overdeveloped) North and (underdeveloped) South. PFP aims to provide socially responsible assistance to pottery groups and individuals in their search for stability and improvement of ceramic production, and in the preservation of their cultural inheritance.

Potters for Peace refers to itself as a "U.S. based nonprofit network of potters, educators, technicians, supporters, and volunteers interested in peace and social justice issues." The organization does most of its work in Nicaragua, however, recently PFP has branched out into Central America, Asia, and in Africa. Potters for Peace is a registered nonprofit organization and donations made by U.S. citizens are tax deductible.

The organization conducts regional sales of Nicaraguan pottery in Denver, San Francisco, and in Yellow Springs, Ohio. PFP also maintains a booth at the annual National Council for Education in Ceramic Art (NCECA) meeting where they educate the industry about Nicaraguan pottery and their role in its development. PFP conducts educational tours to Nicaragua, with visits to San Juan de Oriente, and supports cultural exchanges among Central American potters. PFP also publishes a newsletter twice a year to inform members of events and to report on the organization's progress.

Potters for Peace maintains a website (www.potpaz.org) through which they solicit donations and memberships. The annual membership is $25, and one can also make a donation by printing out a form from the website, and mailing it to the organization. Potters for Peace also advertises T-shirts, books, videos, and posters through the website. All purchases orders, donations, and memberships must be mailed to the organization's address in Arizona. The website does not allow for on-line purchases. PFP does not sell pottery directly through its website but lists places where the pottery can be purchased. Currently only eight retailers in the United States are listed on the website as selling Nicaraguan pottery.

When PFP first began to provide assistance to the potters of Nicaragua it was discovered that the potters didn't need help making pottery, they needed funds to buy supplies and equipment. The potters of Nicaragua were skilled in their craft but lacked the ability to effectively market their products. They needed help in promoting their works and exporting them to the United States and Europe. Potters for Peace developed a brochure and organized tours of the area. Potters for Peace also organized informational visits by retailers from the United States such as Pier 1 Imports, which placed a one-time order for 18,000 ceramic pieces.

One of the newer projects PFP promotes is a ceramic water purification system. The portable unit is a low-cost alternative to more expensive systems, and is aimed at residents of less developed countries and victims of natural disasters. The system costs about $10 and requires no electricity to operate. Replacement clay filters cost around $4 and are replaced once a year. The units consist of a porous clay filter that uses colloidal silver as a germicide and disinfectant. Potters for Peace does not sell the filters but promotes their use and teaches potters how to make the filters in order to increase their income opportunities. Although PFP had a significant role in developing the filters, the organization decided not to patent the process in order to ensure widespread usage.

Potters for Peace now seeks to help the poorer and more remote regions of Nicaragua where access to the international market is almost impossible. Potters for Peace found that the transportation costs of moving pottery from these remote locations was prohibitive, and so the organization encouraged the potters of the remote area to develop ceramic jewelry. The jewelry is sold through PFP and other NGOs and church groups. Potters for Peace seeks to generate employment, and give the poor people of Nicaragua dignity. It is hoped that this will promote peace in a country not known for a peaceful existence.

Charles A. Rarick

Discussion Questions:

1. Select one international trade theory and use it to explain the pottery industry of Nicaragua.

2. Evaluate the mission, activities, and success of Potters for Peace.

3. What suggestions would you make to Potters for Peace in order to increase the effectiveness of the organization?

Sources: Barbaformosa. (1998). The potter's wheel. Barcelona, Spain: Parramón Ediciones; Morrison, M. (2002). Nicaragua. New York: Scholastic; Shields, C. (2003). Central America: Facts and figures. Broomall, PA: Mason Crest Publications; Yetter, L. (1999). Potters for Peace: Throwing clay in Central America. Living Buddhism, October; Internal documents provided by Peter Chartrand, U.S. Coordinator of Potters for Peace, May, 2005; Personal visit to San Juan de Oriente, Nicaragua on June 24-25, 2005; Telephone interview with Ron Rivera. May 23, 2005; www.adifferentapproach.com. Accessed on May 19, 2005.www.potpaz.org. Accessed on May 19, 2005; www.promujer. org. Accessed on May 19, 2005; www.seattleedu/asbe/studytour/nicargua/papers/pottery.html. Accessed on May 19, 2005; www.unido.org/doc/5222. Accessed on May 19, 2005.

Case prepared by Charles A. Rarick and Martine Duchatelet.

EXERCISE 2

WEB-BASED EXERCISE:
NAFTA

Web Address: www.ustr.gov

Purpose: To further your understanding of the North American Free Trade Agreement and to consider the benefits of regional economic integration.

Procedure: Visit the Web page of the United States Trade Representative. Go to the pages on the site devoted to the North American Free Trade Agreement and then answer the following questions.

Questions:

1. What impact has NAFTA had on trade among the three member countries?
2. List at least three benefits of NAFTA as specified at the Web site.

3. Explain your opinion of the benefits and costs of regional economic integration.

EXERCISE 3

THE FREE TRADE AREA OF THE AMERICAS: EXPLORING THE DRIVING AND RESTRAINING FORCES

Purpose: To gain a better understanding of the proposed Free Trade Area of the Americas (FTAA) and to explore both sides of the current debate.

Procedure: Read the background material provided in the exercise and assemble into small groups. Each group will compile a list of driving and restraining forces that impact passage of the free trade area. Driving forces are pressures that make the free trade area more likely to develop. Restraining forces are pressures working against the development of the free-trade area. After compiling the list, the group should reach a conclusion as to which set of forces is stronger.

This exercise requires you to think critically about forces that impact the creation of an area of economic integration.

Background

Economic integration comes in many forms: a free trade area, a customs union, a common market, and an economic union. These forms represent varying degrees of integration. A free trade area like the North America Free Trade Agreement (NAFTA) or the Free Trade Area of the Americas eliminates tariffs among member countries.

In 1994 a free trade area was proposed at the Summit of the Americas, which would include 34 nations in the Western Hemisphere. The free trade area, referred to as the Free Trade Areas of the Americas (FTAA), would build on the North America Free Trade Agreement (NAFTA) to become the largest free trade area in the world. The goal was to achieve tariff-free trade among member nations by 2005, however, that goal was not realized.

Member Countries

Antigua and Barbuda	Argentina	Bahamas
Barbados	Belize	Bolivia
Brazil	Canada	Chile
Colombia	Costa Rica	Dominica
Dominican Republic	Ecuador	El Salvador
Grenada	Guatemala	Guyana
Haiti	Honduras	Jamaica
Mexico	Nicaragua	Panama
Paraguay	Peru	St. Kitts and Nevis
St. Lucia	St. Vincent	Suriname
Trinidad & Tobago	United States	Uruguay
Venezuela		

Supporters of the FTAA point to the increasing market size of Latin America and the fact that economic integration is already occurring in Latin America with the Southern Cone Common Market (MERCOSUR), the Andean Pact, the Central American Common Market, CAFTA, and in the Caribbean with CARICOM.

Opponents of the FTAA point out the difficulties of economic agreement among such a large and diverse group of countries. Economic conditions and income vary greatly among the 34 member countries, as do environmental and labor regulations. Opponents also fear the loss of jobs in wealthier countries.

DRIVING AND RESTRAINING FORCES

List below forces, that are driving economic integration in the Americas, and forces, that are restraining such integration. Or, in other words, list forces that can cause FTAA to occur (driving) and forces that can keep FTAA from developing (restraining).

DRIVING FORCES

1. _____

2. _____

3. _____

4. _____

5. _____

Charles A. Rarick

Restraining Forces

1. _____

2. _____

3. _____

4. _____

5. _____

EXERCISE 4

WEB-BASED EXERCISE: THE WTO

Web Address: *www.wto.org*

Purpose: To gain a fundamental understanding of the World Trade Organization and its function in international trade.

Procedure: Visit the Web page of the World Trade Organization and find the answers to the following questions.

Questions:
1. What is the WTO?
2. When was it established?
3. Where is it headquartered?
4. How many countries are members of the WTO?
5. Explain the benefits of the WTO trading system.

6. What are the common misunderstandings about the WTO? Do you agree with any of these misunderstandings?

Part Three

THE GLOBAL MONETARY SYSTEM

Cases:
E- Cash: Global Currency?
Trading Pesos for Greenbacks
Global Trade Blues
The Mouse That Roared

Exercises:
The Foreign Exchange Market
International Monetary Fund
The World Bank
The Euro

CASE 14

E-CASH:
UNIVERSAL CURRENCY
FOR THE INTERNET?

Prior to the creation of a medium of exchange, primitive commercial transactions were conducted using bartering. A cumbersome and inefficient method, the barter system gave way to the creation of money. Early forms of money included shells, stones, and precious metals. Over time, more sophisticated media were introduced, including paper as a unit of value. Paper money, issued by governments and banks, was later supplemented with checks and credit/debit cards.

During the 1990s a new medium of exchange emerged in conjunction with the increased popularity of the Internet. Electronic cash, or e-cash, was created by a number of companies to facilitate Internet transactions. Although each offering of e-cash was somewhat different, the basic idea included consumers depositing money by various means into an account and, when purchasing online, they would use their "cyberdollars" to pay for their purchases. No checks or credit cards would be needed.

PayPal, which was started in 1998, is used by online auctions, including eBay (which owns PayPal), as a means of paying for transactions. Consumers in over 55 countries, including Australia, China, Germany, and South Korea can bid on items and, if successful, use funds from their PayPal account to settle the transactions. Other companies such as BidPay, 99Bill, and AliPay offer similar services to global customers. In China, 99Bill sells prepaid payment cards that can use for on-line payments, including fees to play video games on the Internet.

E-cash offers a number of advantages to both consumers and Internet merchants. It allows consumers without credit cards to easily make purchases, it can reduce transaction expenses for merchants, and it makes "micropayments" possible. Consumers who do not have credit cards can deposit money with an e-cash distributor and make their purchases without the time delay of sending a payment and waiting for their checks to clear. Merchants accepting e-cash payments are usually charged a lower processing fee than the fee charged by credit card companies. Perhaps one of the biggest advantages of e-cash is that this system makes micropurchases (1/10 cent to $1) more feasible. Such transactions are important for certain services offered on the Internet, such as purchasing information. As the Internet has become a truly global medium of communication and commerce, e-cash has the potential to facilitate transactions across national boundaries and differing currencies. While credit cards are still the most popular method of payment online, many consumers in less-developed countries have not been able to acquire them, making Internet purchases difficult. While the concept of electronic cash offers many benefits to both consumers and merchants, many start-up e-cash companies have either gone bankrupt or shifted the focus of their business.

Discussion Questions:

veshed interest, unfamiliarity, scandal

1. Why hasn't e-cash become a more popular form of payment for Internet purchases?

   low cost

2. How might e-cash help to develop entrepreneurial activities *would not* in less-developed countries? *- less access to the dollar*   *era*

3. Do you think e-cash will ever become a universal currency? Explain.   *- speculative declines*
   - less of sov.
   - concerns on safety

Sources: "E-Cash 2.0," The Economist, February 19, 2000; "Online Payment Firms Target China." The Wall Street Journal, August 11, 2005, R. Buckman; (www.paypal.com).

Case prepared by Charles A. Rarick.

CASE 15

TRADING PESOS FOR GREENBACKS: THE DOLLARIZATION OF SAN MIGUEL

With its economy shrinking and inflation being the highest in the Western Hemisphere, the president of San Miguel has decided that his country should abandon its own currency in favor of the U.S. dollar. The president of this small, South American country reasons that the dollar will bring economic, and perhaps political, stability to San Miguel. He feels that having the American dollar as its official currency will restore investor confidence in San Miguel's economy and force fiscal and monetary responsibility on the part of the government.

Last year, the economy of San Miguel contracted 7% and inflation is currently running at over 60%. The San Miguel peso has lost 20% of its value in the past six months and foreign reserves are rapidly being depleted. It is hoped that by adopting the dollar as the official currency of the country, inflation will be eliminated, foreign investment will increase in the country, and economic growth will occur.

The president is using the example of Argentina as his model; however, he plans to go further than this neighbor did: Argentina now pegs its currency to the dollar on a one-for-one basis. The president's plan calls for San Miguel to slowly replace all its pesos with American dollars and only use its own currency for small transactions. All San Miguel pesos would be exchanged for dollars at a set exchange rate and all financial statements would be issued in dollars. No new national currency would be created.

The idea has the support of the business community and the International Monetary Fund (IMF); however, there is opposition from indigenous groups and others who worry that the plan would have an adverse effect on the poor. Others worry that such a plan would also remove some national sovereignty and put the United States in charge of monetary policy in San Miguel. At present both sides are strengthening their positions. The president and the business community are pushing for a rapid conversion and the opposition is planning demonstrations against the plan. There has been a call for work stoppages and mass protests on the part of the opponents. The president dismisses the concerns of the opposition as foolish and points to Panama, which uses the U.S. dollar as its currency. He states that Panama is a completely independent country with economic stability and that Panama is poised for strong economic development. San Miguel should learn from the Panamanian experience, states the president.

Discussion Questions:

1. How would replacing the peso with the dollar affect monetary policy in San Miguel?

2. What are the advantages and disadvantages of a country adopting the U.S. dollar as its currency?

3. Other than replacing its currency, what else could be done to help solve San Miguel's economic problems?

4. What would you recommend?

Note: This is intended to be a fictional case, however, it is based on an actual recent situation.

Case prepared by Charles A. Rarick.

Charles A. Rarick

CASE 16

GLOBAL TRADE BLUES

Anthony Richardson and Diego Velasquez were sitting at a bar in South Beach, Miami. They had both graduated from Barry University with a B.S. in international business three years before and had remained friendly. Anthony, a native of Jamaica, carried a green card thanks to his mother's remarriage to an American citizen several years ago. Diego, a native of Spain, had come to the U.S. on a student visa and had been one of the few lucky ones to win a green card in one of I.N.S.'s periodic lotteries for all comers without regard to national origin. Both were ambitious and possessed entrepreneurial spirit. Both had started their own businesses about fifteen months prior to this meeting. Both were taking advantage of their cultural backgrounds and their connections in their homelands to foster their business endeavors.

Anthony was exporting sports equipment to Jamaica and Diego was exporting travel services to Western European countries by organizing exclusive, luxury tours for small groups of wealthy Europeans interested in seeing the sights in the U.S. They both felt they had discovered a promising niche in which their businesses could grow and prosper, but, fueled by beer, they both started bemoaning the adverse effects of currency devaluations on their profits.

Anthony has a cousin in Montego Bay, Jamaica, who acts as his agent. He secures contracts for sports equipment (swimming goggles, swimming fins, snorkels and masks, scuba gear, tennis rackets, etc.) with the various resorts and fancy retail shops all over the island. His cousin is successful at acquiring new customers and Anthony is confident that his business is growing. However, as a middleman (he does not manufacture the sporting goods), he pays in U.S. dollars for the goods he exports while he receives payment in Jamaican dollars for the goods he brings to Jamaica. Anthony earns his profit from

74

undertaking the tasks of selecting the goods, organizing for their transport to Jamaica, paying all necessary taxes and tariffs, selecting appropriate clients, and mostly from accepting the risk of exchange-rate fluctuations between the U.S. and the Jamaican currencies. He keeps close watch on the valuation of the U.S. dollar in relationship to the Jamaican dollar.

Exchange Rates – Jamaican Dollars per U.S. Dollar

January 1, 1997	35.03
June 1, 1997	35.09
January 1, 1998	36.59
June 1, 1998	36.47
January 1, 1999	37.16
June 1, 1999	38.80
January 1, 2000	41.37
June 1, 2000	42.24
October 17, 2000	44.00

When he started his business in June 1999, Anthony had priced his goods to realize a net profit margin of 50%, without taking into account the vagaries of the currency exchange rate. He has attempted to reduce uncertainty by locking his suppliers, his transporters, and his Jamaican clients into two-year contracts. These two-year contracts do not allow him to adjust flexibly to the changes in the currency-exchange rate, and Anthony feels that his profits are being squeezed out. Furthermore, another cousin, a talented artist in Kingston, the capital of Jamaica, is pestering him. She calls him a "fat cat" and demands that he help struggling Jamaican artists by purchasing their artwork (mostly paintings and wood carvings of all styles). She even insists that she is doing him a favor because Jamaican art is so well appreciated in the U.S. that it could be sold in art stores in Miami, Fort Lauderdale, and the Palm Beaches for ten times its worth in Jamaica.

Diego's woes are different. He deals with several travel agencies in Western Europe that cater to the discerning wealthy tourist who seeks to discover unusual destinations. Egyptian tombs, Greek or

Roman temples, gothic cathedrals, and medieval castles are run of the mill for such travelers. Diego, as an upper-middle-class, educated Spaniard, understands his clients' taste for a different experience quite well. He offers several successful packages: New York City (museums and Broadway), San Francisco and the wine country, Chicago and the Great Lakes country, the American Southwest (Taos, Mesa Verde, Santa Fe, Albuquerque, Bryce and Zion canyons), the American West (Colorado Rockies, Yellowstone and Grand Tetons national parks), and so on. Because his customers come from various European countries, he formulates his prices in the common currency, the euro. He has observed with great trepidations the recent, accelerated slide of the euro against the U.S. dollar.

Exchange Rates – U.S. Dollars per Euro

January 4, 1999	1.1812
June 1, 1999	1.0449
January 3, 2000	1.0155
June 1, 2000	0.9307
July 3, 2000	0.9526
August 1, 2000	0.9228
October 2, 2000	0.8806
October 17, 2000	0.8499

Diego's profits are threatened by the fact that all his expenses are incurred in U.S. dollars while his revenues are collected in euros. Marketing considerations suggest to Diego that he should keep the tours' prices steady rather than adjust them to reflect the slide of the euro. Diego is aware that he could perform operations on the forward market for the euro to mitigate the effects of exchange rate-risk. The *Financial Times* of the day (October 18, 2000) published the following information for October 17, 2000:

Euro	Spot	1 month	3 months	1 year
U.S. $	0.8499	0.8512	0.8523	0.8621

Anthony and Diego are feeling too mellow to try and sort out their currency exchange- rate woes. They both feel good about having shared their global trade blues with a kindred spirit and they part with the intention of remaining in contact and meeting periodically over a couple of "cold ones."

Discussion Questions:

1. How could Diego use the forward market to protect himself from further devaluations of the euro?

2. Why doesn't Diego consider the futures market?

3. Could Anthony also protect himself by hedging on the forward market?

4. How threatening is the devaluation of the dollar to Anthony's profits?

5. Is there an obvious solution to Anthony's worsening situation?

Sources: JMD to USD: www.patriot.net/~bernkopf; Spot Exchange Rate, Euro Area: www.bog.frb.us/releases/H10/hist/dat96_eu.txt; "Currencies and Money," Financial Times, October 18, 2000; "Euro Markets," Financial Times, October 18, 2000.

Case prepared by Martine Duchatelet.

CASE 17

THE MOUSE THAT ROARED

The world's smallest country, the Duchy of Grand Fenwick, is only 16 square miles. Located on mountainous slopes, it enjoys favorable climactic conditions for the cultivation of grapes. The country is mostly unspoiled by modern standards and wine making is a time-honored tradition, developed into an art. Like most economically backward small countries, Grand Fenwick exports its main agricultural product and imports rudimentary machinery. Its sole trading partner is the United States to which it exports its famous wine, "Pinot Grand Fenwick." Grand Fenwick's official currency is the ecu (E): one ecu is equal to one dollar.

Table 1 summarizes the situation in the U.S. and Grand Fenwick. Inside the table appears the value expressed in Ecus of the resources each country must expand to produce a case of Pinot wine and a machine, respectively. Grand Fenwick's exceptional climate gives it the edge in wine production while the United States' size allows for mass production and economies of scale realized in the machinery production.

Table 1

	Pinot Wine (By case)	Machinery (By machine)
U.S.	E 25	E 200
Grand Fenwick	E 20	E 500

A price for each product established itself on the world markets so that Grand Fenwick was able to subsist on the export of its Pinot wine to the U.S. as long as the conditions in Table 1 prevailed.

But, in the 1950s, wine production in the U.S. underwent major restructuring. Investors poured money into the Napa and Sonoma valleys in California, buying large ranches, planting healthy grapes, and building large cellars and large bottling facilities that Grand Fenwick could not match.

Modern technology allowed for new cost reductions in California wine production. Furthermore, extensive marketing efforts launched a "Pinot Grand Enwick," which for most American wine drinkers was undistinguishable from the foreign "Pinot Grand Fenwick." As a result, the amount of resources needed for the U.S. to produce one case of Pinot wine fell dramatically.

Table 2

Resources Required to Produce 1 Case of Wine and 1 Machine

	Pinot Wine (By case)	Machinery (By machine)
U.S.	E 10	E 200
Grand Fenwick	E 20	E 500

The Duke of Grand Fenwick and his advisors saw bankruptcy looming over their beloved country and decided to declare war on the U.S. This seemingly foolhardy move was actually quite devious: Grand Fenwick counted on losing the war to the U.S. and benefiting thereafter from all the economic aid this generous nation has historically showered on the countries it had defeated.

Discussion Questions:

Looking at Table 1, the initial situation:

1. What rate of exchange between the two goods might prevail?
2. How is an actual exchange rate established on the global market?
3. Which country will likely end up selling its export goods on the global market at the most favorable price?
4. Assuming the actual international prices are E 50 per case of wine and E 600 per machine, what is the exchange rate between the two goods?
5. Show that both nations benefit from trade. Assume that Grand Fenwick has 2,500 ecus worth of resources per year and needs 5 new machines per year.

Looking at Table 2, the subsequent situation:

6. Is there any rationale for the two countries to engage in trade?
7. Would the previous exchange rate established in the initial situation still be acceptable?
8. Assume the new international prices are E 600 per machine, as before, but E 26 per case of wine, knowing that Grand Fenwick needs 5 new machines per year and that, all other things being equal, the annual value of Grand Fenwick's resources is 2,500 ecus, why does Grand Fenwick feel hard-pressed?

Note: Grand Fenwick is a fictional country immortalized in the satirical novel, The Mouse that Roared, by Leonard Wibberley, and in the 1958 classic British movie, directed by Jack Arnold, which starred Peter Sellers in three major roles, plus Leo McKern and Jean Seberg.

Case prepared by Martine Duchatelet.

EXERCISE 5

THE FOREIGN EXCHANGE MARKET: CONVERTING WORLD CURRENCIES

Purpose: To develop skill in determining the value of one currency relative to another. An ability to determine a currency's forward premium or discount is also established through this exercise.

Procedure: Assemble into small groups and answer the five questions that follow using the currency exchange rates below.

EXCHANGE RATES

Country	U.S. $ equiv.	Currency per U.S. $
Britain (Pound)	1.4940	.6693
1 month forward	1.4948	.6690
3 month forward	1.4966	.6682
6 month forward	1.5001	.6666
Colombia (Peso)	.0004756	2102.75
Japan (Yen)	. 009348	106.97

1 month forward	. 009404	106.33
3 month forward	.009509	105.17
6 month forward	.009679	103.31
Saudi Arabia (Riyal)	.2666	3.7505

Questions:

1. How many American dollars can be purchased with 100 British pounds?

2. How many Saudi riyals can be purchased with 100 American dollars?

3. How many Colombian pesos can be purchased with 1 million Japanese yen?

4. How many American dollars would it take to purchase 2 million Japanese yen for a 90-day delivery?

5. Is the forward contract in question 4 selling at a premium or discount? What is the annual premium or discount?

Exercise prepared by Charles A. Rarick

EXERCISE 6

WEB-BASED EXERCISE: THE IMF

Web Address: www.imf.org

Purpose: To increase your understanding of the mission of the International Monetary Fund and how the organization functions.

Procedure: Visit the Web site of the IMF and answer the following questions.

Questions:

1. What is the stated purpose of the IMF?
2. Where is the IMF located?
3. What is a special drawing right (SDR) and a quota?
4. How are quotas determined?

5. Provide your opinion of the statement "The IMF cannot coerce its members to do much of anything."

EXERCISE 7

WEB-BASED EXERCISE:
THE HE WORLD BANK

Web Address: *www.worldbank.org*

Purpose: To further your understanding of the mission of the World Bank and its role in the global economy.

Procedure: Visit the Web page of the World Bank and answer the following questions.

Questions:

1. What is the mission of the World Bank?
2. Who runs the World Bank?
3. What is the difference between the World Bank and the World Bank Group?
4. Briefly explain the role of each of the five agencies within the World Bank Group.

5. Locate two separate World Bank projects in two separate countries and describe these projects.

EXERCISE 8

WEB-BASED EXERCISE: THE EURO

Purpose: To gain a fundamental understanding of the currency of the European Monetary Union, the Euro, and to further enhance your skills in researching the Internet for international business information.

Procedure: Using search engines, such as Google, Yahoo, or others, find answers to the questions below. As with all Internet research inquiries, you must evaluate the credibility of the source. In this exercise you will be asked to assess the accuracy of your sources.

Questions:

1. What is the euro?

2. Which countries have substituted their national currencies for the euro?

3. What is the function of the European Monetary Union and the European Central Bank?

4. What are the pros and cons to a single European currency?

5. Evaluate your Internet sources and explain why you feel each one can be relied on to provide correct information.

Part Four

INTERNATIONAL STRATEGY AND ALLIANCES

Cases:
Wal–Mart or Carrefour?
Brilliance China Automotive
The International Diamond Industry
Groupo Gigante Enters the U.S. Market
The Toledo Bicycle Company
Café Britt: Costa Rican Coffee

Exercise
Overseas Private Investment Corporation (OPIC)

Charles A. Rarick

CASE 18

WAL-MART OR CARREFOUR: WHO WILL BE MASTER OF PLANET RETAIL?

Sam Walton began Wal-Mart, the world's largest retailer, in 1962. Headquartered in Bentonville, Arkansas, Wal-Mart was built on the policies of "everyday low prices" and a 100% customer satisfaction guarantee. Walton provided the lowest prices, on average, among American retailers, and directed the organization to achieve superior customer satisfaction. He had previously worked for the JC Penney Company and it has been reported that Mr. Penney once told Sam that he did not have a future in retailing. Walton's views on retailing were iconoclastic and industry-defining in the United States.

With over 3,000 stores in the United States, Wal-Mart has begun an aggressive expansion into the international marketplace. Wal-Mart has over 1500 stores in Canada, Mexico, UK, Germany, South Korea, China, Brazil, and Argentina. It also operates a small number of stores in a few other countries through joint ventures. Wal-Mart's recent entry into the European market (primarily through acquisition) has caused anxiety, and in some cases, panic among European retailers. Wal-Mart is larger (sales) than its major competitors Carrefour, Metro AG, and Ahold, combined. Approximately 80% of Wal-Mart's stores are in the United States.

Carrefour, the second-largest retailer in the world, was started in France when two brothers, Jacques and Denis Deforey, who were in the grocery business, partnered with Marcel Fournier, who owned a department store. Known for their extreme attention to detail and the ability to cater to local tastes, Carrefour established itself as the major retailer in Europe. Carrefour now has over 6,000 stores in Europe, South America, and Asia, and is planning expansions into the Caribbean, Africa, and the Middle East. Carrefour attempts to localize its operations as much as possible and uses few expatriates. Approximately 80% of store sales come from outside its home country France.

Carrefour's global strategy involves careful study of local markets and careful attention to local customs. For example, in China Carrefour cuts its vegetables vertically, not horizontally, to avoid an image of bad luck among its Chinese customers. Carrefour has been a pioneer in the concept of "store clustering" internationally, altering its product mix, store facilities, and prices to suit different economic regions. Carrefour is the largest foreign retailer in China and sees the Asian market as critical to its continued success. Carrefour has 226 stores in Asia, compared to Wal-Mart's 59 stores. One-quarter of Carrefour's new store growth comes from the Asian market.

Wal-Mart is a much stronger company financially and it has deep pockets for international expansion. Its everyday low price concept has been a very viable strategy and Wal-Mart pioneered creative and successful approaches to supplier management and technology integration. In the United States, Wal-Mart has huge scale economies and excellent logistical operations. In terms of domestic operations, Wal-Mart has a very impressive 22% return on shareholder equity.

Internationally, Wal-Mart has experienced less success. International sales account for only about 20% of Wal-Mart's total revenue, and its return on assets for international operations has been considerably lower than for its domestic operations. In Europe, Wal-Mart faces strong unions, increased regulatory constraints, and weak scale economies. The ability to export its everyday low price concept to Europe is being challenged, especially in Germany. The everyday low price concept has also not been effective in Japan where Wal-Mart operates a joint venture with Seiyu. Many Japanese associate low prices with lower quality goods.

The world's largest retailer hopes to match its domestic success internationally and many analysts believe it has the financial and managerial ability to do so. On the other hand, Wal-Mart lacks the international experience of Carrefour and is a latecomer in many markets where Carrefour is well established.

Charles A. Rarick

Discussion Questions:

1. Which international strategy does Wal-Mart follow? Which international strategy does Carrefour follow? Which do you feel is a better strategy for global expansion?

2. Can Wal-Mart learn anything from Carrefour? Can Carrefour learn anything from Wal-Mart's success? Explain.

3. Which retailer, in your opinion, will win the battle for global leadership?

Sources: "Wal-Mart: Chimera," The Economist, January 29, 2000; "Who's Afraid of Wal-Mart?" Fortune, June 26, 2000; "Wal-Mart at Centre of Prices Probe in Germany" The Financial Times of London, June 28, 2000; "Business: Growing Pains," The Economist, April 16, 2005; Wal-Mart 2005 Annual Report; www.carrefour.com.

Case prepared by Charles A. Rarick.

CASE 19

BRILLIANCE CHINA AUTOMOTIVE

Brilliance China Automotive was established in 1992 to manufacture vehicles in China. The company is incorporated in Bermuda and its initial asset was a 51% equity interest in the Shenyang Vehicle Manufacturing Company. Since 1992 Brilliance China Automotive has expanded into the automotive parts business through equity interests and has established a joint venture with BMW. With sales of RMB 10.1 billion, Brilliance China Automotive produces minibuses, passenger sedan, and BMW 3-Series and 5-Series automobiles.

Brilliance China Automotive's manufacturing unit, Shenyang, was the first automobile manufacturer in China to receive ISO 9000 quality certification. The company established a just-in-time inventory system and employed the latest management practices in an effort to distance itself from the old bureaucratic ways of doing business under the Chinese state system. Brilliance China was also a pioneer in raising capital. It was the first Chinese company to have its stock listed on the New York Stock Exchange (NYSE). The initial public offering (IPO) raised $80 million and on its first day of trading the company's share price closed a $20.125, a 26% increase over the IPO price. It is especially difficult for a Chinese company to list on the NYSE due to the stringent financial reporting requirements. Chinese businesses have traditionally employed a fund accounting system that places an emphasis on the source and application of money. Chinese state-owned organizations do not operate on a model of profitability and, therefore, all financial records of the Company had to be converted to U.S. Generally Accepted Accounting Principles. Even though all of Brilliance's products are produced and sold in China, the Company wanted to secure a deep source of funding and provide a greater sense of legitimacy through its U.S. equity offering.

Brilliance China Automotive produces two models of minibuses, the JinBei and the Granse. The Company also produces its own sedan called Zhonghua and assembles the BMW's through its joint venture. Most of the components for the BMW sedans are imported from Germany and assembled in China under the supervision of 50 BMW expatriates working for the joint venture. Brilliance China Automotive produced over 100,000 vehicles in 2003 which represented a record level of production. The Company produced 75,000 minibuses, 26,000 sedans, and 4,300 BMW's in 2003. Brilliance China Automotive has 8,700 employees. The Company currently has an annual capacity of 120,000 minibuses and 100,000 sedans. Brilliance China Automotive also produces auto components such as engines, moldings, and stamped parts through its equity interests in other companies. The Company has a strategic partnership with Toyota in the production of minibuses and strategic partnerships with Mitsubishi, Johnson Controls, and TRW Automotive in components.

China Brilliance Automotive's corporate strategy is based on the "Four Pillars." The company seeks to maintain its competitive advantage through: 1) maintaining leadership in the minibus sector; 2) stronger brand image, improved product quality, and greater cost efficiencies; 3) leadership in the premium sedan market; and 4) becoming an active player in the Chinese automotive component parts industry. While the Company has done well in its short life, it is a small part of the large and fragmented Chinese automotive industry. At present there are 123 automakers in China, producing 4.4 million cars a year. That number is expected to greatly increase in the coming years as China continues to develop economically. Of the 123 auto manufacturers in China, only two produce more than 500,000 vehicles a year. The top auto producers in China, in order of size are Shanghai Volkswagen, FAW-Volkswagen, Shanghai-General Motors, and Guangzhou-Honda. Brilliance China Automotive does not place in the top ten producers of automobiles in China. Volkswagen began production in China in the mid 1980s and now sells more cars in China than in its home base of Germany. China has become the fourth-largest producer of automobiles, behind the U.S., Japan, and Germany. Production in 2003 increased 36.6% over production levels of 2002. After twenty years of economic reform,

China has developed classes of consumers that can afford to purchase a personal automobile. China has also developed a wealthy class of consumers who prefer premium brands of products, including automobiles. Daimler-Chrysler has announced that it plans to build a factory in China, partnering with Beijing Automotive.

As China's economy continues to grow at a rapid rate, the government has begun to institute macroeconomic polices aimed at controlling the economic expansion. The government has begun to tighten credit including that used for auto financing. Additional austerity measures are expected to reduce overall demand for automobiles in China. In addition, the government has begun to establish stricter regulations on auto emissions and fuel efficiency. These regulations are expected to increase the manufacturing costs of automakers. On top of possible declining sales and rising manufacturing costs, China's entry into the World Trade Organization (WTO) began the process of tariff reductions which protected domestic automakers in the past.

Brilliance China Automotive has planned a response to these environmental threats by 1) implementing cost reduction programs, increasing domestic components, and increasing internal controls; 2) building relationships with foreign partners for new product development and possible export of its products; and 3) targeting specific customer groups such as government agencies, hotel chains, and taxi companies. While no one knows how long the austerity measures will be in place in China, Brilliance China Automotive hopes to emerge more competitive and positioned to grow into one of the leaders of the Chinese automotive industry.

Charles A. Rarick

Discussion Questions:

1. What are the strengths and weaknesses of Brilliance China Automotive? What opportunities and threats does the company face?

2. What strategic direction would you recommend for Brilliance China Automotive?

3. Some critics of free trade argue that open markets benefit developed countries more than developing countries. What do you think?

Sources: *Automotive Brilliance China Sees Danger in WTO Wave*. Reuters, May 16, 2000. K. Kearney; Brilliance China Automotive Holdings Limited. Interim Report, 2004; Brilliance China Automotive Holdings Limited. Annual Report, 2003; *China to Have 14.66 Million Home Sedans by 2010*. Sino Cast China Business Daily News, February 2, 2004; *Competition Heats Up in China's Luxury Car Market*. Beijing Times, October, 2003; *New Policy Needed for China Automotive Industry*. Emerging Market Economy, August 19, 2003; *West Carmakers Grabbing Share of China Market*, People's Daily Online, May 23, 2004.

Case prepared by Charles A. Rarick.

CASE 20

THE INTERNATIONAL DIAMOND INDUSTRY

Diamonds are produced in the earth's mantle when carbon is exposed to extreme pressure. Some diamonds make their way to the earth's surface and become a precious commodity. Since the 1930s the South African company, De Beers has managed to manipulate the world price of diamonds. The long running and successful cartel began when Sir Ernest Oppenheimer, Chairman of De Beers began buying diamonds on the open market during the Great Depression; a time when diamond prices were falling. Since that time De Beers acted as the buyer of last resort for the diamond market and the firm stockpiled billions of dollars in diamonds in its London vaults. The company would buy diamonds from anyone in the world, no questions asked. The rough diamonds were taken to London where they were evaluated and sorted and ten times a year De Beers offers its diamonds to select buyers at non-negotiated prices. Since De Beers controls most of the diamond producing mines in South Africa, Botswana, and Namibia it has significant control over the world's diamond supply. This control is shrinking, however, with increasing diamond production coming out of Russia, Canada, and Australia. De Beers once controlled 80% of the world's diamonds. Now the company control approximately 55% of global supply.

DIAMOND MINE PRODUTION (million carats)
MAJOR PRODUCERS

Botswana	30.4
Australia	31.0
Congo D.R.	25.0
Russia	19.0
South Africa	12.8
Canada	11.2

Another threat to the supremacy of De Beers is the Leviev Group of Israel. Leviev is the world's largest cutter and polisher of diamonds and was once a customer of De Beers. Dissatisfied with the lack of competition in the rough diamond market, Leviev sought out additional sources of rough diamonds and helped the Russian government develop its diamond extraction industry. The company now controls a large part of the Russian supply of rough diamonds and has begun to win favor with major producing countries in Africa by setting up shop in those countries and employing their citizens. Leviev is now both mining and finishing diamonds, and can offer host governments more employment opportunities than De Beers.

Recently concerns have been raised about diamond sourcing, with allegations made that diamonds are being used to finance rebellion in at least two African countries. It is believed that rebels in Angola and Sierra Leone, and possibly the Congo as well have used diamond sales to finance their civil war activities. This trading of diamonds for weapons resulted in a threatened boycott of the product, not unlike the successful boycott of the fur industry that was begun earlier in protest of animal cruelty.

Fearing the "fur factor" and the threaten boycott of its product, De Beers withdrew its buyers from the African countries in question and began to promote "conflict free" diamonds. The company began to certify that its diamonds were not coming from war-torn parts of the world or used to finance rebel causes. Critics argue that "blood diamonds" will simply be funneled out of these conflict areas and through trading centers such as Mumbai (Bombay) where they could be blended with diamonds from legitimate sources.

In response to these concerns, in May 2000, representatives of diamond producing countries in Africa met in Kimberley, South Africa and drew up an agreement to certify that diamonds exported from member countries were not blood diamonds. The Kimberley Process Certification Scheme (KPSC) requires its 43 member countries to establish procedures to ensure that its diamond exports are not funding rebellion, and to package the diamonds in tamper-resistant shipping containers. Member countries are not allowed to trade diamonds with non-member countries. Any member country not in compliance with the agreement will be banned from trading with member countries. Recently the Republic of Congo was de-listed because government officials could not account for a large discrepancy between its diamond exports and its legitimate diamond production. While the civil wars in Angola, Sierra Leone, and Congo have begun to come to an end, other concerns about diamond sourcing has arisen. The United States has passed The Clean Diamond Trade Act prohibiting the importation of any rough diamonds not certified as conflict free. The U.S., along with the European Union, (both members of the Kimberley Process) are concerned that conflict diamonds have been used to fund terrorist activities including terrorist acts by the al Qaeda network.

In addition to the concerns over conflict diamonds, the industry now faces its biggest change due to advances in diamond-making technology. The desire to make diamonds has been around for many years. In the 1950s the first man-made, or cultured diamonds were produced. The process was very expensive and diamond experts could tell if the diamond was natural or man-made. Recent advances in diamond manufacturing have produced man-made diamonds that are physically identical to natural diamonds and almost indistinguishable. Two companies, Gemesis and Apollo are producing man-made diamonds that have the potential to change the diamond industry forever. Gemesis uses heat and pressure to turn graphite into a yellow diamond. Apollo uses a carbon vapor that attaches atom by atom to a thin wafer of diamond to make a clear diamond of any size. While the process of producing man-made diamonds is still expensive, diamonds can be made artificially and sold at prices of at least 35% lower than natural diamonds. Man-made diamonds also provide the advantage of being conflict free and not used to finance rebellions around the world.

In response to these challenges, De Beers has announced a fundamental change in company strategy. The company will shift its focus from supply management and price control to a more demand-oriented strategy. It will begin to sell off its diamond stockpile and promote its image as a quality provider of diamonds. Instead of promoting the industry as a whole, as it has done for years with its successful "a diamond is forever" ad campaign, De Beers will seek to

Charles A. Rarick

differentiate itself from the competition and develop a strong brand loyalty. Under consideration is the possibility of branching out into other product lines such as clothing, watches, and handbags.

Discussion Questions:

1. Do you feel that a global company should change its strategy in response to threatened consumer boycotts? Explain.

2. How important do you feel it is to diamond customers that their purchases be "conflict free?" Will consumers pay more for "conflict free" diamonds?

3. How should De Beers respond to the current threats of man-made diamonds and reduced market control?

Sources: F. Guerrera and A. Parker, "De Beers to Seek Conflict Free Diamond Rules." Financial Times of London, July 11, 2000; "De Beers: All that Glitters is not Sold." The Economist, July 11, 2000; "The Diamond Business: Washed Out in Africa." The Economist, June 3, 2000; "Losing their Sparkle." The Economist, June 3, 2000; "The Cartel isn't Forever." The Economist, July 17, 2004; W. Wallis. "Africaa's Conflict Diamonds: Is the UN-Backed Certification Scheme Failing to Bring Transparency to Trade." Financial Times, October 29, 2003; M. Pressler. "Diamond Lab Produces Bling Bling for a Lot Less." Miami Herald, March 7, 2004; www.kimberleyprocess.com.

Case prepared by Charles A. Rarick

CASE 21

GROUPO GIGANTE ENTERS THE U.S. MARKET

As customers enter Gigante Supermarkets they are greeted by the sounds of Mexican music and the sight of piñatas hanging from the store's ceiling. Customers see signs which read "el mejor precio" (the better price) as they select edible cactus, chili peppers, and fresh-baked pan dulce. These customers are not in Mexico, they are American customers shopping in Southern California. Gigante, Mexico's third largest retailer has begun to move into the United States market with the introduction of stores in Los Angeles, California. California is home to an estimated 11 million Latinos, most of them from Mexico. Gigante is following its customers north and setting its sights on other parts of the United States. The company wants to be the leading supermarket chain in Latino areas across the United States.

Grupo Gigante was started in Spain in 1923 by Losada Angel Go'mez. In 1956 the small business moved to Mexico City, and today the company is still headed by members of the Losada family. Grupo Gigante operates 270 stores in 19 Mexican states and has joint venture agreements with Radio Shack and Office Depot to operate their stores in Mexico. Grupo Gigante also operates 40 Toks restaurants. Sales in 2002 were over $3 billion (USD) and net income was $33.5 million (USD). The company employs over 35,000 and competes in Mexico with Wal-Mart (USA), Comerci (Mexico), and Carrefour (France). In the United States Gigante competes with large domestic grocery chains such as Vons, Albertson's, and Wal-Mart Super Centers. Gigante also must compete with smaller grocery operations that target the Latino market.

Gigante entered the U.S. market in an attempt to capitalize on the increasing number of Mexican immigrants in the United States, and the fact that Hispanics now represent the largest minority group in the country. Numbering 38.8 million, Hispanics have surpassed African-Americans as the largest minority group in the U.S. with 13 percent of the population. That number is expected to rise to 17 percent by 2020. Hispanics generally have larger families, lower incomes, and are more price-sensitive. They generally plan a shopping trip, including a review of specials and the use of coupons. Hispanic consumers tend to be more brand-loyal than non-Hispanic customers. Hispanics visit grocery stores more often than non-Hispanics and spend more on groceries. They tend to place a higher value on eating meals at home and preparing these meals from scratch. While many retailers in Hispanic markets of the U.S. have begun to stock more ethnic foods, and even devote sections of the store to ethnic offerings, Gigante is attempting to reproduce the entire Mexican shopping experience for its customers. Product offerings, ambience, and Spanish-speaking employees make Hispanic customers feel more at home than in a traditional American supermarket.

Gigante is not the only Mexican company with a strategy of moving with its customers. Famsa, a home appliance and furniture company from Monterrey has also begun to open stores in Southern California. Famsa is not attempting to directly compete with domestic firms but rather to concentrate in the Latino market exclusively. As Farmsa's president states "We're not coming to the U.S. to face big companies like Circuit City or Best Buy. Our focus is the Hispanic market." Both Famsa and Gigante have the advantage of having an in-depth understanding of the Hispanic market and how to best serve that market.

Gigante has a competitive advantage not only in terms of differentiation, but also with costs. On average, prices are 15% lower at Gigante than at traditional U.S. supermarkets. Gigante is able to offer these lower prices due to its lower labor costs. Clerks working at Gigante earn an average of $10.29 per hour compared to $17.90 per hour at other California grocery stores. Gigante's meat cutters are paid $7 an hour less than others in the area. The United Food and Commercial Workers union has not fought these lower wages for its members working at Gigante; however, the wage concessions are not expected to be permanent.

As Gigante looks towards expansion, it has targeted the more "mixed neighborhoods" of Southern California; areas when there is a balance between Latino and non-Latino customers. Gigante hopes to begin to attract a variety of customers. It is not unusual for tastes and preferences to cross ethnic lines as different groups become more familiar with each other's cultures. For example, salsa has become the most popular condiment in the United States and its popularity is not driven exclusively by Latin consumers. The company is also eyeing locations in Northern California, Arizona, and Nevada. The company has set an agenda that not only includes continued growth in the U.S. market, but also improvements in store image, technology, and personnel.

As Gigante continues to advance into the U.S. market, the increase in Hispanic population and income has not gone unnoticed by domestic rivals. Both Kroger and Albertson's have begun to experiment with store concepts in Latino areas of Southern California.

Discussion Questions:

1. What strengths, weaknesses, opportunities, and strengths does Gigante face as it establishes itself in the United States market?

2. What strategic direction would you recommend for Gigante as it embarks on an expansion drive into the U.S. market?

3. Do you think Gigante will be successful in the U.S. market? Explain.

Sources: Garcia, K. (2003). *Open Markets: Latino Food has Arrived in Mainstream Stores.* Hispanic Magazine, September; Millman, J. (2001) *Mexican Retailers Enter U.S. to Capture Latino Dollars.* Wall Street Journal. February 8; Ratnesar, R. (2003). *Fresh from the Boarder.* Time Inside Business. April.; www.fmi.org; www.gigante.com.mx; www.hoovers.com/gigante

Case prepared by Charles A. Rarick and Luz Maria Luna.

CASE 22

THE TOLEDO BICYCLE COMPANY:
PEDDLING INTO EASTERN EUROPE

Hans Kohl immigrated to the United States in 1892 and shortly thereafter began to manufacture and sell bicycles out of his Toledo, Ohio home. The company became an overnight success because of the strong demand for bicycles at the time and the exceptional quality of the bike produced by Kohl. The business was later named the Toledo Bicycle Company (TBC) and the company has remained in the hands of the Kohl family up to the present day. By 1950 the company was selling over 700,000 bicycles a year and commanded a 25% share of the market. By 1985, market share had dropped to just a little over 5%, and the company was desperately seeking ways to reduce costs and increase sales. The brand name was still strongly associated with quality bikes by consumers; however, the product was considered stogy.

During the 1970s, new competitors entered the market, producing sporting and mountain bikes. The Toledo Bicycle Company continued to produce its more traditional model, which was sold primarily for the children's market, even though bicycle sales to adults by competitors had been rapidly increasing.

Unable to reduce labor costs significantly in the Toledo plant, the company began to look internationally for a low-cost production site. In 1989 the company entered into a joint venture agreement with a Hungarian bicycle manufacturer. The Hungarian Bike Company (HBC) had a good reputation for quality in Hungary and its labor costs were only a fraction of the current labor costs of TBC. Compared to other Eastern European workers, it was felt that Hungarian workers were less militant and strike prone.

The initial agreement called for TBC to import component parts to Hungary, where the bicycles would be assembled and sold throughout Eastern Europe. TBC would provide component parts and design, and HBC would assemble and market the product. Hungarian managers would run the plant as an autonomous unit. TBC hoped to later export bicycles from Hungary into the United States to be more cost competitive. It was felt that if production costs could be significantly reduced, TBC bikes could be sold through mass merchandisers in the United States and the company could once again regain its leadership role in the industry.

The negotiations for the joint venture agreement became more complex than TBC had planned. The collapse of the Soviet Union brought uncertainty, and in some cases, chaos to Eastern European governments. International joint venture laws were constantly changing and no one seemed to know the specifics of the law. Finally, in 1991, an agreement was reached and production began.

From the start, the joint venture experienced problems with production. Managers of the old Hungarian Bike Company had been trained in a system that rewarded output and paid scant attention to quality issues. TBC was surprised by the low level of quality output at the plant, given the good reputation HBC had in Hungary. When a total quality management (TQM) program was initiated at the plant, only marginal improvements resulted. When the same program had been implemented at TBC in the United States, quality had improved substantially.

Productivity was also a problem in Hungary. Workers were prone to absenteeism and seemed to care little about their jobs. Even though their wages had been raised because of the association with TBC, workers did not appear to be very motivated. TBC estimated that the productivity level at the Hungarian plant was about half the productivity level at the American plant.

In 1992 the Hungarian government increased tariffs on imported parts, raised the value added tax (VAT), and instituted an import-handling charge. These additional taxes significantly increased the costs of production for the Hungarian bicycles.

Faced with further deterioration in its U.S. market share, lower than expected sales in Eastern Europe, and rising production costs, the company went into debt, and by 1995, TBC had declared bankruptcy.

Discussion Questions:

1. What factors make for a good international joint venture agreement?

2. What could TBC have done differently to avoid the problems it experienced in Hungary?

3. What should TBC do to pull itself out of bankruptcy?

Note: Although this case is fictional, it is based on an actual situation.

Sources: "A Bicycle Made for Two," The Economist, June 8, 1991; "How Schwinn Bike Company Pedaled into Bankruptcy," Reuters Business Report, December 18, 1996; Charles Hill, International Business, Boston: Irwin/ McGraw-Hill, 1998.

Case prepared by Charles A. Rarick.

CASE 23

CAFÉ BRITT: COSTA RICAN COFFEE

Known by various names such as mocha, java, or a cup of Joe, coffee is one of the world's most popular drinks. Coffee is also a valuable commodity and the source of income for a number of countries. Coffee is grown mainly in countries located in the equatorial region of the world, between the Tropic of Capricorn and the Tropic of Cancer. Sixty million metric tons of coffee is produced each year in this coffee belt by more than 60 countries. One of those countries is Costa Rica, a country that has traditionally relied heavily on coffee exports as a source of revenue. While coffee is a popular Costa Rican product, it did not originate in Costa Rica or anywhere in Latin America. The origins of coffee can be found in Africa.

HISTORY OF COFFEE

The history of coffee can be traced to East Africa, in present day Ethiopia around the year 600AD when a local goat herder named Kaldi noticed his flock eating berries from a bush. As legend has it, the animals seemed to become energized from the berries and Kaldi himself experienced the same effect after he consumed some of the fruit. Coffee eventually made its way to the Arabian Peninsula. Beginning with the 10th Century, Arabs learned to step coffee beans in water to produce a drink called "gahwa." It is believed that the world's first coffeehouses were established in Mecca and became places where people could play chess and argue politics. The drink grew in popularity as word of its properties spread.

Coffee beans were traded at the port of Mocha in the 13th Century, but the plant itself was prohibited from being exported out of Arabia. In the 17th century a Muslim pilgrim brought coffee seeds back to his home in India and began a coffee plantation. Dutch traders began purchasing coffee plants from India and growing them in Java. Venetian traders then introduced coffee to Europe, and a French naval officer named Captain Gabriel Mathieu de Clieu brought a single coffee plant to the Caribbean. The plant was first introduced in Martinique and from there, coffee plants made their way to Central and South America. Legend has it that from a single coffee plant comes almost all the coffee now grown in the Caribbean and Latin America. Coffee was introduced to North America in the 1660s and coffeehouses quickly sprung up in New York, Boston, and Philadelphia. The Boston Tea party was planned in one of these early coffee houses.

Coffee production began in Costa Rica in 1779. The climate of Costa Rica was ideal for growing coffee beans and the commodity soon became the leading product for export. In order to encourage coffee exports, the government of Costa Rica supplied each family with 25 plants if they agreed to grow coffee. In addition, they were given a tax exemption on all earnings from the sale of the coffee beans. This incentive resulted in most families being engaged to some extent in coffee production. In order to insure that Costa Rican coffee maintained a quality image in the world marketplace, the Costa Rican government passed a law banning the growing of any coffee other than Arabica in the country.

COFFEE PRODUCTION

Coffee is from an evergreen that produces a blossom that hardens and turns from green to bright red in color. The coffee plant belongs to the botanical family called Rubiaceae and the average coffee tree produces about a pound of coffee a year for 25-30 years. The fruit of the coffee tree, referred to as cherries, contains two-sided beans from which coffee is produced. There are two basic species of coffee in the world: Arabica and Robusta. Arabica beans are considered to be the higher quality coffee beans and are grown in higher altitudes. The higher altitude causes the beans to grow more slowly and to develop what is called a "hard bean." Robusta coffee beans can grow in lower altitudes and mature more quickly. The bean is less expensive to produce but gives a less desirable taste. Robusta coffee is often sold in cans in supermarkets and is often the bean found in instant coffee. Arabica coffee plants, while considered superior in taste are more difficult to grow and yield fewer beans per plant. Robusta are easier to grow, yield more beans per plant, and are disease resistant. The Robusta bean produces a harsher taste and is generally not considered appropriate for a premium coffee product. Arabica coffee is grown primarily in Latin America and India. Robusta beans are primarily grown in Africa and South-East Asia.

Coffee beans are usually harvested by hand and dried either by placing them in the sun, called patio drying, or using a mechanical tumbling dryer. After the beans have been dried they are milled which removes the outer skin of the bean and give the bean a shine. The beans are sorted and graded before being sent to market. To turn coffee beans into a desirable drink, the beans must be roasted. The roasting process heats the beans to between 320F and 480F degrees in a steel drum.

Coffee beans are turned into a liquid drink in a variety of ways. All methods have in common the use of hot water to extract the essential oils and caffeol from the ground coffee beans. Coffee can be made using a filter method or a percolator, both traditionally popular in the United States, or consumers can use an espresso machine and force hot water through finely ground and compacted coffee. This method has become increasingly popular in the U.S. and has been popular in Europe for some time. Turkish coffee is made using a cooper pot in which the ground coffee is boiled in the pot, usually three times, producing a very strong coffee.

THE COFFEE INDUSTRY

The coffee industry is very susceptible to commodity price changes. Coffee retailers profit from falling prices, and coffee producers benefit when prices are rising. The coffee producing industry has experienced some difficult years as the price of coffee reached record lows in recent years. Coffee prices were held constant during the 1960s, 1970s, and 1980s as the coffee cartel was able to control supply and maintain price stability. In 1989 the cartel collapsed, causing prices to begin a long and significant drop. Although prices spiked during poor harvesting seasons, the long-run trend was downward from about 1990 to 2004. Increased volume coming from Vietnam and Brazil fueled the price decreases. Vietnam was able to increase coffee production during the 1990s from a small production of 84,000 tons to 950,000 tons, becoming the second largest coffee producing country behind Brazil. Coffee is traded on the New York Coffee Sugar and Cocoa Exchange and the price is volatile.

In addition to increased supply, technological breakthroughs in the processing industry allowed roasters to use more Robusta beans without getting the harsh taste. This change in processing allowed for a greater supply of Robusta beans to be processed. Vietnam and Brazil produce most of the Robusta coffee in the world market. The Big Four coffee sellers in the world, Nestle, Procter and Gamble, Sara Lee, and Kraft had previously blended only a small amount of Robusta beans into the blend of Arabica beans, but now are able to significantly increase the Robusta content.

Worldwide coffee prices continued to fall during the 1990s and in 2001 reached a record low. Sometimes price levels were below production costs. The worldwide coffee glut appears to have now ended with prices being up over 20% in the past year and this increased price trend is expected to increase. Smaller crop yields in Brazil, Vietnam, and Indonesia, coupled with rising demand are driving prices higher. Prices at the supermarket and at coffeehouses such as Starbucks have been rising as commodity prices increase.

Coffee plantations require a labor-intensive work force of seasonal workers to hand pick berries and wash and dry them. Vietnam has a competitive advantage in coffee production over most of the rest of the world. It is estimated that production costs are three times higher in Central America than in Vietnam, for example. The world's largest coffee producing countries can be seen in Figure 1.

Figure 1
Major Coffee Producing Countries
(60 kilo bags, 2003)

Brazil	28,825,000
Vietnam	11,250,000
Colombia	11,000,000

Indonesia	6,464,000
Mexico	4,550,000
India	4,508,000
Ethiopia	4,333,333
Uganda	3,100,000
Guatemala	3,000,000
Honduras	2,913,333
Peru	2,525,000
Cote d'Ivoire	2,325,000
Costa Rica	2,120,000

Source: International Coffee Organization (www.ico.org)

Per capita consumption of coffee has been declining in the developing world but growing in developed countries. Premium coffee sales, using only high quality Arabica beans has grown approximately 40% in the United States. When the world price of coffee was declining, specialty retailers such as Starbucks reaped greater profits. As the price of coffee is now increasing, the additional costs are being passed on to consumers. Coffee demand is relatively constant, however, coffee supply is often unpredictable due to weather conditions.

Some coffee has a worldwide reputation for high quality, including Blue Mountain coffee from Jamaica and Kona coffee from Hawaii. A number of niche coffee products exist including the world's most expensive coffee called Civet. Civet coffee comes from the undigested discharge of the fruit eating civet. The civet is a cousin of the mongoose and lives in South-East Asia. The civet eats coffee beans, the beans pass through the animal undigested, and are then collected by processors. The coffee is very scarce and highly prized for its unique flavor and aroma. Other less exotic specialty coffee includes estate, shade grown, and organic coffee. Estate coffee is coffee from only one plantation. Estate coffee is not blended with beans from other producers and maintains its pure or consistent flavor. Shade grown coffee is grown under shade trees and appeals to consumers who feel this practice is more environmentally responsible in that the practice avoids soil erosion and is also beneficial to wildlife. Some coffee is also certified as "fair trade coffee" meaning that a price baseline is maintained by buyers who insure against falling prices paid to growers. This coffee appeals to consumers who feel that a market based pricing system can at times cause farmers to suffer extreme and unexpected drops in income. Fair trade coffee accounts for only about three percent of the coffee market. Organic coffee is grown without chemicals and fertilizers and appeals to a limited segment of the coffee industry as well. Organic coffee prices generally are fifteen cents a pound higher than non-organic coffee.

CAFÉ BRITT

The Costa Rican coffee industry consists mainly of small farms or fincas. While Costa Rican coffee has traditionally been considered to be a quality product, the country was not well known as a producer of gourmet coffee. Café Britt was founded in 1985, being the first gourmet coffee roaster in Costa Rica. Café Britt was founded by its current president and chairman, Steven Aronson. Aronson, who was an American permanently living in Costa Rica, had studied agricultural economics at the University of Michigan and had been involved in several coffee processing companies in Latin America. The current CEO and general manager is Pablo Vargas, a Costa Rican who holds graduate degree in agricultural economics and business from Michigan State University. Vargas, who has worked for Café Britt for the past thirteen years was responsible for implementing the a quality assurance program, establishing the Internet sales concept, and promoting the retail store concept. The company is headquartered in Heredia, a town near the capital, San José. The privately held company sells the Café Britt brand through the Internet, in its 17 retail stores in Costa Rica, and through hotel chains and restaurants. The company also sells unprocessed coffee (green coffee) to processors. The Company also has three stores at the international airport in San José. Café Britt produces a lower quality brand coffee for the domestic retail market as well. Café Britt Coffee Corporation was incorporated in Curaçao and consists of the following subsidiaries: Grupo Café Britt, S.A. and Finca Tropico, S.A. incorporated in Costa Rica; Café Britt Arabica Marketing, NV incorporated in Curaçao. The Company has recently established operations in Peru to roast coffee and sell chocolates. The company operates a successful Internet site (www. cafebritt.com) where customers can purchase coffee, sweets and nuts, music, and Costa Rican crafts. The Internet site has been highly rated by BizRate for its level of customer satisfaction. Customers can also call a toll free number to order Café Britt products. Shipping costs for orders less than $58 are $6.95 per order and shipping is free for orders over $58. International shipments (outside the U.S., Canada, and Puerto Rico) cost an additional $20.

Figure 2
Sales Distribution

Retail Stores	59%
Supermarkets, Restaurants, Hotels	17%
Internet	10%
Green Coffee	10%
Coffee Tour	4%

Café Britt sells 12 ounce coffee bags retail for $7.95. The coffee is offered in the following verities: Dark Roast, Light Roast, Espresso, Decaffeinated, Shade Grown Organic, Tarrazu Montecielo, and Tres Rios Valdivia. The Company also sells a variety of candies and nuts such as Creamy Coffee Cheros, Chocolate Covered Coffee Beans, and Chocolate Covered Macadamia Nuts. Café Britt promotes Costa Rican artists through the sale of local music and crafts.

Café Britt considers its quality product to be a strong competitive advantage in this highly competitive market. The Company seeks to be a leader in customer service and to provide an exceptional product at a competitive price. Café Britt is ISO-9000:2000 certified and promotes a quality mission statement.

Café Britt maintains a 100% customer satisfaction policy and will replace any product or give a refund if the product does not meet customer's expectations. The coffee is grown in Costa Rica by over 4,000 smaller growers, milled and patio dried, roasted and packed all by Café Britt. Café Britt seeks to capture the higher end of the coffee market and to be identified with Costa Rica. Café Britt is as much about Costa Rican tourism as it is about coffee production. As current CEO Pablo Vargas likes to state "Costa Rica sells Café Britt and Café Britt sells Costa Rica."

Costa Rica is well known as a desirable tourist destination. Each year tourist flock to the country to see it's many natural attractions including volcanoes, rain forests, and wildlife. With one-fourth of the country devoted to national parks and protected areas, Costa Rica has become a popular eco-tourist destination. Tourism growth was strong until 2001 when the terrorism attack in the United States reduced travel to many parts of the world including Costa Rica. Tourism had grown from 435,000 visitors in 1990 to 1,131,000 in 2001. Most visitors to Costa Rica are from the United States, however, significant numbers of visitors come also from Canada and Europe. Increased airline flights, more hotels, and a strong Euro have helped tourism rebound in Costa Rica. Capitalizing on this aspect of the Costa Rican economy, Café Britt conducts a very popular multimedia coffee tour of its facilities. The tour is one of Costa Rica's more popular tourist activities and attracts over 40,000 visitors a year to the plantation. For about $30US tourists are taken from their hotels by bus to the plantation and provided with a highly entertaining introduction to coffee growing and processing. Through this professionally conducted tour, visitors learn about the history of coffee, how coffee is grown and roasted, and what it takes to produce a premium coffee product. Exhibit 5 shows pictures from the coffee tour. Many visitors are introduced to the Café Britt brand through this tour. The tours are heavily promoted and arranged through local hotels in the capital city. Following the tour visitors can stroll through the Café Britt shop at the plantation and purchase products, or use the Internet Café and send electronic Café Britt greeting cards to their friends back home.

Café Britt competes with a number of Costa Rican brands including Bardu Coffee, Café Delagro, Café Rey, Café Volio, Doka Estate Coffee, Dota Coffee, and Kiry Coffee. Another Costa Rican coffee producer, Américo, has established an exhibit in the San José airport and touts itself as the "genuine Costa Rican coffee." In addition, Café Britt must compete with other gourmet brands, each with a particular niche in the market.

Café Britt has done well during its existence, especially when one considers the volatility of coffee prices and the number of competitors the company faces. Café Britt uses generally accepted accounting standards, and its financial statements are audited by KPMG of Costa Rica. Café Britt uses the U.S. dollar as its functional currency.

CAFÉ BRITT LOOKS TO THE FUTURE

With significant gains in sales and profitability in 2004, Café Britt looks towards the future with a desire for further expansion. The Company has increased its production capacity through its expansion into Peru. Café Britt hopes to duplicate its successful business model in Peru. Although not generally known for quality coffee, Peru does have some exceptional quality production and Café Britt hopes to duplicate its business model there using the same tourism link. Café Britt is aware of its dependency on Costa Rican tourism for its continued success and the importance of being identified as "Costa Rican coffee" by tourists.

Charles A. Rarick

Discussion Questions:

1. What are the strengths, weaknesses, opportunities, and threats for Cafe Britt?

2. What could Café Britt do to establish itself in retail stores in the United States? Is this important to Café Britt's continued success? Explain.

3. What advice would you offer Café Britt in order for the company to maintain its leading position?

Sources: Batsell, J. (2004). *Cup by cup, coffee fuels world market from Costa Rican origins.* Knight Ridder Tribune Business News. September 19; Brackey, H. (2005). *Java lover's jolt: Prices going up.* Miami Herald. March 4; Katona, C. and T. Katona. (1992). The coffee book. San Leandro, CA: Bristol Publishing; Mackenzie, C. (2005). *Fair trade price certification spurs debate.* Miami Herald. March 28; Personal interview with Pablo Vargas in Heredia, Costa Rica on April 8, 2005; Stein, N. (2002). *Crisis in the coffee cup.* Fortune. December 9; Teves, O. (2004). *Undigested coffee beans: Good to the last drop.* Miami Herald. December 26; Telephone interview with Steven Aronson. March 28, 2005. www.cafebritt.com. Accessed on February 15, 2005; www.cnn.com. Accessed on October 18, 2002. www.hoovers.com. Accessed on February 15, 2005; www.ico.org. Accessed on February 15, 2005. www.lind-waldock.com. Accessed on February 15, 2005; www.ncausa.org . Accessed on March 25, 2005; www.wto.org - Costa Rica Tourism numbers. Accessed on April 12, 2005.

Case prepared by Charles A. Rarick, Martine Duchatelet, and Anne Fiedler.

EXERCISE 9

WEB-BASED EXERCISE: OVERSEAS PRIVATE INVESTMENT CORPORATION (OPIC)

Web Address: www.opic.gov

Purpose: To gain a better understanding of the functions of this private, international agency and its role in global financing.

Procedure: Visit the web page of the Overseas Private Investment Corporation (OPIC) and answer the four questions below.

Questions:

1. When was OPIC started, where does it get its funding, and what services does it provide?

2. What types of funding are available from OPIC?

3. What protection does OPIC political risk insurance provide?

4. Select a recent OPIC project and briefly explain what it seeks to accomplish.

Part Five

INTERNATIONAL MARKETING

Cases:

N-e-s-t-l-e-s
Frito-Lay Adapts to the Chinese Market
Bradford LTD Learns About Countertrade
Mount Gay Rum
Tonia Motorbikes: A Case of Chinese Piracy
Insulting Islam, One Step at a Time
Plunge Furniture Factory - Lithuania

Exercise:

Marketing to the Mexicans

CASE 24

N-E-S-T-L-E-S
NESTLÉ MAKES THE VERY BEST CEREAL?

Nestle, S.A. is the world's largest food company. This Swiss multinational began in 1866 when pharmacist Henri Nestle invented a formula for use by infants who could not breast-feed. Nestlé's first product, Farine Lactee was sold as an alternative to mother's milk and quickly became a success. In years to follow, the company diversified into other food items. Although Nestle may be best known for its chocolate line, the company markets a wide variety of food products, including frozen foods, coffee, soups, and mineral water, as well as pet foods and cosmetics. Today this food giant employs over 230,000 people worldwide.

During the 1980s the company noticed that Europeans were increasingly purchasing breakfast cereal. Traditionally, Europeans chose to consume other food products for breakfast, such as croissants, jams, cheese, and meats, however, it was becoming clear that a large potential market for Nestle was developing in its own backyard. Europeans were switching to ready-to-eat cereals because of their convenience, low cost, and nutritional value. The American cereal company, Kellogg, had been in Europe for some time; however, sales had not been especially strong. Although Kellogg sold breakfast cereal in over 130 countries, Nestle felt that given its strong brand name and reputation for quality, it could compete with Kellogg in the European market. After all, Nestle was a world-class leader in the food industry and breakfast cereal was a very profitable segment of the market. Entering this market segment seemed logical.

Nestle decided to enter Spain first. The company developed a breakfast cereal that would best be eaten with warm milk. The cereal was of a harder substance than the competing brands, and considered appropriate for the Spanish market based on limited market research.

At first the cereal sold well; however, after just a few years, sales began to fall and channel members refused to handle the product. The cereal sold in Spain, which was designed for use with warm milk, was extremely hard if eaten with cold milk.

Undaunted by its lack of success in Spain, Nestle next moved into France. France turned out to be a more difficult market than Spain. Strong competition from Kellogg, high shelf-stocking fees, and production problems dogged Nestle in France. Nestle had decided to produce the cereal in a Swiss plant and ship the product to France. Cereal production was given a low priority in the Swiss plant and production was unreliable. At this time, market research was indicating that Nestle cereal was seen as inferior to Kellogg's. Nevertheless, Nestle continued its European expansion, utilizing a pan-European view of the market. Mass production and product standardization were seen as effective ways to combat the competitive pressures it faced from the American companies.

In the late 1980s General Mills decided to enter the European market. Like Nestle, it lacked a first mover advantage in the European cereal market and would have to develop production, marketing, and distribution capabilities on the continent. By this time Nestle was losing money in all cereal markets, so a partnership seemed like a good solution to the problems facing the two companies. Nestle would convert some production capacity to General Mills products, provide a recognized brand name, and move the product through the channel of distribution. General Mills would breathe life into the failing Nestle cereal business by providing technical expertise in the areas of production and marketing.

At present, Nestle still has not been able to establish itself as a major producer of breakfast cereals anywhere in the world. Although Nestle has been very successful in many major food groups, success in independently producing and marketing a cereal line has evaded the company. Nestle recently began the acquisition of Ralston Purina and had expressed an interest in acquiring Quaker Oats. Some observers speculate that Nestle could purchase the ability to be a leader in the breakfast cereal line.

Charles A. Rarick

Discussion Questions:

1. Specifically, what mistakes did Nestle make in its marketing of cereal in Europe?

2. Why has Nestle, the world's largest food company, been unable to develop a successful line of breakfast cereals?

3. Do you think the acquisition of American companies with cereal experience will successfully establish Nestle as a global player in this market? Explain.

Sources: Nestle's corporate web site (www.nestle.com); Hoovers (www.hoovers.com); "Competition: Europe Cooks Up Cereal Brawl," Fortune, June 3, 1991; "Nestle Unfazed by Unilever/Bestfoods/Link," Reuters, June, 7, 2000; "Nestle Mulls Quaker Oats Bid as Potential Suitors Withdraw," Independent, November 25, 2000; "Nestle Buys Ralston Purina," Miami Herald, January 17, 2001.

Case prepared by Charles A. Rarick.

CASE 25

FRITO-LAY ADAPTS TO THE CHINESE MARKET

In the 1930s, two men in different parts of the United States began businesses that would eventually come to dominate the global snack food market. In 1932, Elmer Doolin, an ice cream salesman, stopped for lunch at a local San Antonio café. He noticed a package of corn chips at the café and purchased it for five cents. This small purchase would come to change his career and his life. The chips Doolin purchased were made from corn dough used for centuries by Mexicans to bake bread. Impressed with the product, Doolin sold his ice cream business and purchased the corn chip producer's business for one hundred dollars. The brand, Frito, was created in the kitchen of his mother, along with the early production of the corn chips. Doolin would bake the chips at night and sell them during the day. Early sales were in the range of $8-10 a day. As business expanded, the company was moved from San Antonio to Dallas. Frito became a major chip producer in the Southwestern United States.

Around the same time, an entrepreneur in Tennessee named Herman W. Lay was selling potato chips produced by an Atlanta company. Lay sold the chips from his personal automobile until 1938 when the chip manufacturer fell on hard times. Lay managed to buy the business and changed its name to H.W. Lay and Company. The company's products became popular with consumers due to their good taste and convenience making Frito-Lay the dominant producer of snack foods in the Southeastern United States.

After World War II, the two companies began to cooperate in the area of product distribution. At this time they were still limited to their respective geographic markets, with Frito in the Southwest and Lay in the Southeast. In 1961, the two companies merged to form

Frito-Lay, Inc., and in 1965 the company was merged again, this time with the Pepsi-Cola Company. The Pepsi-Cola Company became PepsiCo and consisted of the Pepsi-Cola Company, the Frito-Lay Company, and Tropicana Products. The company now also markets the popular brands Quaker Oats and Gatorade.

Although the U.S. market is the largest market in the world for snack foods, due to its saturation, Frito Lay has expanded significantly into international markets. The company tries to capitalize on its economies of scale and global brand image to compete with local brands. The typical entry strategy is to first learn which company is the leading snack company in the foreign market, and then attempt to purchase that company. If that fails, Frito-Lay aggressively competes against that local company. Frito-Lay's international operations add $9 billion to PepsiCo's $25 billion revenue. International markets have in many cases been more profitable for PepsiCo than the domestic market of the United States.

Pepsi entered China in 1981 to sell soft drinks, and since that time has invested more than $1 billion. In 1994 Frito-Lay entered the Chinese market with its popular Cheetos brand snack. Potato chips were not introduced into the Chinese market until 1997, due to the Chinese ban on potato imports. Frito-Lay had to establish its own farms in order to grow potatoes acceptable to company standards. Early adaptation to local markets required Frito-Lay to make significant changes. For example, Frito-Lay's Cheetos sold in China do not contain any cheese due to the propensity of the Chinese to be lactose intolerant. Instead of cheese flavoring, Cheetos is offered with barbecue or seafood flavoring. In addition, the packaging was made smaller so that the price would be more acceptable. Other international adaptations had previously been made in other markets by Frito-Lay, including the popular Thai product, Nori Seaweed Chips.

Frito-Lay found that the Chinese market was not a single entity. Regional tastes and preferences had to be considered and products altered accordingly. Chinese living in Shanghai, for example, prefer sweeter foods, and Chinese living in the Northern region prefer a meaty taste. Frito-Lay also has found that having a good understanding of culture helps sell products. The Chinese belief in the Great Unity, or yin and yang, have marketing and product development implications. Yin and yang are the opposing forces in the universe and seek balance. The Chinese also seek balance, including balance in their foods. Fried food is seen as hot and not appropriate in the summer months so Frito-Lay developed a new product, cool lemon potato chips. This product consists of chips dotted with lime specks and mint and packaged with cool climate images to connote winter months.

Promotion in China has required other adaptations, including advertisements showing the peeling of potatoes to indicate the product's basic ingredient. Promotion in China has successfully related collectivist tendencies of the Chinese people and the desire of the Chinese to try new products outdoors, in a conspicuous fashion. Early adopters in China want others to see their consumption of Western products. As with many Western products, young consumers are the first to try the product, and in the case of Frito-Lay, the focus has been on young women. As Jackson Chiu, sales director for Frito-Lay states: "We market to girls and the boys follow." Frito-Lay has been very creative in its promotion efforts in China, however, one advertisement resulted in a small problem. Using the picture of Mao Zedong's cook in its promotion resulted in the company being ordered to offer an apology and to pay the cook 10,000 yuan (1,200USD) for violating a Chinese law that requires getting permission before using someone's picture.

Frito-Lay's entry into the Chinese market has also caused some controversy. Some critics charge that companies like Frito-Lay have caused the Chinese diet to become unhealthy. Many Chinese can remember when food was rationed, long food lines existed, and consumers were offered little choice. Today the Chinese have a large variety of food options, and snack foods are a popular choice. As a result of their dietary changes, the Chinese have become more overweight. In the past ten years, the percentage of the Chinese population considered overweight has risen from almost none to a little under one third of the population. A common way of greeting someone in Chinese is the English equivalent of "Have you eaten yet." The Chinese are now able to answer yes more often to that question, and many are selecting foods that are considered by some to be unhealthy.

Concerned with the health effects of its products, not only in China, but also in health-conscious markets such as the United States, PepsiCo has begun to change its product offerings. Based on medical advice, PepsiCo has divided its products into three groups: 1) "Good for you" foods such as Gatorade and oatmeal; 2) "Better for you" foods such as Nacho Cheesier Baked Doritos; 3) "Fun for you" foods such as Pepsi Cola. The good for you foods are naturally healthy or engineered to be healthy. The better for you foods contain more wholesome ingredients or have reduced fat and sugar. The fun food isn't considered to be especially healthy. PepsiCo is moving product development towards the "good for you" and "better for you" groups. According to nutrition expert, Professor Marion Nestle of New York University, "Frito-Lay products are still high in calories, salt, and rapidly absorbed carbohydrates." For now the Chinese do not seem too concerned and Frito-Lay continues to develop this rapidly expanding market.

Discussion Questions:

1. Evaluate the approach Frito-Lay used as it entered the Chinese market. Would you consider the approach to be ethnocentric, polycentric, or geocentric? Explain your answer.

2. Is the company being socially responsible in your opinion by selling products that may be considered unhealthy?

3. What lessons can be learned by examining the experiences of Frito-Lay in China?

Sources: Author unknown. (2004). *Frito-Lay Sees Crunchy Business for Chips Here*. The Economic Times, June 3; Author unknown. (2004). *Chairman Mao's Cook Wins Lawsuit vs Pepsi*. China Economic Net, July 23; Flannery, R. (2004). *China is a Big Prize*. Forbes, May 10; Kurtenbach, E. (2004). *Urban Chinese Struggle with Battle of the Budge*. LaTimes.Com, July 18; Parker-Pope, T. (1996). *Custom-Made: The Most Successful Companies Have to Realize a Simple Truth – All Consumers Aren't Alike*. Wall Street Journal, September 26; Sellers, P. (2004). *The Brand King Challenge*. Fortune, March 21; www.abcnews.com *Using Potato Chips to Spread the Spirit of Free Enterprise*, September 9. 2004; www.fritolay.com. Accessed on July 12, 2004. www.pepsico.com; Accessed on July 12, 2004.

Case prepared by Charles A. Rarick.

CASE 26

BRADFORD LTD LEARNS ABOUT COUNTERTRADE

Bradford Ltd. manufacturers cement, the gray talc-like powder that is used to make concrete when water, sand, and aggregate (stones) are added. Cement is treated as a commodity type product, and Bradford is looking to expand its markets by exporting cement to Russia.

Mark Miller, Bradford's CEO is directing his team in establishing a trading relationship with Hydzik's Development, a major building contracting company located several miles from St. Petersburg. Myron Sczurek is Hydzik's CEO and is working with Mr. Miller to "cement" a deal. All of the specifics related to the transaction have been agreed upon and they are now at the final stage and trying to reach agreement as to form of payment.

Hydzik's Perspective:
1. Desire to pay in rubles (the Russian currency)
2. Desires to take title of cement shipment upon arrival in their facility near St. Petersburg
3. Desires to keep transaction as simple as possible; a handshake would be nice
4. Expresses a strong belief in a growing and stable Russian government and economy

Bradford's Perspective:
1. Mr. Miller fears the dollar/ruble exchange rate is unstable and that it will deteriorate
2. Wants Hydzik's to take title of the cement when it leaves U.S. port
3. Fears a handshake may not be sufficient

4. Doesn't share Mr. Sczurek's optimism regarding the stability of the Russian government or economy

The Proposed Solution:

After several days of discussion, Mr. Miller and Mr. Sczurek both feel that the trade is in both parties best interests; a win-win situation. They both agree that a possible solution includes the use of "countertrade" as a form of payment, and that Hydzik's will take title at the U.S. port. Mr. Sczurek offers to pay for the cement by shipping an equal value of Vodka for the cement. The first shipment of cement is to have a market value of $1,000,000 to which Hydzik's will ship $1,000,000 worth of vodka to Bradford. Mr. Miller left the meetings to discuss the offer with his staff to draw-up a counteroffer and is to get back to Mr. Sczurek by the end of the week.

Discussion Questions:

1. Which party do you believe benefits most from the proposed solution and why?

2. If the quantity of vodka is determined by fair market value in U.S. dollars ($1,000,000) at the time of the trade, is the $1,000,000 in cement protected from fluctuations in the currency exchange rate in this proposal?

3. If you were Mr. Miller, where would the favorable F.O.B. (U.S. port or Russian port) and why?

4. You work for Bradford and are charged with writing the counterproposal for the amount and value of the vodka needed to "cement" the deal. How would you approach reaching this value and how would you justify it to Hydzik's Development?

Case prepared by Jack Kleban.

CASE 27

Mount Gay Rum:
The World's Oldest Rum Maker Looks
to the Future

Once the drink of choice among sailors and pirates, rum is undergoing a transformation. Rum is an increasingly popular alcoholic beverage, and major producers who have pioneered new rum products and flavors are shaping its image. While the Caribbean is home to more traditional rum makers, increased competition from Latin America and Asia threaten to disrupt the economies of the rum producing countries.

RUM AND ITS HISTORY

Rum production can be traced to ancient India and Egypt. Both countries had developed a sugar-based alcoholic beverage many years before the New World was discovered. On his second voyage to the New World Christopher Columbus brought sugarcane from the Canary Islands. The crop flourished in the hot, humid environment of the Caribbean. The crop became a major export for the various colonies of the Caribbean. When it was discovered that a by-product of sugarcane, molasses, could be fermented and distilled, a new alcoholic drink was born. The new drink called rumbullion, or sometimes "kill devil" was a favorite of sailors who noticed that the drink held up better during long voyages than beer, or even water. In fact, the drink got even better with age.

Eventually the drink became known as rum and was widely produced throughout the Caribbean. Rum production developed in the Caribbean with the development of the sugar plantations. In order to make rum, one begins with sugar cane. The juices from the plant are extracted by pressing the sugar cane stalk. Some rum

130

producers prefer to use molasses instead of sugar juice. Molasses is the product of the sugar refining process. Yeast is added to the sugar cane or molasses and allowed to ferment. The "sugar wine" is then boiled, while the vapor is collected and condensed (distilled). The product is then aged anywhere from one to thirty years or more. Most rum is aged in oak barrels that once held whiskey or bourbon. After aging, the rum is blended and bottled.

There are many different types of rum products. White rums are not aged in oak casks, and may not be aged at all. They are usually used as mixers for drinks such as pina coladas or daiquiris. Golden rums, or regular rums, are aged from 6 months to 2 years. Dark rums, or premium rums are aged for two years or more, and superpremium rums are aged much longer. The dark color of rum comes from the oak barrels in which the rum is aged. Rum quality is based on age, but four other factors are also important in determining quality. The quality of inputs, type of fermentation, degree of distillation, and blending skill are also important to producing a quality rum product. Uniform standards do not exist in the industry, so wide variation exists among the rum producing companies and countries. Rum drinkers generally prefer a darker, aged product. However, individual tastes vary among the rum consuming population.

Recently spice rums have been developed in which the rum is mixed with cinnamon, pineapple, or banana. Some producers, such as Angostura of Trinidad have begun marketing tropical, fruity rums such as mango and passion fruit, hoping to attract younger, female customers. Bacardi has begun to offer many varieties of flavored rum including vanilla, raspberry, and coconut. Flavored rums have become very popular and now account for over 30% of all rum sales. The variety of product offerings has increased not only with flavoring, but also with mixtures, such as Bacardi's new Ciclon product which is a mixture of rum, tequila, and lime.

THE RUM INDUSTRY

Structurally the rum industry is a very fragmented industry. Many rum producers are small, family run businesses. Rum is distilled in many parts of the world; however, most well-know brands come from the Caribbean including the world's most popular brand Bacardi of Puerto Rico. Other well known brands include Captain Morgan and Castillo also of Puerto Rico, Appleton of Jamaica, Malibu and Mount Gay of Barbados, Barbancourt of Haiti, Flor de Cana of Nicaragua, and Royal Oak of Trinidad. Cuba produces 34 different brands of rum, none, however, can be sold in the United States. Through a French partner, the Cuban government is selling the much sought after Havana Club brand in Europe.

Rum is produced in many countries outside the Caribbean including India. The UB Group of India recently began to export Indian Rum to the United States and the United Kingdom. Rum is even produced in the United States, although in small quantities. For example, New Orleans Rum is a niche player in the industry producing handcrafted, single barrel, aged rum. While many small players exist in the industry, Bacardi is the dominant firm and market leader.

Rum sales have increased in recent years, making rum one of the hottest categories in the industry. Increased popularity of rum is attributed to the increased variety of flavored products offered, the increasing tendency to mix rum with other products, and the "fun in the sun" image projected by rum as Latin drinks such as the mojito have become more popular. While Bacardi is the market leader, rum production in the Americas did not begin in Puerto Rico, but in Barbados.

BARBADOS

Barbados played an important role in the development of the rum industry in the Americas. The small island state of just over 270,000 inhabitants traces many of its customs and practices back to its colonial influence. Barbados was under British rule from 1627 to its independence in 1966. Sugar production was central to the economy of Barbados for many centuries and an important export for its colonial power. Soon after sugar farming began, rum making in Barbados was developed as a by-product. Sugar and rum production became critical to the economy of Barbados. Today tourism is much more significant to the economy of the island. Barbados enjoys a relatively high standard of living and a well-educated citizenry.

Barbados is one of the most affluent countries in the Caribbean and it has developed an advanced telecommunications infrastructure and IT industry. Barbados is a member of the World Trade Organization (WTO) and the Caribbean Community (CARICOM). The country is known for its banking and insurance industries, but perhaps is better known for its rum. The oldest and most popular brand of rum produced in Barbados is Mount Gay Rum.

MOUNT GAY RUM

Recently, Mount Gay Rum celebrated its 300th year of producing its sugar-based alcoholic beverage, making Mount Gay the oldest rum maker in the world. It is generally believed that rum was first produced on the Mount Gay Estate in 1663, however, written records date back only to 1703. Nevertheless, the written record still makes Mount Gay the longest lasting rum producer.

Mount Gay Rum Estate is located in a northwest parish of Barbados, once known as Mount Gilboa. After several previous owners, John Sober brought the property and distillery and hired Sir John Gay Alleyne to manage the operations. After the death of Sir John, the site was renamed Mount Gay in his honor. The plantation was later purchased by a businessman named Aubrey Ward, who introduced Mount Gay Rum to the global marketplace. In 1989, the Ward family sold a majority interest in the business to the French company, Remy Cointreau; yet the family still maintains involvement in the plantation and a financial interest in the company.

Mount Gay Rum uses molasses, not sugar juice to make its rum. Molasses derived from Barbados sugar cane is mixed with pure Barbados water and distilled in two separate batches. Part of the molasses mixture is placed in a Coffey still to produce a single distillate that has a strong alcohol content. The other part of the mixture is placed in a copper still to make a double distillate, lower in alcohol but more robust in flavor. The two distillates are aged separately in oak barrels once used to age Kentucky bourbon. Once matured, the two distillates are blended together to produce Mount Gay Rum products.

Mount Gay Rum produces its traditional rum called Mount Gay Rum Eclipse, a longer aged rum called Mount Gay Extra Old, and a brandy-tasting rum called Mount Gay Rum Sugar Cane Brandy. Mount Gay also produces a clear, non-aged rum used for mixed drinks. In addition, the company has recently introduced two new products to the U.S. market. The introduction of vanilla and mango flavored rum in the U.S. is an attempt to capture the expanding flavored rum market. Mount Gay products are sold internationally through distributors in Australia, Hong Kong, Denmark, Italy, Mexico, the United States, and the United Kingdom. The largest market for Mount Gay Rum is the United States, however, the company reports that it has strong sales in Canada, the Caribbean, and Europe, and that those sales are getting even stronger.

Mount Gay Rum has been associated with sailing for centuries. Barbados is a difficult island from which to sail across the Atlantic due to its prevailing winds and currents. As a sign of sailing ability, sailors would buy a barrel of Mount Gay Rum before returning to Europe. The possession of this rum indicated that the sailor had visited the island and had the skill to make the transatlantic voyage from Barbados. Today Mount Gay Rum keeps the tradition alive by sponsoring over 100 regattas worldwide. The regattas allow Mount Gay Rum to promote its products in various parts of the world.

FUTURE CHALLENGES

Mount Gay Rum faces increasing challenges in order to retain its independence. The dominance of Bacardi in the market and many small producers makes it difficult to compete. Mount Gay Rum has relied on tradition as a competitive advantage in the past but that may no longer be enough. The increasing marketing sophistication of Bacardi and fragmentation of product categories places smaller producers at a disadvantage. In addition, with falling trade barriers, Caribbean countries are facing increased competition from Latin American and Asian companies.

The West Indian Caribbean countries, of which Barbados is a member, recently received a 70 million euro grant from the European Union (EU) to help make the Caribbean rum industry competitive. The grant is the result of an agreement between the U.S. and the EU, which removes trade barriers in the areas of spirits and telecommunications. It is feared that the Caribbean countries will not be competitive against larger producer countries such as Brazil and countries that subsidize their rum industries. The Caribbean rum industry employs over 50,000 people and the EU grant to the 15 Caribbean countries is intended to guard against a reduction in employment in the industry. The majority of the grant will be used for production upgrades, but a smaller portion of the grant is to be used to help smaller companies develop business and marketing plans to help them compete in the changing industry.

As Mount Gay looks to the future, it must consider the current trends that may help or hinder its competitive position. The increasing popularity of rum is a positive trend, however, beverage trends can be short-lived and Mount Gay must be aware of the increasing market power of its biggest competitor, Bacardi.

Discussion Questions:

1. Discuss the strengths, weaknesses, opportunities, and threats facing Mount Gay Rum.

2. What do you recommend as a competitive advantage for the company?

3. Develop a marketing plan for Mount Gay Rum that you feel will help the company to stay competitive.

Sources: Author Unknown. (2002). *Caribbean rum makers narrow definition of drink*. EFE World News Service, October 28; Author Unknown. (2004). *Fine rums are at their best when served in a snifter or just over ice.* Cigar Aficionado, August; Author Unknown. (2004). *UK, US consumers to taste Indian rum from UB group.* Asia Pulse News, April 6; Broberg, M. (1989). Barbados. New York: Chelsea House Publications; Cioletti, J. (2004). *Here are a few more colors to add to the palette.* Beverage World, July 15; Miller, K. (2004). Business Barbados. St. Thomas, Barbados: Caribbean Business Publications; Percival, D. (2003). *Adding punch to the Caribbean rum industry.* The Courier ACP-EU. May-June; Plotkin, R. (2004). *Moving on up: The rum category continues to grow, on the strength of an approachable taste, great mixability, new flavor introductions, and popular image.* Beverage Dynamics, July-August; Turrettini, J. (2004). *Their man in Havana.* Forbes, February 16; http://www.countrywatch.com. Accessed on October 9, 2003; http://www.ministryofrum.com/rum101.html Accessed on October 9, 2003; http://www.rum.cz/galery/cam/ht/barb/index.htm. Accessed on October 9, 2003.; http://www.mountgay.com. Assessed on October 9, 2003.

Case prepared by Charles A. Rarick.

CASE 28

TONIA MOTORBIKES: CHINESE PIRACY

Tonia Motorbikes is the third largest manufacturer of motorized scooters in Japan. The company sells its product, a 125cc vehicle in Japan, Taiwan, Korea, Vietnam, and other Asian markets.

In an effort to reduce labor costs and to penetrate the Chinese market, Kenichi Hoskia, CEO of Tonia, decided to establish a manufacturing operation on the Chinese mainland. Tonia invested $17 million in a state-of-the-art production facility. The Chinese government had insisted on Tonia making a major commitment in order to enter China, including the establishment of a facility equipped with Tonia's most advanced manufacturing technology.

Tonia formed a joint venture with China's Happy Motors, a large, state-owned motorbike manufacturer. Tonia was required to share its technology secrets with Happy as a condition of the joint venture agreement. At first Kenichi resisted; however, the Chinese government assured him that it was in the best interests of both partners to keep the information secret. The Chinese government guaranteed that no one outside the partnership would be allowed access to any of Tonia's trade secrets. Since this guarantee came from high levels of the Chinese government, Kenichi felt more comfortable letting Happy Motors gain insight into the recent advances Tonia had made in small engine design. The thought of a market with 1.25 billion consumers was also a factor in his decision to share critical trade information.

After only five months of producing motorbikes in China, a Tonia employee noticed the Tonia 125 model being sold over the Internet for $2200. Since the machine sold for $3,400 in Japan and $2,600 in China, the employee questioned how a new bike could be sold so cheaply. Further investigation led Tonia to Yiwu, China, where the seller was located. It was learned that Yiwu is the counterfeit capital of China, a place where counterfeiters from all over the country come to distribute their goods. Upon investigation, Tonia employees learned that the motorbikes being sold under the Tonia brand name were indeed counterfeit products.

With the help of an investigator in China, Tonia learned that not only were counterfeit bikes being sold in China, but that they were being exported to other Asian countries and some were even being exported to the United States and Europe. It was obvious to Kenichi that someone at Happy Motors had sold Tonia's technology. Not only was Tonia losing sales due to the counterfeit goods, but Kenichi also worried that if the quality of the product were inferior, consumers in important markets would be lost for future sales. Kenichi feared that if this situation were left unchecked, the potential existed to ruin the strong brand name Tonia had established.

Kenichi continued to investigate the source of the counterfeited goods but was unable to determine where the products were being manufactured. Rumor had it that a former Taiwanese counterfeiter, who was expelled from Taiwan when the government cracked down on product piracy, had moved to the Guangdong province of China and was manufacturing Tonia brand scooters there. It was also rumored that this individual had connections with Chinese government officials; however, there was no proof that these rumors were true.

After six months of investigation, Kenichi still could not determine the source of the counterfeit bikes and it was becoming clear that further investigation would probably not reveal the source. Kenichi did learn that, regardless of official government policy, product piracy was rampant in China. Weak laws, poor enforcement, and light penalties made counterfeiting a very lucrative and attractive business in China. Kenichi sat in his office and pondered his next move.

Discussion Questions:

1. Do you find it conceivable that state-owned enterprises in China are engaging in product piracy? Explain.

2. What effect has China's entry into the World Trade Organization (WTO) had on product piracy?

3. What should Kenichi do about this problem?

Note: This case is fictional; however, some source material is from "China's Piracy Plaque," <u>Business Week</u>, June 25, 2000.

Case prepared by Charles A. Rarick.

CASE 29

INSULTING ISLAM, ONE STEP AT A TIME

Pegasus Footwear was an international manufacturer, well known throughout the world for its product design and marketing savvy. Products were designed at company headquarters in the United States, and Pegasus used an extensive system of contract manufacturing to produce a variety of mostly athletic shoes sold throughout the world.

Charles Clark, or C.C., was the regional manager in charge of Pegasus operations in Southeast Asia. Clark, a British citizen, was responsible for manufacturing and marketing in the entire region. C.C. had been with Pegasus for 10 years and was recently promoted to his present position. The position was seen as a very important one, since most of the contract manufacturing for Pegasus occurred in this region of the world. C.C. was a graduate of Oxford University and began work at corporate headquarters in Los Angeles shortly after receiving his M.B.A. from Stanford. His management style was often described as visionary; however, some of the local managers felt that C.C. possessed a somewhat condescending attitude toward employees from less-developed countries.

C.C. and his team in Southeast Asia were considered very successful by top management back at corporate headquarters. As a result, C.C. earned an unusual degree of autonomy for his group. C.C. oversaw the manufacturing operations in the region (which employed over 1,000 people) and was primarily responsible for the marketing of products that were manufactured in the region. Most of the products, however, was sold in the United States and Europe, and responsibility for marketing in these regions was held by the respective regional managers. All product design was created in the Los Angeles office.

When C.C. arrived in his office on Tuesday morning, he received word of a problem. Storeowners in Indonesia were reporting problems with aparticular shoe that had recently been designed by Pegasus. The shoe called AirBurner, was upsetting Muslim consumers who objected to the design found on the outer heel of the shoe. The design (Figure 1), which spelled "air," was written to resemble fire, but some consumers felt that the design spelled "Allah" in Arabic (Figure 2). Since the shoe is considered by many to be the dirtiest part of clothing, it was considered a major insult to find the word for Allah, or God written there. Storeowners tried to explain that the word was not "Allah" but rather "air," written in flaming letters. Most consumers were not satisfied with the explanation.

C.C. asked for an accounting of the number of shoes produced with the design and was told that 100,000 pairs had already been produced, and that more were being made. One-fourth were to be sold in his region and the rest were on sale in other parts of the world. Although each shoe had a direct cost of production to Pegasus of $6.75 and a recall of all 25,000 pairs in his region would not significantly affect profitability, CC decided not to recall the controversial shoes. He stated: "Pegasus is proud of the fact that we have never had a product recall and we don't intend to start one with this silly design issue. The design clearly spells the word air and it should not be an insult to anyone." C.C. felt that the whole issue would "blow over" in a few days and that a recall would just tarnish the image of Pegasus Footwear.

The problem did not go away and on Thursday C.C. received an urgent call from an employee in Indonesia who informed him that angry crowds were damaging stores, that carried the shoe. Newspapers in the country had reported the story and implied that the product was part of an America plot to discredit and insult Muslims. An international Muslim organization was now calling for a worldwide boycott of all Pegasus products and there was fear that the problem would spread to other countries with significant Muslim populations. C.C. had just been told that the CEO of Pegasus Footwear was waiting on the telephone to speak with him and that she was quite upset about the whole affair.

Discussion Questions:

1. What went wrong in this situation?

2. Do you think that an early recall of the product would have headed off the problem?

3. What would you recommend to C.C. and Pegasus?

Note: This case is based in part on an actual situation; however, it is a fictionalized account and not intended to represent the facts of the real case.

Case prepared by Charles A. Rarick.

Figure 1

PEGASUS DEIGN

Figure 2

WORD ALLAH IN ARABIC

CASE 30

PLUNGE FURNITURE FACTORY - LITUANIA

Plunge Furniture Factory, Inc. (PFF), a privately owned company in Plunge, Lithuania, specializes in building custom-designed kitchen and bathroom cabinets and furniture. It employs 50 people, including managers, and was initially established in 1989. The top management team consists of Jonas Lapas, general manager (CEO), Petras Vilkas, senior manager, and Jurgis Berzas, executive manager. By post-Soviet standards, the company has been quite successful; not only has it survived the difficult early post-Soviet years, but it has experienced steady growth. After the breakup of the USSR, many private firms were established and most of them failed.

While multinational and other foreign firms have entered the market, restrictive and protective legislation discouraged many firms from investing in Lithuania. Additionally, many foreign investors considered investing in Lithuania as a very high-risk venture. As the political and economic situation became more stable, and more realistic laws that favored foreign investment were passed, foreign investment started to grow, with Europeans investing considerably more than U.S. firms. Many of the local firms could not survive the foreign competition because of the commonly held attitude by consumers that foreign goods are superior to locally produced good.

Jonas Lapas was one of the first investors in PFF and is very proud of its success. He has been approached by IKTO, a large international manufacturer of modular Scandinavian-style furniture. IKTO has already purchased eight small furniture-manufacturing facilities in Lithuania, and it is common knowledge that IKTO plans to open a facility in the free trade-zone in Klaipeda, Lithuania's major port on the Baltic Sea. IKTO wants to purchase PFF, which Jonas and the other top managers are very hesitant to sell. However,

IKTO has also proposed a private branding arrangement to PPF. This would entail shifting production to standardized, modular-style furniture, something that would not be that difficult to do. IKTO would guarantee them higher sales than PFF now has and the contract would be for five years, after which either side could renegotiate the deal.

Jonas Lapas, Petras Vilkas, Jurgis Berzas, and Antanas Upe (the fourth major shareholder but one who does not work for PFF) will be meeting tomorrow to discuss IKTO's proposal. Jonas knows that, regardless of what PFF does, IKTO will expand in Lithuania and the rest of Eastern Europe because of the availability of relatively cheap labor. He is also concerned that by agreeing to a private-label arrangement, PFF might lose its independence and this could be a very risky proposition. Jonas thinks that an outright sale might be more feasible. He must decide before the meeting which course of action he should propose. He also must determine what the selling price of PFF should be if the other owners decide to pursue this course of action. Lastly, Jonas must decide whether PFF should pursue a long-term private branding arrangement with IKTO, and if so, what conditions should be applied to this type of an arrangement.

Lithuania's population stands at 3.7 million and its agricultural and industrial sectors account for 9% and 28% of GDP, respectively. It has relatively limited natural resources; forests cover about 30% of its 65,000-square-kilometer territory. Upon regaining its independence in 1991, Lithuania was left with remnants of 50 years of central planning and integration with the countries of the former Soviet Union, including a distorted relative price structure, severe macroeconomic imbalances, and an economy biased heavily toward agriculture and light industry. Independence brought with it a severe terms-of-trade shock, as Russia increased the prices of oil and other raw materials exported to Lithuania to world market levels. Under Soviet rule, these items had been priced artificially low. This resulted in high inflation and a breakdown in trade relations that led to a sharp initial decline in output and living standards.

The government also started a parallel program of structural reforms that began with extensive liberalization of domestic prices, financial markets, non-agricultural foreign trade, and capital flows.

Lithuania's enterprise and private-sector development reforms have in some respects been models of such reforms for all the post-Soviet countries. By 1999, the privatization program had successfully transferred assets into private hands, with nearly all small businesses and some 60% of industrial enterprises privatized through a voucher scheme. While most long-term fundamentals remain sound, Lithuania's short-term path was fundamentally altered by the August 1998 crisis in the Russian Federation. Trade with the Commonwealth of Independent States (CIS) fell in 1999. In spite of increasing trade flows with the West, GDP growth slowed to a still solid 5.1% for 1998, before actually turning negative in the first quarter of 1999. The government is presently trying to do whatever it takes to achieve membership in the European Union (EU). The country is pursuing candidacy for membership and hopes to achieve full membership status in the early part of the next decade. Thus, the government is pursuing policies to bring Lithuania in accord with EU directives in a broad range of areas.

Under the Soviet system, the central planners in Moscow decided where, how, and when products would be produced within the USSR. Factories in Lithuania produced a variety of goods, including highly sophisticated products for the Soviet military. Only the planners in Moscow had access to the whole picture and coordinated the supply chain from start to finish. The heads of the government-owned enterprises in Lithuania received their raw materials and supplies without knowing the source of supply; upon completion of the manufacturing process, the goods were loaded into trucks or rail cars and left the plant without the local managers knowing where this output was headed. Goods destined for local consumption were the exception to these rules. With independence, Lithuanian firms were now on their own. They have to scramble to locate supplies as well as customers; something they had no experience doing.

PFF employs 50 people and was established as a privately held corporation. During Soviet times, it had been a branch of Minija, a large government-owned enterprise that had branches throughout Lithuania. Minija specialized in producing all sorts of folk art: crosses, carved wooden roadside crosses, walking sticks, and the like. The Plunge branch specialized in producing carved telephone shelves and desk calendar holders. With the introduction of economic reforms in the 1980s, Minija started downsizing and selling some of its branches. Jonas Lapas, a manager at Minija's Plunge branch, recruited two other managers, two woodworkers who worked in the factory, and Antanas Upe, a friend who was an executive at another company, to join forces and buy the Plunge branch. These men formed a cooperative and became joint owners of this cooperative. The owners soon changed the cooperative into a privately held corporation. Two of the owners sold their shares, leaving Jurgis Lapas, Petras Vilkas, Juozas Berzas, and Antanas Upe as co-owners of the new enterprise.

The men decided early on that they would be manufacturing kitchen and bath cabinets. They did not see a financially rewarding future in the manufacture of handmade folk art products. The technology they had just purchased consisted of woodworking equipment, and the new owners knew that the equipment could easily be refitted for cabinet making. They believed that there existed a considerable transfer of skills between the two production processes. Both required excellent woodworking skills and both were very labor intensive. Most of the cabinets that the firm initially sold were hand-carved with traditional Lithuanian motifs, while all their competitors made standard cabinets from plywood covered with a thin brown-colored veneer called "Finnish."

At first, PFF made only the standardized cabinet set that was popular in the Soviet Union, using the same process that the other kitchen and bathroom cabinet makers used, except that the company was able to differentiate itself by offering three colors in addition to the usual brown. PFF then started making its cabinet doors out of solid wood. Today PFF makes kitchen and bathroom cabinets in a wide variety of sizes and shapes, all meeting EU market standards. All cabinets are custom ordered and no standardized sets are manufactured.

When PFF made its first standardized set of kitchen cabinets, the set was brought to Vilnius (the capital) and displayed on Antanas Upe's front lawn. The set sold very quickly and people started ordering more sets. Each of the six founders also had a kitchen and bathroom set made for their home. Word-of-mouth advertising led to orders and the company grew. The foreign exchange store in Vilnius started carrying the cabinets. However, only consumers having access to large amounts of foreign exchange could purchase these cabinets. Soon Vilnius Furniture, Klaipeda Furniture, and Sauliai Furniture (Vilnius, Kaunas, Klaipeda, and Sauliai are the largest cities in Lithuania) started carrying PFF's products. The target market was the very affluent and well-connected consumer. Some competitors tried copying PFF's high-gloss finishing style. but were not able to match PFF's quality. Today PFF has no local competitors manufacturing these high-gloss colored cabinets but foreign competitors have started to enter the market.

As was customary in the former USSR, PFF did not use any advertising except for displaying the product on Antana's front lawn and showing off the installed cabinets in their homes to friends. Yet everything the company initially produced sold. By 1998, PFF was selling average of 100 sets a month. PFF's target market is still the affluent consumer. Its products are out of reach of most consumers since the amount of disposable income that most Lithuanians have is quite limited; additionally, people are not used to installment buying. Most could not get a loan and others are very concerned about their ability to repay the loan. Many do not like the idea of paying interest and will try to save their money to make cash purchases, thus avoiding any interest payments.

PFF management feels that it has no local competitors that can match its quality. They proudly tell their customers that each unit that they produce is made with the same care that they would take if they were "making it for their own home." In 1997, PFF was the only Lithuanian manufacturer using the colored high-gloss laminate process. Others who tried were unsuccessful because they were unable to duplicate PFF's quality standards. However, Finnish, Swedish, Norwegian, and German firms have entered the market with a wide variety of high-quality products. Jonas Lapas believes that PFF's products and these new foreign competitors' products are of comparable quality. However, since the imported cabinets are priced considerably higher than PFF's cabinets, Jonas thinks that PFF will fare well against these competitors

In 1996-1997, the number of stores carrying PFF's products

increased to six and the foreign-currency store no longer existed. Additionally, a building supply center in Kaunas that serves as a broker for building materials also takes custom orders for PFF cabinets to be used in new construction. PFF has started advertising in the mass media, using television, radio, newspaper, and magazine ads to promote its products. It takes part in Lithuanian trade shows whenever possible. Trade shows in Lithuania are widely attended by the public and builders.

As Jonas sits in his office, he tries to come up with recommendations for tomorrow's meeting concerning IKTO. The economy has taken a turn downward and a drop in orders has occurred. Jonas believes that this is just a temporary drop and that sales will increase as the economy improves. However, some of the owners think that selling to IKTO would be a wise decision or at the very least that, PFF should consider leasing some of its production facilities to IKTO. IKTO, however, is not interested in a partial arrangement; it wants the whole manufacturing facility converted to the manufacture of IKTO products. It would prefer to use PFF because of its skilled work force and reputation for high-quality work, but IKTO can purchase or setup manufacturing facilities in Lithuania on its own.

Discussion Questions:

1. What difficulties do companies in countries formerly organized as centrally planned economies face as they attempt to compete in the global marketplace?

2. Create a marketing plan for Plunge that will allow the company to compete with a larger, more established producer.

3. Should the owner of PFF sell out to IKTO? Explain.

Sources: www.neris.mii.lt/history/html, accessed June 26, 2000 ; www.lrytas.lt.html, accessed March 27, 2001; www.worldbank.lt.html, assessed March 10, 2001.

Case prepared by Birute Clottey.

EXERCISE 10

MARKETING TO THE MEXICANS

Purpose: To determine the suitability of a promotional campaign developed in one country for use in another. The exercise is designed to highlight potential differences that should be considered when developing a multinational advertising campaign.

Procedure: Read the short incident below and in small groups discuss why the recommended promotional strategy may not be effective. Also provide suggestions for changing the advertising campaign to be more successful in Mexico.

Incident: The CEO of a successful online investment brokerage firm has decided to enter the Mexican market. He discusses his views with you concerning the firm's promotion in this new market. The CEO feels that the same advertising copy can be utilized, except that Spanish will be substituted for English. The advertisements typically emphasize the firm's low commission structure and operating efficiency. Many of the ads feature a young American couple outsmarting older couples who use traditional brokerage services. The promotional material uses irreverent humor to show that investing wisely leads to long-term financial gain.

Appreciation is expressed to Leticia Ramos who provided assistance in creating this exercise.

Part Six

IMPORT/EXPORT, LOCATION DECISIONS, GLOBAL MANUFACTURING

Cases:
Moonbeam Electronics and Free Zones
Red Dragon Enterprises: Cheap Chinese Labor?
Rocko Handbags
Samuel Bonnie: International Entrepreneur
Mighty-Mart's Contract Manufacturing Issues

Exercise:
Where Do I Find Global Customers?

CASE 31

MOONBEAM ELECTRONICS:
PROFITING FROM A FOREIGN TRADE ZONE

Located in Southwest Missouri, Moonbeam Electronics is a manufacturer of small electrical appliances, such as toasters, toaster ovens, can openers, mixers, and blenders. Moonbeam assembles these products in its Springfield, Missouri facility using a number of foreign suppliers for component parts. Virtually all products are assembled from parts from Japan, Taiwan, Korea, and China.

All of Moonbeam's production occurs in the Springfield facility, and the company employs over 400 people. Although labor costs might be lower in Mexico or Asia, Moonbeam has never considered moving its production operations out of the country. Wages and benefit costs are moderate and the work force is productive. Moonbeam exports approximately 25% of its production output to Latin America, Europe, and Asia. The company hopes to increase its export potential with some product design changes and increased international marketing efforts.

Jim Harrison, vice president of logistics for Moonbeam, has been communicating with an old college friend who recently took a job at the Toyota production facility in Kentucky. Jim's friend told him that Toyota utilizes a foreign trade zone (FTZ) and that Moonbeam could benefit from one as well. After further discussions on the telephone, Jim decided to fly to Kentucky to see the Toyota facility and learn more about the FTZ concept.

Jim learned that Toyota imports from Japan component parts for its automobile manufacturing, and that by utilizing a FTZ the company avoids paying any customs duties on the component parts until the cars leave the FTZ. If the autos are exported out of the United States, then Toyota pays no tax on the component parts at all. It was explained to Jim that an FTZ is an area in the United States, that is considered to be international territory, and, therefore, U.S. customs duties do not apply.

Jim has further learned that there are two types of foreign trade zones, a general-purpose trade zone and a subzone. The general-purpose trade zone operates for the benefit of several different companies and the subzone is established for one company's use exclusively. Toyota has a subzone for its production operations in Kentucky. From his visit Jim has decided that there are three benefits to operating in an FTZ: (1) delay of payment of custom duties, (2) possible elimination of custom duties, and (3) the bypassing of U.S. Customs regulations. He is confident that Moonbeam can realize all three benefits, but he wants to further investigate this idea before he formally presents a proposal for adoption to senior management.

Discussion Questions:

1. Research foreign trade zones and determine if Jim is correct in his assertions concerning the potential benefits.

2. Specifically, how might Moonbeam benefit from the establishment of an FTZ? Are there any disadvantages?

3. Would you recommend that Moonbeam establish a subzone? Explain.

Sources: G. Hanks and L. Van "Foreign Trade Zone", Management Accounting, January 1, 1999; J. Daniels and L. Radebaugh, International Business, Upper Saddle River, NJ: Prentice Hall, 2001.

Case prepared by Charles A. Rarick

CASE 32

RED DRAGON ENTERPRISES:
CHEAP CHINESE LABOR?

Rex Adams is about to leave China and may never return. He has experienced difficulties that he never imaged he would find in a foreign joint venture. His company, Batrionics hoped that China would provide a source of lower cost manufacturing; however, what he found was corrupt government officials, dishonest managers, and poor quality products.

CHINA

The Chinese called their country the "middle kingdom," meaning that China was at the center of the world. For centuries China was in fact the world's leading civilization and sought to keep foreigners out by building a wall thousands of miles long. Although China is officially a communist state, since 1979 the country has been moving towards a capitalistic economy and now eagerly invites foreigners into its economy. The "iron rice bowl," where all workers in China were guaranteed a job, is being replaced by a market-driven system. Although China still has many state-owned enterprises, economic reform is moving rapidly as China becomes a major player in the global marketplace. China became a member of the World Trade Organization in 2001. Having the largest population of any country, with over 1.3 billion, China is often seen as a country with enormous market potential. The cost of labor in many parts of China represents some of the lowest labor costs in the world. China represents the fasting growing economy in the world and many foreign companies have invested in the country in recent years. The large population, and the hope of tapping into that market, as well as those who are looking for a low cost manufacturing location lure many investors.

While many investors have found success in China, a number of foreign investors have experienced great difficulties. Batrionics was one those companies which experienced difficulties.

BATRIONICS

The company was established in 1984 by two Australians as a small manufacturer of laptop computer batteries. Batrionics produced replacement laptop batteries at a cost lower than the original manufacturer and quickly became successful. The batteries were first produced in Australia, and then in Taiwan. When one of the founders died of a sudden heart attack, the remaining founder, Rex Adams, took total control of the business. He expanded the product line into a number of different types of industrial batteries. The industrial battery market is a very competitive one; a market where small price differentials make all the difference. Early in the business the founders learned that if they hoped to be competitive, they would have to move their manufacturing operations out of Australia. Taiwan proved to be a good choice, having much lower production costs and an ability to produce a quality product. The wholly-owned operation in Taiwan was satisfactory for a number of years, however, increased price sensitivities in the market caused Rex to consider other manufacturing locations. An obvious choice was China. Rather than completely shutting down the manufacturing operations in Taiwan and moving them to China, Rex decided to enter into a joint venture agreement with a Chinese manufacturer, and to gradually reduce the company's operations in Taiwan.

RED DRAGON ENTERPRISES

After doing some investigation, Rex discovered a small manufacturer of batteries and related industrial products in China called Red Dragon Enterprises. In addition to producing small batteries for the consumer market, Red Dragon also manufactured automotive batteries, watch batteries, switches, timers, electrical cords, smoke alarms, and air purifiers. The company was eager to find a foreign partner who could provide capital for expansion and help the company improve its quality. Red Dragon was considered a quality producer in China, but its products were not of a high enough quality to be sold outside China, with a few exceptions.

The owner of Red Dragon was Tsang Wai. Tsang was a self-made man. After the death of Mao Zedong in 1976, Tsang saw an opportunity in China. With the death of the communist leader he began to manufacturer small electrical products at home, using scrap material from the state-owned factory where he worked. Although this practice was strictly illegal at the time, Tsang did not let that stop him. He moved his manufacturing operations out of his small home when the Chinese government began to allow small businesses to operate legally. At that point he was able to hire workers and expand the product line. Tsang's sales and profits grew rapidly, and being very frugal, he was able to put much money back into the business and grow the company even more. Red Dragon was a respected brand in China but the company had not been successful in exporting its products to the United States and Europe. Some of Red Dragon's products, such as the smoke detectors and water purifiers were sold in some Southeast Asian countries. The company's batteries, however, were not seen as being competitive against international brands.

Rex Adams heard about Red Dragon and was interested in the company because of its experience in producing some of the batteries his company sold. While he was aware of the problems of poor quality, Rex felt that he could install new procedures in the company and improve the company's ability to produce quality batteries. He wanted to find a company that was struggling, and where improvements could be made, because he felt that he could leverage his company's knowledge and skill against the joint venture partner. When Rex approached Tsang, he found a highly motivated and energetic man who was very interested in expanding his operations and becoming a global player. Rex at first referred to Tsang Wai as Mr. Wai, forgetting that in China, the family name comes first and that Tsang Wai would really be Mr. Tsang. The two men got along well, even though Tsang's English proficiency was limited. Tsang had a young assistant who spoke English and who helped him to communicate with Rex. The young assistant would never make eye contact with Rex, and at times, Rex wondered if he was really translating correctly. At one point Rex put his arm around the young man and asked if he was being fair in his translating. His level of discomfort made Rex wonder even more about the translation.

AGREEMENT IS REACHED

After a number of trips to China, and many days spent negotiating, the terms of the joint venture were agreed upon. When Rex asked Tsang to sign a contract, he refused. He told Rex that the entire relationship should be based upon trust, and that a contract only represented "paper trust," and would be meaningless. Rex was going to be investing a significant amount of money in the joint venture and felt very uncomfortable doing so without a formal agreement. He told this to Tsang and finally Tsang replied, "OK, we put dragon blood on paper." Not really sure what he meant, Rex felt that this implied that a contact would be created. After still more discussion, and at times argument, the two men agreed to have a simplified document drafted, one which was much more general and open-ended than Rex had planned. He had heard that the Chinese did not like contracts, and that business relationships in China were based on trust and "face" more than legal documents. Although feeling very uneasy about the lack of a detailed formal contract, Rex nevertheless signed what amounted to a general letter of intent. Tsang told Rex that he had recently visited a fortuneteller and that she told him that the joint venture was going to be a "big success." Tsang told Rex that his future in China was bright and that the joint venture would bring both of them good fortune.

At the insistence of Tsang, the joint venture was named Red Dragon Enterprises. Rex had reservations concerning the name, feeling that this would create confusion and not clearly separate the joint venture from Tsang's business. Tsang insisted on the name, telling Rex that the name brought good luck to him and anything else would "encourage evil spirits." The manufacturing operations were located in Nanjing and the agreement would have to be approved by local government officials, or so Rex was told. After Rex had his bank in Australia wire his company's investment to China, Rex and Tsang went to see the government official. Rex was pleased that the government official, Lee Yi, spoke English well. She explained some conditions that would have to be met in order for Batrionics to operate in China. The conditions appeared reasonable to Rex and the meeting went smoothly. Official approval of the joint venture would be made by a committee, Rex was told, and would probably take a few weeks. Rex felt that he was on his way to securing a low cost base of manufacturing.

After two weeks, Rex became concerned when there was no word yet about the government approval of the joint venture. Rex had stayed in China waiting for approval and was getting anxious. Tsang had already begun to spend some of the capital Rex had provided for the partnership, and it was an uncomfortable feeling having the money spent without official approval of the project. Tsang told Rex that there would not be any problems and that the two should continue to plan for expansion. After four weeks of being in China and still no approval, Rex demanded that he and Tsang go to the government official and see what was causing the delay. When they were finally able to get an appointment with Ms. Lee, her disposition did not appear to be as pleasant as before. She told Rex that sometimes these approvals take longer than expected and she felt that the problem with approval was an inadequate level of infrastrure at Red Dragon. When asked for details, Lee told the men that the electrical and water systems of the manufacturing facility were not acceptable, based on government standards. She recommended that Rex hire a contractor to make improvements to these two systems. Rex was concerned that this would delay expansion even further, but Lee told him that she had the name of someone who could do the job quickly and get the plant approved. Rex asked for the name and made the necessary arrangements. Minor improvements were made to the Red Dragon facility, yet the costs appeared not to be minor. Rex agreed to pay the entire costs of the improvements yet he felt that the joint venture was being exploited by the local government.

After another week of waiting, official approval came for the joint venture. Rex was very happy and Tsang commented that although Rex thought it took a long time, it really was expedited because he, Tsang, had "guanxi' or connections. Rex didn't think the process went very quickly and dismissed the guanxi claim. Over the next couple of months Rex made many trips to China and brought managers from Taiwan with him from time to time to consult with the managers at Red Dragon. Additional equipment was purchased, and it finally began to appear that the venture was moving ahead. Tsang informed Rex that the joint venture would need additional capital soon. This came as a complete surprise to Rex as he had planned on not providing any more capital at all for the project. Tsang explained that costs had been higher than expected and that unless additional capital was provided, the quality improvements Rex had demanded could not be achieved. Rex reluctantly agreed to provide more capital.

With a business to oversee in Taiwan, Rex left China and spent the next three months between Taiwan and Australia. He left Tsang in charge of the Chinese operation. Tsang made regular reports to Rex, and the reports were always very favorable. Production was increasing, quality was improving, and Red Dragon was about to embark on an international sales drive. Rex began to plan a reduction in the Taiwanese operations as he was going to soon be receiving batteries from China. One of most trusted managers from Taiwan, Chen Wah was asked to visit the Chinese facilities and to measure the progress Red Dragon was making in being able to supply Batrionics with the needed batteries. It was planned that when the facilities in Taiwan were phased out, Chen would still be employed by Batrionics and would help manage the Chinese joint venture.

BAD NEWS FROM CHINA

Chen traveled to China and made a shocking report to Rex. He had found that the batteries being produced by Red Dragon for Batrionics were not being made of sufficient quality and that production levels were well below what Tsang had reported. Chen also reported that Tsang told him that the joint venture was again almost out of money and would need an additional capital infusion. Rex told Chen to stay in China and to find out all he could about what was happening there. After another week, Chen reported back to Rex that inventory was missing and that he felt some of the managers at Red Dragon had been stealing the product and selling it through Chinese distribution channels. Chen confirmed that the bank account of the joint venture contained almost no funds. Rex decided that he would have to go back to China and see the problems for himself.

When Rex arrived in China, he met with Chen who provided him with the facts that clearly showed that much of the joint venture's inventory was missing. Chen did some checking and found that the products had been sold inside China. It was easy to identify the products made by the joint venture because the products were produced using the new equipment and the equipment left an identifying mark. When Rex presented Tsang with these facts, he said that employees had stolen some of the inventory and that they had all been fired. When asked what happened to the funds in the joint venture bank account, Tsang replied that mistakes had been made in accounting and that he would be investigating what had happened to the money. Rex was very unhappy with the answers provided by Tsang and he lost his temper. He accused Tsang of stealing the money and dealing with him in bad faith. Tsang said nothing and simply looked towards the floor. Rex decided that it was time for legal or governmental action.

Making an appointment with an official at the office of the Commission for Foreign Economic Relations and Trade, Rex hoped to get Chinese governmental help in solving his problems with Tsang. Rex and Chen visited the office of Mr. Wu, who listened to what the two had to say about the situation and he reviewed the joint venture agreement between Batrionics and Red Dragon. He seemed sympathic; however, he offered little advice. After a long period of silence he suggested that Rex hire a consultant, a former official from the Commission to help solve the problems. Rex told Mr. Wu that he was done hiring people recommended by Chinese government officials and that he was going to seek legal assistance in the matter. Both Chen and Mr. Wu recommended against legal action, telling Rex that the joint venture agreement was too weak to be enforced in his favor.

Rex left the government offices wondering how he had ended up in this situation. He knew that other foreign firms were operating in China, and he assumed that they were not experiencing all of these problems, so he wondered why he had such difficulties. Rex had to decide if he should cut his losses and leave China for good, or if he should try to work with Tsang and attempt to salvage the situation.

Discussion Questions:

1. What mistakes did Rex Adams make in his Chinese joint venture?

2. Do you think the problems Rex Adams faced in China are unique or common? Explain.

3. What should Rex do now?

Sources: Ahlstrom, D. M. Young, and A. Nair. (2002). *Deceptive Managerial Practices in China: Strategies for Foreign Firms*. Business Horizons, November-December; Harris; P. Moran, and S. Moran. (2004). Managing Cultural Differences. Burlington, MA: Elsevier; Li, J. (2000); Passport China. Novato, CA: World Trade Press; www.worldfactsandfigures.com/countries/china

This case was prepared by Charles A. Rarick.

CASE 33

ROCKO HANDBAGS, LTD.:
PROFITING FROM SELLING BELOW COST?

Rocko Handbags manufactures and sells a variety of upscale purses, totes, and other handbags under its popular label. An enterprising young woman named Natalia Martinez, who developed a popular purse, invented the name Rocko, and developed a European flavor for the brand. She had formed the company five years ago and it has done well, commanding a premium price for its products, which are especially popular among teenagers and young women.

At present, the brand is only sold in the United States and Canada. All products are manufactured in the company's Georgia plant, but Rocko has created the illusion that the products are really Italian designer bags. Natalia's promotion message emphasizes European style and quality even though each bag carries a label identifying that the product is "Made in the U.S.A." Savvy promotion has kept the European image alive and it has served the company well.

Natalia wants to develop this image and strong brand loyalty internationally. She hopes to duplicate her domestic success by first entering the Latin American market and later Asia. Through personal contacts, she has been introduced to the senior buyer for a major retail chain in Brazil who expressed interest in carrying the popular Pippi bag. This bag is especially popular among American teens, and the Brazilian buyer feels that it probably would be equally popular among young women in Brazil.

Natalia has just received an offer from the Brazilian retailer to supply 20,000 Pippi bags at a price of $ 8 per unit. Natalia is surprised and disappointed by the offer, since the Pippi bag is sold to retailers in the United States at $22 per unit. After consultation with Rocko's accountants, Natalia learns that the $8 offer is below the cost of production. The total production cost per unit for the

Pippi is $10, and in addition, the accountants worry that not only will Rocko lose $2 for each of the 20,000 units, but also the premium image may be jeopardized if the offer is accepted. There is concern that the product would be sold in Brazil at a price considerably lower than the average U.S. retail price of $35 to $45.

Natalia does not see how she can accept the offer; however, she does want to enter the South American market as soon as possible. Her accountants advise against the move at this time based on their financial analysis (shown below). Although the Georgia plant (operating at 70% capacity) could produce the additional units at this time, Natalia is concerned with the potential loss of profits and prestige.

Pippi Product Line
Cost Analysis

Total Fixed Cost (salaries, depreciation, utilities): $500,000

Variable Cost per Unit:

Direct Labor	**$3.00**
Direct Materials	**2.00**
Total per Unit	**$5.00**

Average Volume - Units per Year:	**100,000**

Average Fixed Cost (500,000/100,000)	**$5.00**
Variable Cost	**$5.00**
Cost per Unit to Produce	**$10.00**

Discussion Questions:

1. Will Natalia lose money if she accepts the Brazilian offer? Explain.

2. What factors other than costs and revenue should be considered in this case?

3. What would you recommend to Natalia?

Case prepared by Charles A. Rarick

CASE 34

SAMUEL P. BONNIE:
INTERNATIONAL ENTREPRENEUR

Emily Devine could not stop starring at the customer sitting at table five. She knew it was wrong to stare, but she could not help herself. Ever since the man walked into the café on South Beach, where Emily works to pay for her MBA classes, she could not shake the feeling that she knew this man's face. He was very handsome, perhaps he was a model, or better yet, an actor or musician. It was not unusual to see rich and famous people in the café on Miami Beach. The man was reading some papers that looked very much like a business plan, and Emily nearly dropped the food in his lap as she read over his shoulder while placing his order on the table. All she managed to see was the letterhead SPB International. Again Emily could not help but feel like she knew that name. "Oh well" sighed Emily, "I better forget about him and get back to my work or I will be looking for a new job."

It was not until that night when Emily was researching a paper her economics class that it dawned on her who this man was. "Where did I put that magazine?" she wondered as she searched the piles of books and journals cluttering here desktop. Finally she found it, last month's issue of *Young Entrepreneur*, and there he was on the cover. She recalled reading the article last month and thinking how he was so good-looking, charming and smart. Emily decided that this is whom she would write her report about and sat down to reread the story of SPB International founder, Samuel P. Bonnie.

Samuel P. Bonnie, Sam to his friends, was just an ordinary guy. He liked to hang out with friends, fish, surf, and when he had a little extra time on his hands, he dappled with molecular chemistry. It was on one of those rainy afternoons in South Florida that Sam made what turned out to be the greatest mistake of his life. It seems that he was fooling around with the properties of foam rubber in order to come up with a better beer coolie to keep his beer cold when he went out fishing. (You know those foam rubber things that people stick beer cans in; they usually have advertising on them.) Sam was trying to develop a liquid that could be put on the foam rubber that would increase its insulation qualities. Sam told the story this way:

> "I was working in my garage lab, and had just put the foam rubber into a tub of the chemical compound when I heard Jack at the door. You all know Jack, Jack Hughes the "American Dream Boy" who won the Gold Medal in cycling at the Olympics in Sydney. I met him when he was in Florida training for the Olympics. Anyway, Jack, who had stopped his training ride because of the rain, and I started talking and watching TV. I think the Wimbledon tournament was on, and I forgot about the experiment in the garage. About an hour later I remembered and ran out to the garage to take the foam rubber out of the solution. The strangest thing had happened. The foam rubber had become hard and what was more peculiar, it had somehow lost over ½ of its weight. About that time the rain had stopped and Jack decide he was going to head home before it started up again. He was putting his bike helmet on when I got a crazy idea…"

The article recalled how Sam spent the next few weeks fashioning a bicycle helmet out of foam rubber and treating it in the same solution. Jack tried the helmet and liked it so much that he wore it to train, and eventually in the Olympics where he won the Gold. There was a great deal of talk in the cycling world (where events can be won by fractions of a second) about "Mr. Hughes' New Helmet." The article went on to quote Sam on his strong beliefs about social welfare. Emily read this with fascination.

> "It has always bothered me to see companies become rich off the blood and sweat of the third world people. Now do not get me wrong I am not saying that companies should not do business in the third world, I just believe that if they do they should be ethical. Pay the workers a wage that will

house and feed a family and do not hire children to work
when they should be going to school. I mean this is not
rocket science, just treat people with basic respect."

Young Entrepreneur told of how SPB International's plant was one
of the first to receive SA 8000 certification for socially responsible
manufacturing. SA 8000 certification indicates to the world that
the manufacturer who possesses this certification has passed an
independent audit of employment practices in areas such as health
and safety, discrimination, free association, child labor, working
conditions, compensation, and management systems. Employers
who are SA 8000 certified agree to pay a living wage, refrain from
engaging in forced or child labor, allow employees to join labor unions
if they desire, and provide fair and humane working conditions and
supervision. The article described how SPB International had recently
built a school and a medical clinic at the plant. These facilities were
free to workers and their families, as well as other local people.

Jessica Francis and Bryan Saba, the senior partners of Francis &
Saba Consulting, had advised SPB International as it was starting
out. They both were greatly impressed by Sam's business savvy.
"Sam brought us in to advise on several aspects of the business, but
in actuality we just confirmed most of his decisions" Saba said when
interviewed for the article. "It was amazing," gushed Francis, "I have
never seen a new comer to an industry make all the right decisions."
Francis and Saba had analyzed the bicycle helmet industry. They
had discovered that the global market was $230 million and that
there were seven firms in the industry with the top 4 firms claiming
$195 million or 85% of the market. Francis and Saba had considered
advising Sam not to enter such a concentrated market. "We had
prepared our report advising Sam to sell his patent to one of the big
boys in the market and to live well on the proceeds until Congress
changed everything", Francis remembered.

Jessica Francis was referring to the Bicycle Helmet Act of 2000.
In an attempt to lower the staggeringly high number of deaths caused
by head trauma resulting from bicycle accidents, and under extreme
pressure from the insurance lobby, the United States Congress passed
a two-pronged law. The law provided that any state that failed to pass
legislation requiring every cyclist to wear a helmet would lose 85% of

all federal highway funds it currently received. The bill also allows for tax incentives for companies that produce helmets.

Most of the states were quick to respond, passing laws that fined un-helmeted cyclists from $500 to $5,000. Many of the states offered subsidies to low-income cyclists that would pay up to half the price of a helmet. Sam recalled what happened next.

> "The American market was going to explode, and here I was sitting on a new formula that could produce better lighter helmets at a fraction of the cost. I had to get into the market. But you cannot wade into a market like that a little at a time, you have to jump in, and jump in big. You know like a cannonball. I knew that the current firms in the industry were not going to make it easy for me. But I was the man who designed the helmet that won the Gold Medal and I think maybe I was just too dumb to be scared. I took all of my savings and got a loan from a buddy of mine who had gotten rich during the dot com boom. (He was one of the few who knew when to get out.) I found a place where we could get the helmets produced and then with the help of Jack as a spokesman I started getting these things on the market."

"Boy" Emily thought, "I can't believe this guy. He is so smart and socially minded, yet he is so humble too." Emily read the conclusion of the article, which outlined the success of SPB International. SPB International has already claimed ten percent of the American market and according to Sam they are now looking at new markets.

> "We may have gotten lucky with the timing on this thing but the truth is we have the best product on the market. If it weren't for Congress, we might not have gotten this big this fast, but I think we would have gotten here eventually. We are now moving into the European market. Jack has done a good job as spokesman here in the US for us but in Europe he is very well known, so we are talking to the better known champions of last year's *Tour de France* about endorsement deals. I expect our sales to become huge in Europe. Besides expanding geographically, we are now looking at branching out into the production of motorcycle

helmet industry and construction hardhats.
And you know, I still need to work on that beer coolie..."

Emily decided that she would use this company as the subject of a paper she needed to write for her economics class. As SPB International expanded, Sam was looking for additional locations in which to establish manufacturing operations. Emily knew from the article that SPB was considering three countries: Indonesia, Cote d'Ivoire (Ivory Coast), and Moldova. An initial investigation into the backgrounds of these countries produced the following information:

	INDONESIA	COTE D'IVOIRE	MOLDOVA
Population	201M	16.4M	4.28M
Population Growth Rate	1.5%	3.8%	.1%
Main Religion(s)	Islam	Islam, Christian, Indigenous	Orthodox
Government	Republic	Republic	Republic
GDP	$142B	$10.4B	$1.5B
Per Capita GDP	$684 US	$660 US	$354 US
Life Expectancy	62 years	46 years	67 years

As Emily looked over these data it became clear to her that there were perhaps more things to consider in a location decision.

Discussion Questions

1. Is Sam's attitude about social welfare and corporate responsibility typical of an entrepreneur? Is it desirable? Explain.

2. What additional information should Emily consider in her analysis for country selection?

3. Which country should SPB International chose for its next manufacturing facility?

Sources: Baye Michael, (2000) Managerial Economics & Business Strategy. Boston, MA: McGraw-Hill Higher Education; Pfeffer Jeffrey, (1998) The Human Equation. Boston, MA: Harvard Business School Press; Social Acc ountability International's website: http://www.cepaa.org; State Department Country Background Notes: http://www.state.gov.; Van Horn, James, (2002) Financial Management & Policy. Upper Saddle River, NJ: Prentice Hall; World Facts and Maps, Rand McNally 2000 Millennium Edition.

Case prepared by Michael Wilcox, Martine Duchatelet, and Charles A. Rarick.

CASE 35

MIGHTY-MART'S CONTRACT MANUFACTURING ISSUES

Mighty-Mart is a large retail chain that operates over 1,000 stores in the United States and Canada. The company has experienced phenomenal success over the years in terms of growth and return on shareholders' equity. The firm has gained market share over its competitors through a strategy of low-cost leadership and dedication to customer service. Mighty-Mart prides itself on its ability to reduce costs and to pass those savings on to customers. The company has been a model of efficiency among mass merchandisers, and its ability to control costs has given it a strong competitive advantage.

Mighty-Mart was founded in 1968 in a small town in eastern Kentucky by Jimmy John Whitlow. This now-deceased, decorated, war veteran left a legacy of uncompromising business principles, which included complete customer satisfaction, low-cost business operations, and a strong commitment to buy from American suppliers.

Anne-Marie Bradford is a well-known television personality who has developed a loyal following through her unwavering commitment to traditional American values. Most TV viewers see her as a kind-hearted and wholesome individual. Anne-Marie's early morning TV program promotes health, fitness, and family values. She also has a newspaper column, which provides advice on marriage, family, and wardrobe decisions. So it seemed logical for Mighty-Mart and Bradford to team up to market a line of women's apparel under the Anne-Marie name. Although Mighty-Mart did prefer to source its products domestically, increasingly it has begun to rely on foreign suppliers.

Under a contract manufacturing arrangement with China's Yellow Dragon Enterprises, Mighty-Mart and Anne-Marie developed the product line, which would be sold exclusively in Mighty-Mart stores.

The cost of production in China was much lower than anywhere else, and Yellow Dragon had developed a reputation for quality. Under the manufacturing contract, Anne-Marie approved all product designs and Mighty-Mart handled the administration of the business relationship. Yellow Dragon Enterprises acted as an independent contractor; however, Mighty-Mart dictated what to produce, when to produce it, and, in many ways, how to produce the products. Day-to-day management of the operations was left to Yellow Dragon.

Although some Chinese manufacturers had been known to violate the human rights of their factory workers, Mighty-Mart was confident that it could force Yellow Dragon to follow Chinese labor laws and treat the employees well. Mighty-Mart had emphasized that it wanted nothing to do with any business that violated basic workplace rights. As a form of control, Mighty-Mart engaged one of the big U.S. accounting firms to audit Yellow Dragon employment practices over the term of the contract.

The U.S. auditors visited Yellow Dragon factories from time to time and often found labor violations. None of the violations were considered to be of a serious nature and most involved the lack of payment for overtime. Yellow Dragon had been reluctant to pay overtime for Saturday work, which was mandated under Chinese law. A few safety violations were uncovered as well; however, Yellow Dragon always corrected the problems uncovered by the auditors and Mighty-Mart was unconcerned with the problems the auditors discovered.

Late one afternoon, Dexter Lewis, CEO of Mighty-Mart received an urgent call from Carol Dempsey, director of external relations for the company. Dempsey explained that she had just received a call from an international labor watchdog group that was accusing Mighty-Mart of running a sweatshop in China. A representative from the International Organization for the Elimination of Sweatshops (IOES) had been told that an angry group of Yellow Dragon employees had stormed the local labor office in the Guangdong province of China, demanding that employment conditions at the company be improved. The workers accused the company of numerous unfair labor practices, including fines, beatings, and underpayment for hours worked. Lewis told Dempsey that she should look into the matter further, and he expressed concern that this incident could tarnish the company's image.

While Dempsey investigated the matter further, IOES alerted the media about the working conditions in "Mighty-Mart's Chinese sweatshops" and public criticism grew against the company and Anne-Marie Bradford. After a week of being attacked in the media, Anne-Marie went before her television audience and tearfully explained that she had no idea that her popular clothing line was being manufactured under sweatshop conditions. She assured the audience that she and Mighty-Mart would end their relationship with Yellow Dragon Enterprises and that her clothes would never again be made under such "horrible" working conditions.

An investigation by the IOES concluded that workers at Yellow Dragon had been working under sweatshop conditions. The IOES stated that the accusations against the company were true and that Mighty-Mart and Anne-Marie Bradford should be ashamed to have allowed these things to happen. According to the IOES, workers had routinely been beaten by company guards, denied overtime pay, forced to work 16 hour workdays, and exposed to unsafe conditions. Management fined workers who spoke out against the company and even refused to allow them to leave company property when they were not working. Yellow Dragon charged workers excessive prices for company housing and food, and sometimes had children as young as 10 years old working in unsafe factory conditions. Many of the charges against the company violated Chinese labor laws.

It was learned that Yellow Dragon had deceived Mighty-Mart and the auditors, sometimes in elaborate fashion. For example, the company had created showcase factories for the auditors to inspect, when most of the clothes were being produced in other factories under less desirable conditions. The company warned employees against speaking to the auditors unless they had good things to say about the company. Threats, beatings, and fines kept Yellow Dragon employees from informing the auditors about the real working conditions of the company.

Although Mighty-Mart had been duped by Yellow Dragon, a number of public interest groups began to speak out against the company. Mighty-Mart was accused of negligence in the control of its foreign manufacturing arrangements. Many in the press questioned the effectiveness of self-regulation of foreign manufacturing and they demanded more government regulation and social accountability.

Discussion Questions:

1. Is Mighty-Mart and/or Anne-Marie Bradford responsible for the working conditions at Yellow Dragon Enterprises? Explain.

2. Can a process of self-regulation ensure that labor rights will be upheld in foreign manufacturing operations? Explain.

3. What should Dexter Lewis do to solve this problem?

Note: This case is fictional; however, it is based on a similar situation as reported in D. Roberts and A. Bernstein, "A Life of Fines and Beatings," Business Week, October 2, 2000.

Case prepared by Charles A. Rarick

EXERCISE 11

WHERE DO I FIND GLOBAL CUSTOMERS?

Purpose: To give students the opportunity to explore means of acquiring international sales and to decide when going global is in the best interests of a company.

Procedure: Read the incident that follows and then research ways in which a small business can find assistance in exporting its product. List and explain at least five means of acquiring foreign buyers, then decide if the business profiled in the incident below is ready to engage in exporting activities.

Incident: Sofia Payne is an artist and entrepreneur. While in high school, Sofia began creating metal artwork as part of an art class. She found the work so exciting that she decided not to attend college; instead, she began to work full-time on her creations. At first she made her artwork in the family garage and sold the products at local arts and crafts fairs. Sofia's artwork became popular in her hometown of Atlanta, and she was able to move out of the family's garage and into her own studio. Her business is quite successful, and she now focuses on creating metal horses, which she sells in galleries across the country. Her most popular item is a life-size model, which she sells for $10,000. While the item has sold well, it has a limited market in the United States, and Sofia hopes to be able to find additional customers internationally. Sofia does not know where to look for international customers and she is seeking your advice.

This exercise was inspired from the work of Dr. Harry Joiner.

Part Seven

INTERNATIONAL HUMAN RESOURCE MANAGEMENT AND CULTURE

Cases:
Trying to Do Business in Mexico, Gringo Style
Kidnapped in Colombia
Ed's Big Career Move
Canada Timber: Negotiating with the Japanese
A Naïve Sahab in India
Au Revoir, Mrs. Williamson

Exercise:
Hofstede's Cultural Classification Model

CASE 36

TRYING TO DO BUSINESS IN MEXICO, GRINGO STYLE

Ted Dorman was looking forward to his new assignment as plant manager at a newly formed American-Mexican joint venture in Guadalajara, Mexico. The American company, Sterling Metal, produced hardware and decorative fixtures for furniture manufacturers in the United States and Mexico. The new joint venture was an attempt to lower labor costs by operating in Mexico.

Ted had worked at Sterling Metal since graduating from college with a degree in accounting. He had worked his way up in the company through accounting, and eventually shifted his career focus to production. Ted found the challenges of managing the production function very interesting, and he was successful in this area. His position at the new company, SterMexicana, would be a promotion for him, and he looked forward to the opportunity of building a new company.

Although Ted had not worked outside the United States before, he felt confident that his managerial abilities would transfer "south of the border." He and his wife enjoyed vacationing in Cancun and they both liked Mexican food, so the idea of spending a few years building a new company in Mexico appealed to him. Ted's wife, Kim was not as excited about the move, since she and their two small children would have to leave family and friends. Kim would also probably not be working in Mexico, as she had done in the United States.

Before the move, both Ted and Kim read travel books on Mexico and visited Guadalajara to select suitable housing. While Kim had reservations about the move, she felt that it would be a good opportunity for Ted and that she and the children would learn to adapt to their new surroundings. After all, she reasoned, they were only planning on living in Mexico for two years; just long enough for Ted to get the plant up and running and profitable. None of the Dorman's spoke Spanish fluently; however, Kim thought that she could get by, since she had taken three years of Spanish in high school. She had heard that Guadalajara was home to a large expatriate community, and that she could isolate herself and the children from Mexican culture if she felt the need. Ted would be working with English speakers mostly, and many people at the plant could do translating for him. A number of SterMexicana managers had been to the United States and were familiar with its culture. Ted and Kim concluded that cultural adaptation would not be difficult, and no matter how hard the assignment, its short duration was manageable.

When the family arrived in Guadalajara, Manuel Angel Menendez Mata met them at the airport. Manuel would be Ted's Mexican counterpart, acting in the official capacity of assistant plant manager, and unofficially as a cultural mentor. Ted and Kim were surprised by the warmth and friendliness of Manuel and his wife Adriana, and they felt very welcomed by their new Mexican friends. Over the next few days Manuel and Adriana helped the new expatriates get settled in and familiar with their new home. Ted appreciated the personal attention Manuel was giving him and his family; however, Ted was anxious to begin discussing the needs of the new business. It sometimes seemed to Ted that Manuel didn't care to discuss the business or that he was very excited about the new opportunity. Manuel seemed more interested in showing Ted and his family the city and discussing its history, politics, and culture.

Once the Dorman family had settled in, Ted was able to turn his attention toward the business. He had many matters to attend to, including a review of the preliminary work Manuel had done in securing the facility, hiring a work force, and establishing an organizational structure. Manuel explained what he had done and how it would work well. He predicted that the new plant would be fully functional in less than two weeks. Ted was very impressed with Manuel's work and looked forward to the opening of the plant.

During their many conversations, Ted felt that Manuel was very friendly and polite, but that he was a bit too formal and not very relaxed. Manuel wore a suit and tie, even when Ted told him that a more casual form of dress would be appropriate. Ted stated that he had no intention of ever wearing a tie the whole time he would be in Mexico. Manuel sometimes referred to Ted as "Mr. Dorman," even though Ted had instructed him to call him by his first name. During their meetings with outside business associates, Ted noticed that Manuel was even more formal. Manuel, who had visited the United States many times and spoke English very well, understood that Americans were more relaxed when it came to such matters, but he was not happy when Ted began to call him "Manny." Manuel was also unhappy with Ted's refusal to recognize his title, "Licenciado" (licensed one), and that he sometimes referred to him as Senor Mata.

Although things seemed to be progressing toward the opening of the plant, Ted began to worry that Manuel's estimate of when the plant would be functional was too optimistic. Manuel insisted that everything was on schedule and that there would be no problems. It did, however, become obvious as the days went by that the plant was not going to be ready, as Manuel had promised. Ted felt that he had been misled by Manny and that he would have to explain to his superiors back in the U.S. why the plant was not going to open on schedule. Manuel finally admitted that some problems had developed with work permits, but he assured Ted that the plant would be operational in an additional week's time. The plant finally opened, five weeks past the scheduled date.

This delay had caused tension between Manuel and Ted, and Ted felt that he could not trust Manuel. Manuel felt that Ted was too impatient, and that he was not sensitive enough to the problems sometimes found in conducting business in Mexico. Manuel complained to a friend that Ted was trying to do business in Mexico, "gringo style." He offered as an example the failed attempt Ted had made to establish a business relationship with a new supplier. Manuel had arranged for a business lunch between Ted, himself, and representatives from a well- respected metals supplier. Manuel explained how Ted offended the Mexican businessmen by attempting to get down to business quickly. The supplier's representatives felt that Ted was too concerned about business matters, especially price, and that he was rushing to close a deal. They were also offended when

Manuel offered to take the visiting businessmen on a tour of the city and show then some important cultural sites and Ted refused to come along. Ted later told Manuel that he felt that the suppliers were not really serious about getting SterMexicana's business, and that, if they wanted to do business with the company, they would have to send only one representative to his office with samples and a price list. Ted told Manuel that he would no longer spend hours discussing politics, sports, and history without any consideration given to the actual business deal.

The plant had been functioning for about six months without any serious problems when Ted received word from corporate headquarters that the plant needed to improve its efficiency. The quality of the product was considered acceptable, however, the American managers were disappointed with the productivity of the plant. Sterling's main incentive for investing in Mexico was the desire to reduce its labor costs and improve its overall operational efficiency. Ted worried that his career mobility was in serious jeopardy if he did not make major improvements. With this in mind, Ted began to look more carefully at Manuel's work.

From the beginning Ted had turned over to Manuel the day-to-day responsibility for running the plant, but he now felt that he would have to intervene and make some significant changes. After analyzing the situation Ted concluded that three major changes should be made. He proposed to Manuel that an incentive pay system be introduced, that a more participative approach to decision making be implemented, and that a number of workers be fired.

The productivity level of the plant was considered low by American standards, and Ted felt that there was simply no incentive for workers to do more than the minimum level of work. He proposed a pay-for-performance plan in which workers would essentially be paid on a piece-rate basis. The workers would also be given more responsibility for planning and organizing their work, and, in some cases, even planning their own schedules. Ted felt that a more flexible scheduling system would eliminate the excessive time off requested by many workers to handle family matters. Ted also created a list of the lowest-performing workers and instructed Manuel to fire all of them immediately. Since the unemployment rate was much higher in

Mexico than in the United States, Ted reasoned that he would have no problem replacing the workers.

Manuel was stunned by what he was hearing from Ted. Manuel was upset, first, that Ted had chosen to invade his areas of responsibility, and he was further upset by Ted's recommendations. Manuel felt that Ted was being too aggressive and insensitive in labor relations matters, and that his recommendations would not be successful in Mexico. He told Ted that there would be problems with these proposed changes; however, Ted did not seem to want to listen.

Although Manuel did not agree with the recommendations, he did as Ted had instructed and began by firing some of the employees Ted had targeted as low performers. He then implemented the pay-for-performance plan and attempted to explain how it would work. Most workers felt confused by the complex, flexible working-hours plan, which involved basic quotas, a two-tiered pay system, and a time borrowing option, which could be used for personal time off, such as doctor's appointments. Manuel simplified the plan so that workers could go home when they had met their quota, or they could continue to work for additional compensation at a slightly lower per-unit rate. Ted felt that workers would be willing to work longer hours even at a reduced rate if their total compensation would rise. After all, he reasoned, "Mexico is a dirt-poor country and people really need money." Finally, Manuel told the plant supervisors about the plan to empower factory workers and allow them some of the decision-making authority that the supervisors had exercised in the past.

Ted had high hopes that his recommendations for change would produce significant improvements at SterMexicana. He was aware that Mexican culture was different from his; however, he felt that business activities were for the most part universal and that efficiency was not a cultural issue. Ted felt that the proposed changes would result in an immediate improvement in overall operating efficiency.

Slowly, however, Ted began to realize that problems were developing with his recommendations. The first problem he confronted was notification that severance pay would have to be paid to the employees he had recently fired. Ted was unaware, and Manuel did not mention, that Mexican law does not operate the same way as U.S. law, in which workers are considered to be hired at will and subject to at-will termination. Ted was also surprised to learn that not all the employees he had targeted for termination had, in fact, been fired. After investigating the situation further, he discovered that five of the employees whom he had instructed to be fired were still working for the company. Ted was shocked to learn that the five employees were close relatives of Manuel. When confronted with this fact, Manuel just shrugged his shoulders and told Ted that he could not bring himself to fire them.

Although Ted was upset with Manuel's insubordination, he was far more concerned with the lack of any productivity gains at the plant. He was told that most workers did complete their tasks more quickly under the incentive plan; however, they elected to go home rather than work additional hours for more money. Ted was confused by this behavior so he asked some of the supervisors to explain it. They didn't provide satisfactory answers so Ted decided that he should conduct interviews with the employees themselves. Working through an interpreter, Ted asked workers about their jobs and what he could do to make them more productive. He was frustrated by the lack of responses he was getting from the employees. When Ted probed more deeply he discovered that the supervisors had not implemented the participative management practices he had ordered.

Faced with poor operating results during the first year of operation, Ted wondered if the decision to take the job in Mexico had been a mistake. To make matters worse, Ted's family was very unhappy about living in Mexico. Ted had been working long hours at the plant and had basically discounted the complaints he had heard from his wife and children. At this point he began to feel that perhaps they were right in their frequent criticisms of Mexican culture. With over a year left in his assignment in Mexico Ted felt frustrated and wondered what he should do next.

Charles A. Rarick

Discussion Questions:

1. What mistakes did Ted make in his management of SterMexicana?

2. Is Manuel responsible for any of the difficulties presented in the case?

3. What should Ted do now to correct the situation?

Sources: R. Malat, Passport Mexico. San Rafael, CA: World Trade Press, 1996; P. Beamish, A. Morrison, and P. Rosenweig, International Management. Chicago: Irwin, 1997; R Sanyal, International Management: A Strategic Perspective. Upper Saddle River, NJ: Prentice Hall, 2001; J. Scarborough, The Origins of Cultural Differences and Their Impact on Management. Westport, CT: Quorum, 2001.

Case prepared by Charles A. Rarick

CASE 37

KIDNAPPED IN COLOMBIA

Although Melissa Woodruff still felt compassion for the people of Colombia, she now realized that she made the biggest mistake of her life when she encouraged her husband to accept a temporary assignment in Medellin. As she reflected on that decision, she felt as if she would never recover from the Colombian experience.

Melissa and Dan Woodruff met in college and married as soon as Dan graduated. Although the couple wanted to start a family, they decided that it would be best to wait until Dan became more established in his career as a marketing manager with Carolina Textiles. The couple settled into a nice home in South Carolina and Melissa was able to complete her undergraduate degree in fashion merchandising. Melissa wanted to design women's clothing, but she had difficulty securing a position with an established company. She instead began to design and manufacturer her own line and sold the garments on ebay. Although she didn't make much money, she greatly enjoyed the challenge of designing a piece of clothing and seeing its actual completion. Dan did well in his career at Carolina Textiles and the couple thought that they might spend their entire lives in the tranquil surroundings of the small South Carolina town where Carolina Textiles was headquartered. However, that vision was not to be.

After working for Carolina Textiles for only five years, Dan was offered an opportunity which he never envisioned. The firm offered Dan the opportunity to manage a large manufacturing arrangement, which the firm had recently established in Colombia. In an effort to reduce labor costs, Carolina Textiles had contracted with a local textile manufacturer in Medellin, and the company needed someone to manage the day-to-day operations, and to protect Carolina Textiles interests in Colombia. Colombia was seen as one of the desirable locations for foreign manufacturing in that Colombia, along with Bolivia, Peru, and Ecuador were part of the Andean Trade Preferences Act. The Act was amended in 2003, which provided for textiles to be brought into the United States, duty-free, provided that the products were manufactured with U.S. cloth. The city of Medellin seemed like a good choice in that the city had a long history in textile manufacturing. Many of the local manufacturing facilities in Medellin operate in free trade zones, or "Plan Vallejo," and they export much of their output to the United States. The industry was well developed and accustomed to exporting.

Dan, and especially Melissa were at first hesitant about spending two to three years in Colombia. Not only would they miss their friends in South Carolina, but they were aware of the political violence in Colombia. After a visit to Medellin, and after much discussion, the couple decided to give it a try. Melissa reasoned that the experience would be good for Dan's career, and he would be getting a promotion along with the assignment. The couple was still young and could start a family after the assignment. The fact that the couple could easily afford to have a maid who would also cook for them was appealing. Melissa also felt that she could continue her design business, and perhaps, even expand it with the abundant manufacturing facilities in Medellin. The couple sold their home in South Carolina, said good-bye to friends, and headed for the challenges which awaited them in Colombia.

Dan and Melissa settled into a rented three-bedroom home in the suburbs of Medellin. For the most part the couple enjoyed living in the "City of Eternal Spring," however, life in Medellin was also stressful. Without much international travel experience, and only a very basic proficiency in Spanish, the couple experienced a significant degree of culture shock. Melissa would email friends about how different it was living in Colombia; from seeing all the armed guards at the mall, to the ability to purchase medicine at a pharmacy without a prescription. Everyday presented its own set of challenges for Dan and Melissa but the couple adjusted fairly well. Dan was busy with work and Melissa was scouting out new ways to establish her design business.

Dan and Melissa had been warned about the political troubles and violence in Colombia. Before leaving the United States they read much on the history of Colombia. They were especially interested in the revolutionary groups that operated against the government. Dan and Melissa learned that Colombia was still a divided country with the smaller, but dominate population of European descent often in conflict with the larger population of mixed ethnicity. The two rival political groups which developed in Colombia, the Conservatives and Liberals had fought in a bloody civil war called "La Violencia" which began in 1948. The main revolutionary group, the Revolutionary Armed Forces of Colombia or FARC developed out of the frustration of some members of the Liberal party. In the 1980's FARC began to fund its revolutionary cause by taxing the illegal drug industry of Colombia. The group continued to control an increasingly larger share of the country and now claims over 40% of Colombia. FARC also began to diversify its source of funding through the kidnapping of prominent Colombians and expatriates. While the kidnapping threat worried Dan and Melissa, they reasoned that neither one of them was a likely target for kidnapping since they were "just average people." They did not limit their outings and generally tried to blend into Colombian society including frequent attendance at the bullfighting events in the city.

The couple felt acclimated to the culture, for the most part, after about six months. Melissa enjoyed getting dressed up and shopping. She enjoyed buying gifts to send back home to friends. The couple developed a daily routine in which Dan would leave for work every weekday morning at 8:30 A.M. driving himself, and Melissa would begin her day on the Internet, answering emails and developing business ideas. Although the couple did not have the opportunity to make many American friends, they did enjoy the company of a few Colombian couples from Dan's work. Melissa truly enjoyed these friendships and developed a degree of sympathy for the less fortunate members of Medellin society. Sometimes she would open her wallet and drop a large cash roll (large by Colombian standards) into the hat or canister of street beggars. This made her feel as if she was making a big difference in someone's life, something she felt she could not do in the United States.

The compassion she felt towards the Colombian people was not tempered even when her purse was snatched in the local market. While she had the equilivant of about $200 U.S. in the purse, she was more concerned about replacing her credit cards and identification. This made shopping difficult in that she would have to carry cash for all transactions, including larger transactions. The purse snatching worried Dan, but he reassured himself that petty crime was a problem in Colombia and that the couple would just have to be more careful. The event passed quickly, and was almost forgotten when a very impressive article was written in the local newspaper profiling Dan and Carolina Textiles. The article was clipped and mailed back to a number of friends in the United States. The couple felt as if they were making new friends in Colombia and that Dan's career was heading in a very positive direction.

All of this, however, was about to change. On a particularly spring-like day, as Dan left for work he had much on his mind. There were a number of improvements he hoped to suggest to the contract manufacturer, including the addition of a more efficient computerized layout pattern for cutting cloth. As he drove the usual route to his office he was reviewing the different supplier options for the new software, and he kept thinking about the recent article about himself in the newspaper. Suddenly his thoughts were interrupted as the vehicle in front of him came to a stop and the driver opened the hood of the car. A second vehicle moved very and very closely behind Dan's new 700 series BMW, so close in fact that Dan was concerned that the two vehicles would crash. Dan motioned to the driver of the van behind him to move back. Instead four armed men wearing handkerchiefs over their noses and mouths got out of the van, grabbed Dan, and placed a cloth sack over his head. They pushed him into the back of the van and quickly took off. Dan, unable to see what was happening, and unable to understand much of what was being said was confused and scared. Surely he thought to himself, "I'm not being kidnapped. They must have made a mistake." Unable to see, and having some difficulty breathing Dan tried to speak to his captors in English, but he got no response. Dan kept asking them "what's going on" and trying to assure them that they must be making a mistake. After a few hours of riding in the back of the hot van and having no water, Dan was hopeful when the van stopped and the door opened. He hoped the ordeal was coming to an end. Unfortunately for Dan, the ordeal was just beginning. He was placed inside another vehicle and it was the beginning of a very long drive into the remote areas of Colombia - an area Dan and Melissa had planned on visiting some day, although under very different circumstances.

Back at home, Melissa was very busy planning her day when someone knocked at the door. Adriana, the housekeeper answered the door as usual and came very quickly calling for Senora Woodruff. She said a man had left this note for her and she seemed very upset. Melissa was confused as she opened the paper she had been given. The note, written in broken English, stated that her husband had been kidnapped and that she should get a short-wave radio. The note indicated a frequency to use with the radio and the times to use it. It was signed "Gabino." Melissa asked Adriana what this all meant and she told her that Senor Woodruff had been taken by FARC and that he was in great danger. Melissa was beginning to become very upset, however, she retained her composure and called Dan's office, hoping it wasn't true. When Dan's assistant told her that he had not yet arrived, she immediately called his mobile phone. There was no answer. Melissa was now frantic. She called Dan's assistant again and explained what had happened. The assistant, Manuel Chacon told her to stay calm and that he would immediately come to the house. Melissa asked Adriana if she should call the police and Adriana told her that it would not be advisable.

When Manuel arrived he told Melissa to remain calm. He had already contacted Carolina Textiles and told them what had happened. Manuel told Melissa that, unfortunately, kidnapping of foreigners was common in Colombia, but that Dan would be released as soon as Carolina Textiles paid the ransom that would be demanded by FARC. Manuel assured Melissa that no harm would come to Dan and that he would be released very soon. Manuel told Melissa that there was nothing that they could do at this time but purchase the short-wave radio and wait for the designated time to contact the kidnappers. He also advised her to pray for a safe and quick return of her husband. Melissa decided to call her parents whom she had little contact with since moving against their wishes to Colombia. It would be a difficult call but she needed their support.

In quick time Manuel purchased the short-wave radio and set it up in the Woodruff's home. He was in constant contact with Carolina Textiles and he relayed their concern to Melissa. Manuel also had to report to Melissa that Carolina Textiles did not have ransom insurance and that this made the situation more difficult. He reassured Melissa that once the kidnappers learned of this fact they would release Dan, maybe with a "token ransom payment." Melissa, after contacting her parents got their pledge to help pay the ransom.

Three very long days passed before Melissa and Manuel were able to make contact with Gabino, the FARC negotiator. Manuel explained how Dan was not a wealthy man and that the company he worked for did not carry ransom insurance. Gabino told Manuel that unless a $2,000,000 US ransom was paid for Dan they would never see him alive again. Manuel again insisted that this was not possible, however, Gabino was unsympathic. The first contact ended without any hope of agreement. Manuel was instructed to try again, once he had arranged for the money transfer. Manuel assured Melissa that the demands were just typical bargaining and that if she could raise about $50,000 US the matter could be settled. Melissa knew that she could raise that much with their savings and the help of her parents. Dan's parents were deceased. Manuel told Melissa that he would seek the help of Carolina Textiles.

With the help of Manuel, Carolina Textiles decided that they should contact a kidnapping and ransom expert to help with the negotiations. Since they did not carry kidnapping and ransom insurance they would have to pay the costs of the negotiator but it was felt that this was a small price to pay for their employee's safety. The external negotiator would not arrive in Medellin for three days, enough time for Manuel to try again with Gabino. On the second attempt at negotiation the same situation arose. Manuel told the kidnappers that they should release Dan since he was not able to pay the ransom and Gabino continued to make threats. Manuel offered the $50,000 with an expectation that the negotiators would agree to a quick resolution. Gabino told Manuel, with Melissa listening, that for $50,000 he would cut off a certain body part from Dan and mail it to Dan's wife. Melissa became frantic and the second session ended very badly.

During all this time, Dan was still traveling with his captors deeper into the Colombian jungle. The first few days he was riding in several vehicles but afterwards he was on foot, always chained to his captors. Dan tried repeatedly to explain that he was not an important person and that no sizable ransom could be paid. He truly believed that the captors would release him, even if in the middle of a jungle, once they believed their effort would not result in a ransom. Although Dan was optimistic that he would be released, he felt very helpless and vulnerable. He worried how Melissa would be handling the news of his abduction. Although exhausted and poorly fed, Dan continued to insist that he be released. Each day brought increasing frustration for Dan, and Melissa.

Melissa began searching the Internet for information about kidnapping. She learned that on an average day 10 people are kidnapped in Colombia. She also learned that in most cases the kidnappers would eventually settle for 10-20% of the original demands. The prospects for a safe return of the hostage were not very good if the negotiation was not conducted properly. Further searching revealed that many companies, which operate in countries with a high probability of kidnapping, carry kidnapping and ransom (K&R) insurance. The policies typically cover the ransom payment, consultant fees, and transportation needed to deliver the ransom and return of the hostage. It appeared that many companies which carry K&R insurance do not advertise the fact for fear that their employees will more likely become targets of kidnapping. Melissa began to wonder if Carolina Textiles did in fact have K&R insurance but it was not being disclosed at this time.

Melissa heard a knock at the door and a man entered. It was Charles Griffith, a security consultant hired by Carolina Textile to help negotiate the release of Dan. Charles introduced himself and appeared to have great confidence in his abilities. He told Melissa not to worry, and that he had successfully handled the negotiations for two other expatriates, one in Mexico and one in Venezuela. He did state that because Carolina Textiles had no K&R insurance it would make the negotiations more difficult. Melissa told Charles that she had read on the Internet that the typical settlement was between

10-20% of the initial demand and that she could probably raise that amount with the help of the company. Charles just responded by saying "we will see."

Charles began the negotiation process with Gabino and the first session did not go well. Gabino at first refused to talk to him and asked to speak with Manuel. Charles informed him that he, Charles, would be handling the negotiations from now on. The communication ended when Charles asked for proof that the rebels did in fact have Dan and that he was alive. Melissa began to worry that Charles was not the right choice for the negotiation sessions and confided this to Manuel.

Days went by and there was no response from Gabino. Feeling frustrated, Melissa asked Manuel to once again attempt to contact Gabino. He agreed and they decided that they would tell Charles that he should defer to Manuel, at least for a while. Charles strongly opposed this suggestion but agreed to let Manuel do the next session due to the strong insistence of Melissa. He encouraged Manuel to explain that a new negotiator was working for the family.

For Dan, boredom was becoming a major issue. He spent his days at a rebel camp, chained either to a tree or to his bed. Dan would often think of Melissa and the various trips they took together back in the United States. He sometimes replayed movies he had seen in his head to relieve the boredom. The heat, lack of food and water, and constant boredom were beginning to fray his nerves. His frequent outburst caused some guerrillas to threaten him with death. All the rebels carried assault rifles and machetes, and some of them appeared to enjoy the possibility of doing harm to Dan. On a couple of occasions Dan attempted to befriend some of the younger rebels by explaining, in broken Spanish, that he and his company were trying to help the Colombian people by creating jobs. It didn't seem that this mattered to the rebels.

Back in Medellin, with Manuel again doing the negotiations it appeared that progress was being made. Gabino told Manuel that it might be possible to release Dan if $1,500,000 could be paid quickly. While it was impossible for Melissa to raise that much money, even with the offer of $100,000 from Carolina Textiles, at least the kidnapper's demands were being reduced. Manuel also was able to have proof delivered, via a photo of Dan holding a copy of El Tiempo (a daily Colombian newspaper) and he seemed to be developing some rapport with Gabino. Charles, while listening to the negotiations offered suggestions to Manuel, but he was becoming increasingly dissatisfied with the role he was playing.

Charles reported back to Carolina Textiles and expressed his concerns with the fact that Melissa was insisting on having Manuel do the negotiating. Charles expressed his doubts that Manuel could ever reach a settlement. The CEO of Carolina Textiles, Ben Goodin called Melissa to persuade her to allow Charles to take over the negotiations. Melissa insisted that Manuel was better suited for the negotiations and that the life of her husband was at stake. Mr. Goodin was not about to press the issue further, and so he wished Melissa luck and asked that he be kept informed. When news got back to Charles that he was not going to be doing the negotiations he decided to leave Colombia. He did offer suggestions to Manuel and told both Manuel and Melissa that the process could take some time.

Every third day Manuel attempted to contact Gabino. Most of the time there was only static over the airways. The process continued for five long months and it was clear that Melissa was feeling the strain. While Carolina Textiles continued to pay Dan's salary, Melissa felt as if they could do more. Not much progress was being made, however, Gabino did agree to reduce the ransom to $1,000,000. This amount was still much more than Melissa could raise. It appeared to her that time was running out and that there was little hope of rescuing Dan.

It was during one of the darkest periods when a bright spot developed for Melissa. A reporter from the BBC was doing a story on Colombian kidnappings and he interviewed her for the story. Once the article was published, Carolina Textiles developed an increased interest in Dan's safety. Mr. Goodin told Melissa that the company was prepared to help with the ransom to the tune of $250,000 and that he would be sending yet another security expert down to Colombia to help in the negotiations. Melissa felt that the $250,000 may be enough for the rebels, and she could even add more from their savings and the contributions from her parents, if needed. Mr. Goodin insisted that the new security expert would be making the new offers and that he would be more successful than Manuel had been.

Upon hearing the good news, Manuel and Melissa contacted Gabino and told him that the company was prepared to make a final offer of $250,000 and that a new negotiator would be contacting him to arrange for the transfer of funds and delivery of the hostage. Gabino did not share the excitement of Manuel and Melissa and all he said to them was that the amount was "not sufficient." Although somewhat surprised by the reaction, Melissa and Manuel maintained their optimism and awaited the arrival of the new negotiator.

Melissa and Manuel met the new security expert at the airport. Frederick Hervitz was a very experienced hostage negotiator and he wasted no time in telling Manuel and Melissa what they would be doing. Frederick insisted that he, and he alone, would be talking to Gabino. Melissa felt confident in Frederick's abilities and was optimistic that the ordeal would soon be over. Manuel agreed that Frederick should take over the negotiations. He was impressed with Frederick and besides; the whole process was becoming a strain on him personally. Manuel and Melissa told Frederick what they had done and what they had accomplished. He told them that they had made many mistakes.

Frederick attempted many times to reach Gabino, but each time all he heard was static. Frederick at first assumed that Gabino was just making it difficult on him in order to raise the ransom, and lower the expectations of Melissa and the company; however, the long silence did begin to worry Frederick. Weeks went by and there was no communication with Gabino. Mr. Goodin telephoned Melissa and told her not to worry, that Frederick would be bringing Dan home soon.

The words of Mr. Goodin were all too true. After six months of enduring the ordeal, Melissa received a call from the American embassy in Bogotá. It was bad news. Melissa was informed that a body, that appeared to be her husband had been discovered in a remote northern province of Colombia. Melissa was devastated. She couldn't speak. She thought, surely it is a mistake, but deep down she feared it was true. Frederick arranged a flight to Bogotá for Melissa, Manuel, and himself. Melissa positively identified the body, although

Dan looked much different to her than the last time she saw him. He was dirty, had a long beard, and he looked much older. The cause of death was not readily apparent. It deeply saddened Melissa that the last days of Dan's life were spent in such dire conditions.

As Melissa prepared to take the body of her dead husband back to the United States for burial, she couldn't help wonder what went wrong and why the negotiations were unsuccessful. She loved the Colombian people she had met, and she hated the country. Melissa deeply regretted the decision to become an expatriate in Colombia.

Discussion Questions:

1. Were Dan and Melissa foolish in accepting the assignment in Medellin given the current state of danger?

2. What mistakes, if any, did Dan and Melissa make concerning their safety in Colombia?

3. What mistakes, if any, did Dan make during the hostage ordeal?

4. Were there any mistakes made during hostage negotiations?

5. Do you think the situation would have ended differently if Carolina Textiles had K&R insurance?

SOURCES: DuBois, J. (1994). *Cultures of the World: Colombia*. New York: Marshall Cavendish; McDermott, J. (2002). Colombia's Most Powerful Rebels. *BBC News*. January 7; McDermott, J. (2002). Analysis: Colombia's Security Crisis. *BBC News*. May 4; www.countrywatch.com/colombia. Accessed on July 22, 2003.

Case prepared by Charles A. Rarick

CASE 38

ED'S BIG CAREER MOVE

As his plane lands at the Santa Maria International Airport in San Jose, Costa Rica, Ed Moore reassures himself that he made the right decision in accepting his first international assignment in this Central American country. The new job will be a promotion, the first time Ed will be entirely responsible for an entire plant, and it will give him international experience, which he hopes to use to continue his advancement in the company.

Ed Moore has worked for his present employer, Jestin Apparel, for 16 years. Ed is viewed as a loyal employee and he prides himself on the fact that he has worked for Jestin longer than he has been married to his wife, Susan. Susan and their two children (Eddie, age 10, and Jessie, age 13) are not as enthusiastic about the idea of living in Turrialba, a rather isolated town about a two-hour drive from San Jose. Although Turrialba is in a beautiful area of the country and offers abundant hunting and fishing opportunities for Ed, Susan worries about the ability of the children to adapt to the isolation. In fact, since the children do not speak Spanish, it will be necessary for Eddie and Jessie to attend school in San Jose, which requires a long bus ride daily. Both Ed and Susan want their children to become "citizens of the world" and they both feel this opportunity may be good for personal development. Although the family vacationed in Europe once before, their international experience was very limited and none of the Moore family members speak another language.

Ed will be the new plant manager for the Costa Rican manufacturing facility of Jestin. This plant sews together pre-manufactured garments and exports the finished product back to the United States. The previous plant manager relocated to San Salvador to open a new, larger facility for Jestin. Most of the 230 employees are young females, although a number of young men and older women are also employed at the plant. The workers receive an hourly wage which is considerably higher than the average wage in Costa Rica. By most reports the workers are happy with their jobs at Jestin. Turnover at the plant is mainly due to young women getting married and starting a family, or young men moving to the capital for better wages.

Although the quality and efficiency of the plant are considered acceptable by management, Ed has been instructed to try and improve both areas. Ed is known as a rather tough manager, who feels that the best way to motivate employees is through a combined program of threats and incentives. Corporate management felt that Ed's somewhat autocratic style of management would be effective in Costa Rica.

Susan was employed in the United States as an assistant human resources manager, even though she had no formal training in that area. She enjoyed her job and she was hoping that she would be able to work in Costa Rica in a similar capacity. The Turrialba plant already had a bilingual HR manager who was familiar with Costa Rican labor laws and regulations; however, it was felt that perhaps Susan could first learn Spanish and then assist the HR manager. Ed's salary as plant manager will be more than their combined incomes in the United States, and the family will be provided with free housing, a maid, and company provided transportation. The family will live in extreme luxury by local standards.

As the plane touches down in San Jose, Ed remembers the trip the family made to Costa Rica three months earlier. The company had sent the family to Costa Rica to preview the country and to acquaint them with Costa Rican culture. The Moore's enjoyed the cultural tours and the whitewater rafting experiences, however; the children still protested against the move. Leaving friends in the United States is not easy, and they know that they will be giving up the comforts they have become accustomed to in the United States. Ed hopes the assignment will only be for a couple of years, although no plans have been made for his repatriation back to the United States.

As the plane comes to a halt at the gate, Susan looks at Ed and the worry in her face tells him that not all the Moore's are confident that the decision was a good one.

Discussion Questions:

1. What stress factors will Ed and his family likely encounter in this new assignment?

2. How significant a factor will family happiness be when it comes to Ed's success in this new job?

3. How do you think the Costa Rican employees will respond to Ed's management style?

4. Was Ed the best choice for the position? What criteria should be used in selecting expatriates?

5. What could Jestin do to increase the probability that this international assignment will be successful?

Case prepared by Charles A. Rarick.

CASE 39

CANADA TIMBER:
NEGOTIATING WITH THE JAPANESE

Tim Wilder, CEO of Canada Timber, was excited as he hung up the telephone in his office in Vancouver, British Columbia. Tim had just received a call from Akiko Morita, who represented the Japanese furniture manufacturer, Bonsai. Morita informed Tim that Canada Timber was being considered as a major supplier to Bonsai. He told Tim that Canada Timber's reputation as a supplier of quality hardwoods was of interest to Bonsai. Canada Timber exported its products to the United States, Mexico, and several European countries; however, the company did not have customers anywhere in Asia. Tim was excited about the prospect of exporting to Asia.

After several long-distance telephone calls and several more faxes, it was decided that Tim and two of his associates would travel to Japan in order to close an initial sales contract. In addition, Tim asked his brother-in-law, Johnny Sharkey - an attorney, to accompany them, and to act as their legal representative. The two associates Tim selected to join him on the trip were a production supervisor from Canada Timber and another member of the management team. Bill Hudak, production supervisor was a long-term employee of Canada Timber. His knowledge of hardwoods and the production procedures of Canada Timber made him an obvious choice for inclusion on the negotiating team. Tim also asked Kevin Peterson, a regional salesperson, to go along as well since Kevin was married to a woman of Japanese descent, and Tim felt he would make a good impression on the Japanese. None of the Canada Timber employees, or Johnny, spoke Japanese. Kevin knew a few words in Japanese and was somewhat familiar with Japanese culture.

The Japanese had faxed a number of documents to Tim concerning the meetings. Tim was very impressed with the degree of detail provided by the Japanese, including the names and qualifications of the people they would meet during their visit to Japan. A detailed agenda was provided, and the Japanese made all the arrangements for transportation and lodging for the Canadians.

After an exhausting flight, the Canadians arrived in Japan and were greeted by Akiko Morita and other representatives of Bonsai. The Japanese bowed and handed Tim their business cards. Tim, exhausted from the flight, took the business cards from each Bonsai representative and quickly stuffed them into his shirt pocket. After a brief conversation, the Bonsai employees took the Canadians to their hotel to rest. They would be back in the morning to escort them to Bonsai headquarters. The Canadians were very tired but excited to be in Japan. They rested a bit, and then spent the rest of the afternoon and early evening walking the streets of Tokyo.

When Tim and his associates arrived at Bonsai headquarters they were presented with a gift from the company president, Mr. Ono Kusushi. John was unsure if he should open the gift or not, so he decided to thank Mr. Kusushi for the gift and to stuff it into his briefcase. Once again a number of business cards were presented to John and the others, and at this point, Tim remembered that he had forgotten to bring his business cards along. He apologized for the oversight and once again quickly collected the cards from the Japanese.

The meeting began with Mr. Kusushi asking, through an interpreter, how the Canadians liked Japan so far. Tim and the others expressed an appreciation for being in the country and pointed out that Kevin had been to Japan previously while visiting the family of his Japanese wife. The Japanese remained silent as the Canadians told of how they had explored the city the night before and commented on how crowded the city was compared to Vancouver. Tim, who is a very tall man, stated that he felt like a "giant among men in Japan."

It appeared to Tim that the Japanese were very interested in the Canadians' perceptions of the country, and that they would begin to discuss business if he would offer some compliments. Tim thought about the situation and offered some positive comments on the food and drink they had enjoyed in their hotel. Tim then quickly began to discuss business, pointing out how Canada Timber was a quality leader in supplying hardwood products to several countries. He went on at great length about the positive attributes of his company and how it would be a good business decision to select Canada Timber as a supplier.

Bonsai had faxed some preliminary estimates of their wood needs and Tim had prepared a detailed report, which he presented at the meeting. At the end of the report, Tim provided details on costs, and then asked Mr. Kusushi if the numbers were acceptable. A long period of silence began. Tim and the other Canadians began to feel a bit nervous after a few moments had passed and he again asked, through the interpreter, if the price was acceptable. Mr. Kusushi smiled and laughed a bit without saying a word. He then looked at one of the members of the Japanese negotiating team and the two spoke in Japanese without the conversation being translated. At this point Tim interrupted by saying that perhaps the price could be a bit lower if needed. More silence followed and Tim became increasingly nervous. He began to speak, this time addressing the translator and asking if anything could be done to "seal the deal today." He pulled a contract out of his briefcase, lowered the price by 10% and asked Johnny to explain the important points of the sales contract. Mr. Kusushi sat quietly as Johnny explained the details of the contract to the Japanese. Tim and Johnny were concerned that Mr. Kusushi did not say much and that he never made good eye contact with them. After the details of the contract were explained, one of the more senior Japanese representatives suggested that the group take a short break. Tim thought this was a good sign and agreed. He stood up to shake the hand of each Japanese employee as they left the room. When he approached Mr. Kusushi, he gave an especially firm handshake and a pat on the shoulder. He told Mr. Kusushi, referring to him as Kenichi, that he was certain the two could work out a favorable arrangement, and that Canada Timber was prepared to do whatever was necessary in order to become a Bonsai supplier.

When the meeting resumed, Tim was informed that he and his associates were invited to tour one of Bonsai's manufacturing plants, which was located a few hours from Tokyo. Tim happily accepted the invitation, and the Canadians were off to the plant. After much formality once arriving at the plant, the Canadians were given an extensive tour. Tim and Bill Hudak asked many questions about the operation and they felt that they now had a better understanding of the material requirements needed by Bonsai. After the plant tour, the Canadians were taken back to their hotel and told that a Bonsai representative would pick them up in the morning and bring them back to company headquarters.

That evening the four men discussed what had happened during the day and how they should proceed. Kevin felt that everything was on schedule for the Japanese and that it would simply take more time in order to close the deal. He explained that silence was a negotiating tactic of the Japanese, and that Tim should not make any more concessions on price. Tim agreed that the price was already low and that not much profit would be made. However, he felt that if he could get the Japanese to sign a contract, and that if they liked the product, they would be able to do further business under better financial conditions. The four men generally agreed that they should seek a commitment from the Japanese in the morning.

The following day, however, would be no more successful for Tim and his team. After many hours of explaining once again how Canada Timber was the right choice, and that the price was very low, Tim was beginning to get frustrated. He felt that the Japanese were holding out for a lower price, and so he decided to offer a 15% reduction in order to end the negotiations. After the offer Tim slouched down in his chair and decided that he would use silence to his advantage. Tim sat silently and stared at Mr. Kusushi. It seemed like an eternity to the Canadians before someone from the Japanese side finally spoke. One of the senior Japanese employees suggested that the negotiations end for the day and that they resume the following morning. He further suggested that all members of the two teams go out in the evening to experience Japanese culture. At first Tim thought that he could take no further delays, but he then reasoned that he might be able to reach an agreement with the Japanese in a more informal setting.

During dinner Tim continued to press Mr. Kusushi for a decision. Mr. Kusushi politely said that he thought Canada Timber would be a good partner for Bonsai, yet made no commitment. After dinner, the Japanese took the Canadians to a very popular bar in Tokyo and all participants drank heavily. After a few hours Tim moved close to Mr. Kusushi, put his arm around his neck and told him that he was his new friend. Tim told Mr. Kusushi that he was going to give his new friend the best price he possibly could and that meant that he was going to make a final offer of a price reduction of 20%, if he would agree to the deal right now. Mr. Kusushi laughed and responded in English "yes." Tim was finally convinced that the team had closed the deal and that a contract would be signed in the morning.

On the following morning, Tim had Johnny prepare a revised sales agreement with the discounted price. Although the price was much lower than Tim had hoped for, and near his break-even point, Tim, nevertheless, felt that a long-term association with Bonsai and the potential for additional sales in Asia would be beneficial to the company. He was also happy to be able to return to Canada soon. Once again the Canadian team was met at the hotel and driven to Bonsai's headquarters. Tim entered the meeting room surprised not to find Mr. Kusushi present. When he asked the whereabouts of Mr. Kusushi, he was told that he had been called out of town unexpectedly and offered his apologies. Tim was told that Mr. Kusushi would return tomorrow. Tim immediately approached Akiko and told him that Mr. Kusushi had agreed to the terms listed in the sales contract he was holding in his hand. He asked if someone could sign the agreement so that he and his associates could return home. Tim was told that Mr. Kusushi would need to approve any supplier agreements and that it was impossible to do so today. Tim was very upset and it showed. His face was red. He believed that the Japanese were stalling in order to gain additional concessions. Tim moved very close to Akiko and told him that an agreement had been reached and that he should immediately telephone Mr. Kusushi to confirm. After raising his voice, Akiko telephoned Mr. Kusushi and told him of the situation. Upon his return, Akiko said, "Please excuse, Mr. Wilder-san, but we will probably need to wait just one more day." Tim, feeling as if were being manipulated, stormed out of the office, and, along with his negotiation team, headed for the airport.

Charles A. Rarick

Discussion Questions:

1. Evaluate the selection of negotiators from Canada Timber. Were any mistakes made in the selection?

2. What differences in culture between the Japanese and Canadians can be found in this case?

3. What could have been done differently in order to produce a more desirable outcome?

Sources: D. Engel and K. Murakami, Passport Japan. Novato, CA: World Trade Press, 2000; J. Scarborough, The Origins of Cultural Differences and Their Impact on Management. Westport, CT: Quorum, 2000; and R. Sanyal, Upper Saddle River, NJ: Prentice Hall, 2001.

Case prepared by Charles A. Rarick and Gregory Winter.

CASE 40

A NAÏVE SAHAB IN INDIA

It was the opportunity of a lifetime, or so Brian Moseley thought, as he accepted a managing director position for Aspen Automotive's new acquisition in India. Aspen Automotive was a supplier to American automobile manufacturers. The company supplied various component parts for the American automakers, and the recent acquisition of an Indian brake-pad company was seen as a keen strategic move for the company. The Bindi Brake Company was an established manufacturer of automotive brake pads that supplied a few European car companies with a high-quality product. Competition in this market is fierce, and Bindi experienced difficulty in recent years competing with American and Japanese firms. Aspen thought it could capitalize on the experience and low costs of production found in the New Delhi operation, and it sent Brian Moseley, an experienced automotive engineer, to India in order to "make the Indians efficient."

Brian and his family quickly adapted to India. Although many expatriates from developed countries experience overwhelming culture shock, the Moseleys' assimilated well into the expatriate community of New Delhi. With the help of personal assistants and children in private schools, the Moseleys' could separate themselves from most of the challenges of everyday life in urban India. Although they sometimes missed some of the luxuries they had taken for granted back in the United States, they enjoyed the standard of living they were experiencing as privileged expatriates in India. Brian knew that his job responsibilities were to turn around the newly acquired Indian operation, and that if he did this within two years, he would be promoted and moved back to U.S. He felt that this assignment could greatly advance his career.

Managers at Aspen's corporate headquarters felt that the introduction of certain Western managerial practices would be beneficial to Bindi and improve overall efficiency and profitability. Brian was selected to direct the organizational change effort because of his past record of accomplishments in the U.S. and abroad. He had been successful in the turnaround of troubled parts-manufacturing plants in Louisville, Kentucky, and Toledo, Ohio. Additionally, he had worked internationally in Canada, Mexico, and Brazil. Aspen felt that his M.B.A. in management from Michigan State, coupled with his previous domestic and international experience, made him a suitable person to direct the Indian productivity improvement strategy.

Although Bindi produced reasonably high-quality brake components, and labor costs were exceptionally low, the overall efficiency of the operation was considerably below that of other Aspen plants. Top management felt that if the Indian operation could match the level of efficiency of even the least efficient American plant, the acquisition would be a success. After an initial plant visit, top management concluded that the plant was crippled with bureaucracy and that there was no incentive for exceptional performance. Aspen managers observed what they felt were too many Bindi employees drinking tea and socializing instead of working at a brisk pace. They were also shocked to find that no Bindi employee ever received a performance review and that pay for performance was never even considered by past management. Bindi employees were seldom discharged, even when they were clearly not well suited to their jobs and performed poorly. Pay increases and other rewards were administered on the basis of seniority. Employees were often hired, not based on their abilities or potential, but because they were related to a current employee of Bindi. The number of sick days and personal days requested was well above the average of the other Aspen plants.

Brian was directed to make the India subsidiary more like the rest of the Aspen corporate family. For the first three months, Brian did little more than observe and learn about Bindi's current managerial practices. He spoke with managers and employees alike, and made mental notes of the conversations. Brian identified employees whom he felt should be replaced and employees whom he felt had the greatest potential for advancement. After this initial three-month investigation, Brian met with his senior managers at Bindi and proposed that they collectively formulate a turnaround strategy. All of Bindi's managers were Indians and most had been educated in Indian universities. One manager, Rajan Patel, had studied in London and received a postgraduate diploma from the University of London in economics. Brian felt that Rajan was one of the most promising candidates for advancement, and he hoped that Rajan would take the lead in structuring the change management program.

Although Brian had hoped that the Indian managers would formulate a plan for change among themselves, he increasingly became frustrated after a month when no one came forth to recommend a plan. Brian suggested to the group that they consider changes such as pay-for- performance programs, annual performance reviews, management by objectives, and perhaps a 360-degree performance appraisal program. In his view, if the group emphasized performance appraisal, many of Bindi's efficiencies would disappear. Brian believed that most of the employees had the potential for great improvement, and that all they needed was a better system of management. A more scientific and objective approach to management, coupled with a more participative approach, would succeed in increasing the efficiencies and ultimate success of Bindi.

Over the next several months, Brian became increasingly dissatisfied with the progress of the Indian managers in coming up with any constructive plan for changing Bindi's managerial practices. Highly frustrated, he sometimes angrily criticized members of his managerial team in front of their subordinates. The relationship between Brian and the managers became increasingly strained; he was being referred to behind his back as "sahab" or "big boss." A throwback to the British colonial days, this term was used in some instances to refer to a manager who had little understanding of Indian culture.

One of Brian's biggest critics was Rajan Patel. Rajan often criticized Brian's managerial style as being too direct and forceful. On at least one occasion, Rajan referred to Brian's tactics as "culturally imperialistic," asserting that Brian was too immature to be the managing director. He was concerned that Brian was trying to change India's culture to fit an American model of management. Although educated in the West, Rajan did not feel that Indian employees were receptive to many Western managerial practices, which ran counter to basic Indian cultural values. He openly questioned Brian and Aspen's approach to changing the corporate culture of the Bindi Brake Company.

After seven months in India, Brian decided that if change were to occur, he would have to be the one to initiate that change. He called his senior managers into his office one morning and told them of the following changes that were to be effective immediately. First, Brian announced that C.P. Rao would replace Prakash Nur, the assistant plant director and the most senior manager. Rao was a young engineer, educated at an American university, and a person who Brian felt would be best able to implement his vision of change at Bindi. Second, Brian announced that performance appraisals would begin immediately and that at least two employees in each work group would be eliminated in the interest of organizational efficiency. Third, a new plan of 360-degree feedback would be implemented: Subordinates would evaluate their superiors, and annual compensation increases would be contingent on these reviews. No annual increases in compensation would be automatic, and all raises would now be based on merit. Finally, all personal assistants (chaprasi) would be fired and their responsibilities assumed by the managers themselves. Even though the salary expense of the personal assistants was small, Brian felt that it created an unnecessary level of administration, and no other Aspen unit allowed such positions.

At first, the Indian managers seemed stunned by Brian's mandates. No one spoke, and a dead silence filled the room. When Brian asked for feedback on his "recommendations," the managers looked down at the table in front of them and said nothing. Prakash, who got up and left the room, broke the silence. Later, a few of the managers politely told Brian that the ideas were too bold and too sudden a change for Bindi. Brian angrily responded that the change was long overdue and that anyone who would not go along with the new plan should leave the company.

Much grumbling was heard at Bindi over the next few days, as the managers announced the changes. Brian learned that Prakash had resigned and that Rajan was telling everyone about his dissatisfaction with Brian's managerial style. Brian decided to talk individually with all the managers, starting with Rajan. The meeting was less than cordial, and ended with Brian's warning Rajan that he'd "better come on board soon" or he too would be replaced. During subsequent meetings with all the Indian managers, Brian tried to convince them of the urgency and necessity of these proposed changes. At times, it seemed as if they agreed with him and he felt that change would finally occur. After all, when asked directly, no one actually refused to implement the changes.

After a week in which no changes were taking place, Brian reasoned that it might take a little longer than he thought due to cultural constraints. However, he worried that Rajan might be trying to sabotage the change effort. Brian kept a close eye on Rajan, and one morning he was told that Rajan would not be in the office for a week because his brother was getting married in Bombay. Brian was suspicious, checked the personnel records, and discovered that Rajan did not have any brothers. He waited for Rajan to return and then asked him where he had been. Rajan replied that he had attended the wedding of his brother in Bombay. Brian, outraged by the lie, immediately fired him on the spot. Rajan left without a word to Brian.

Although things seemed to be a bit tense at Bindi, Brian told himself that change is difficult and that the long-term consequences would be good for Aspen, Bindi, and India. He continued to quiz the managers on their progress in carrying out the change efforts, and was told that all changes were being implemented, as he had instructed. But further investigation revealed that no changes were being made. Brian called for another meeting of his managers and was shocked to learn that a number of them had decided to quit rather than attend the meeting. Included in the group who resigned were C.P. Rao, whom Brian was convinced would be a leader in making his vision of change a reality at Bindi. Brian sat alone in his office, wondering if change would ever come to the Bindi Brake Company.

Discussion Questions:

1. Evaluate the managerial style of Brian Moseley and explain how it fits with Indian culture. Be specific in identifying any mistakes Brian made in managing Indian workers.

2. Rank the following principals and justify the ranking in terms of responsibility for the lack of change at the Bindi Brake Company: Brian, Rajan, Aspen, the Indian manager.

3. What could each of the above-named principals have done differently to avoid this situation?

4. What should Brian do now?

Case prepared by Charles A. Rarick

CASE 41

AU REVOIR, MRS. WILLIAMSON

Margaret Williamson, age 50 has just returned to London from Paris, where she worked for the past six months as a marketing specialist for a British and French joint venture called EUROi. British computer manufacturer RoyalPC formed the joint venture with a French ISP called Internet du France (IDF). The two companies hope to capitalize on their particular strengths and grow a Pan-European Internet service. EUROi competes in Europe on the basis of price, and has positioned itself as an alternative ISP in an already crowded market. EUROi targets the 16 to 24 year-old market by offering programming that appeals to a more youthful market. The company also offers subscribers sizable discounts on Royal personal computers.

Margaret began her career at Royal fifteen years ago as a secretary. As a recently divorced mother of two, Margaret entered the work force for the first time and displayed a strong work ethic. Although she did not attend college, Margaret is a very intelligent individual and a quick learner. These traits did not go unnoticed at Royal, and she was promoted out of the secretary pool and placed into the Marketing Department. Margaret advanced in the department, gaining a reputation for handling difficult assignments. With a strong devotion to her children and her work, she chose not to remarry. With her children now grown she became interested in an international assignment.

Her colleagues viewed Margaret as an effective manager. She was seen as fair to all, conscientious, a good decision maker, and very loyal to the company. Because of her abilities, she was selected to act as marketing liaison between her company and the French partner in the newly formed joint venture.

Mrs. Williamson, as she prefers to be called, is a refined British lady. She possesses excellent manners and prides herself on her personal composure. Her ability to remain calm and level-headed in tense situations would be challenged when she moved to Paris for her new assignment.

Georges DuPont, age 35 is director of marketing for EUROi. DuPont, a graduate of the prestigious Ecole Nationale d' Administration, comes from an elite French family. Somewhat of a renegade, Georges refused to work in the family business after college. He instead, found employment in a number of computer-related businesses. DuPont became fascinated with the creative side of the computer and Internet business. He had been at IDF for four years, and was highly regarded as an effective manager and creative promoter. As marketing director of the joint venture, DuPont was given the responsibility of working with Williamson to find a way to increase revenue for EUROi. DuPont prides himself on his literary and artistic skills and enjoys engaging others in verbal debate.

From the start of their working relationship, problems surfaced between Margaret and Georges. At first, small personal habits of the two seemed to cause friction. Margaret often remarked that Georges never smiled at her, and Georges called Margaret's personality as "interesting as a bottle of cheap California wine." Over the early weeks of the relationship, the situation deteriorated further. Margaret was convinced that Georges was an incompetent and lazy manager. She felt that Georges was too autocratic and did not delegate enough responsibility to lower levels in the organization.

Margaret further complained to her superiors back in London that Georges frequently broke company policy, canceled meetings with little notice, took two-hour lunch breaks, and never admitted his mistakes. She felt that he did not respect her as an equal partner; in fact, she felt that he actually resented her help in promoting the joint venture.

To add more tension to the already strained relationship, Margaret learned that Georges (a married man) was having an affair with his secretary, Giselle. This fact came to light when Margaret found out that the two of them were going to a resort in the south of France for three weeks of vacation. Margaret was offended by Georges's lack of morality, which included his affair with Giselle as well as his advances to other women in the company.

Georges was equally unimpressed with Margaret. He felt that she was uneducated, insensitive, and too concerned with money and company regulations. Georges frequently joked to others about the way in which Margaret dressed. He felt that she had no taste in fashion, and that this alone made her abilities in the company suspect. Georges was unhappy that Margaret forced everyone to communicate with her in English. Although she spoke little French and Georges and most others spoke fluent English, he resented this, nevertheless. When Margaret requested that she be referred to as "Mrs. Williamson," Georges just rolled his eyes and muttered something in French that Margaret did not understand. He seldom used either her first or last name in conversations with her.

The workplace tensions continued for some time, with Georges and Margaret frequently disagreeing and complaining about each other. It was known throughout EUROi that the two did not get along, and their strained interactions were often the butt of jokes around the company. Georges tried to avoid Margaret as much as possible, which put her in the awkward position of having to go through Giselle to communicate with him. Margaret did not like to deal with Giselle because of her "illicit" behavior with her boss.

The situation finally came to a head when a creative team was to be assembled to design a large advertising campaign for EUROi. Margaret had already developed a plan to assemble the team and empower them with the responsibility of creating a more youth-oriented advertising theme. Margaret had identified five people whom she felt would be best suited for the project. Her plan was to allow these people to work independent of management in creating a new series of advertisements. Margaret felt that a more creative approach to promotion was needed, and she wanted this team to develop a breakthrough design for the promotional strategy.

When Margaret approached Georges with her idea, he refused to accept it. He told Margaret that he felt the current campaign was effective, but admitted that he could see a need for some improvement. Georges recommended that he solicit the advice of a few key people and that he create the new ad design. After all, he was the director of marketing for the new company. Margaret tried to explain to

Georges why her plan was better, and that a similar approach had been successful with RoyalPC. Georges just stared at the ceiling, smoking his cigarette. Margaret wasn't even sure if he was listening to her.

After a few weeks of attempting to convince Georges that her plan was better, Margaret decided that she needed help from London. She arranged for a video conference call to be held between London and Paris, in which she and some senior managers at Royal would discuss the issue further with Georges. Margaret sent an e-mail message to Georges, informing him of the conference but received no response. After two days, she asked Giselle if her boss knew of the proposed meeting and if he could attend. Giselle just smiled and responded that he could attend the meeting, if he desired to do so. Margaret sent a memo to Georges indicating the date and time of the conference call and emphasizing the importance of his presence at the meeting.

On the day of the meeting, Margaret searched for Georges. Even though the meeting wasn't for a few hours, she wanted to make sure he would attend, and she thought that perhaps she could even get him to change his mind before the call took place. Giselle told Margaret that he would be in the office soon and that she would remind him of the meeting.

As the 1:00 PM hour for the meeting approached, Margaret was frantic. She phoned Giselle and demanded to know where Georges was and when he would be in the conference room. Giselle responded that she didn't know where he was and that she really didn't care. When Giselle rudely hung up the phone, Margaret was convinced that Georges would not show up for the meeting. She decided, however, that she might be able to use this to her advantage.

The call from London came precisely at 1:00 PM, with just Margaret sitting in the Paris office. She explained to the people in London that Georges was not present and that she had no idea why he was not there. She went on to tell the London managers that she was not surprised by Georges's behavior; he continually expressed contempt for her, and he had an apparent disregard for the welfare of EUROi. Margaret went on for over 30 minutes detailing Georges's shortcomings, when suddenly he entered the room with three other EUROi employees. Georges apologized for his tardiness but explained that he and the others had been across town working with marketing personnel from a very popular magazine targeted toward the 16 to 24 age group in Europe. Georges was very excited about what this "team" had accomplished, and he wanted the London managers to know the details.

The video call went on for another hour with the three EUROi employees explaining with charts and figures how the association with the youth magazine would be beneficial to the company. They proposed new creative advertising designs and an association with the popular magazine. The team appeared to have been well prepared for the meeting. Georges, who spoke with great confidence and enthusiasm, directed the entire presentation. From the questions asked by the London managers, it was clear that they felt Georges's plan was superior to the one proposed by Margaret. When the presentation was completed they thanked Georges and his team and quickly approved the plan.

At that point Margaret rose from her chair, red-faced and very angry. She appeared at first barely able to speak, but when she began, she angrily accused Georges of undermining her authority. Margaret called Georges a "sneaky bastard," and for the next five minutes vented her frustration at Georges, who sat quietly staring at the ceiling, smoking his cigarette.

Finally the most senior London manager interrupted Margaret and politely asked if Georges and his team could leave the room for a moment. Georges got up and began to leave, but before he left he stopped, smiled at Margaret, and said, "au revoir, *Mrs.* Williamson."

Charles A. Rarick

Discussion Questions:

1. What role does culture play in the interpersonal difficulties found in this case?

2. Who is more to blame; Georges or Margaret; for these difficulties?

3. What advice would you give a British expatriate going to France?

Sources: N. Joseph, Passport France. Novato, CA: World Trade Press, 1997; and J. Scarborough, The Origins of Cultural Difference and Their Impact on Management. Westport, CT: Quorum, 1998.

Case prepared by Charles A. Rarick

EXERCISE 12

HOFSTEDE'S CULTURAL CLASSIFICATION MODEL COUNTRY-RANKING EXERCISE

Purpose: To develop a better understanding of cultural differences and how they affect international management. This exercise uses the model developed by cross-cultural researcher Geert Hofstede and tests your knowledge of eight different cultures.

Procedure: Read the brief description of each element of Hofstede's framework and individually rank each of the listed countries from high to low on the four dimensions of the model. The country highest on a dimension receives a ranking of 1, and the country lowest on the dimension receives an 8. Assemble into groups and discuss your rankings. As a group, develop another ranking, again using 1 = highest and 8 = lowest. Finally, answer as a group the three questions at the end of the exercise.

Hofstede Model:

Working with IBM employees, Danish psychologist Geert Hofstede discovered four dimensions on which cultures differ. Although the sample was limited in terms of representation (employees of IBM), it was an extensive empirical study of individuals from many different cultures, and it stands as the most popular cross-cultural framework involving managerial issues. Hofstede discovered that cultures differ in terms of power distance, uncertainty avoidance, masculinity-femininity, and individualism-collectivism.

Power Distance: The degree to which unequal power is accepted and valued by a society

Uncertainty Avoidance: The degree to which a culture feels comfortable with uncertainty. In high uncertainty avoidance cultures, people do not value ambiguity

Masculinity/Femininity: The emphasis a culture places on values that have been associated with males and females. Masculinity is associated with aggression, materialism, and achievement. Femininity is associated with cooperation, compassion, and human development.

Individual/Collective: The primary focus a society accords either the individual or the group. Individualistic societies value individual rights and responsibilities; collective societies value group achievement and harmony.

Country Ranking

PD	UA	M	I

USA
Sweden
Mexico
Peru

Costa Rica
Japan
Germany
Australia

PD = power distance
UA = uncertainty avoidance
M   = masculinity
I   = individualism

Discussion Questions:

1. In which country do you feel a participative management style would have the greatest acceptance? Which country would be the least accepting? Explain.

2. In which countries would a company policy of financially rewarding individuals based on their performance be most effective?

3. In which countries would managers be expected to give precise directions to their employees?

Exercise prepared by Charles A. Rarick

Part Eight

INTERNATIONAL FINANCE, ACCOUNTING, AND TAXATION

Cases:
Wilson International
"Baa"d Pricing Policies
"Baa"st Transfer Price
Diving into a Tax Haven

Exercises:
Exercise in International Accounting
OECD

CASE 42

WILSON INTERNATIONAL: INTERNATIONAL CAPITAL BUDGETING

Wilson International is a chain of over 100 luxury hotels found mostly in developed countries. George Wilson, a former Chicago sales representative who frequently traveled internationally, started the company. As an international business traveler, Wilson found that hotel quality varied from country to country. He quit his very successful sales job and started a hotel in Dublin, Ireland, a country known for its extensive bed-and-breakfast industry. Wilson felt that business travelers needed a greater selection of hotels in Dublin, particularly in the higher-priced market. The Wilson of Dublin was an immediate success with business travelers and, with the help of a venture capitalist, George was able to expand his hotel concept to 20 countries.

Wilson has always sought hotel opportunities in more developed countries in Europe and Asia. George and his associates felt that the problems found in less-developed countries presented too much risk for his company; thus they avoided most countries of the world. Because the countries in which Wilson operates are considered politically stable and present little political risk, the investment decisions are normally made on the basis of revenue projections using a net present value approach. The firm's cost of capital is used as a means of discounting expected cash flow. If the net present value (NPV) of the investment is above zero, the hotel is constructed. This approach has worked well for the company over the years.

With the possibility of market saturation beginning to rise, George is considering an opportunity to expand into other markets. He has been approached by a trade representative of St. Charles, a small and moderately industrialized island in the Caribbean, who proposes that Wilson International build a business hotel in the capital, Dominic.

The trade rep has assured George that an additional hotel is needed in the capital due to the country's expanding industrialization. St. Charles has always enjoyed a brisk tourist trade, and now the country is diversifying its economy into light manufacturing.

Multinationals from the United States and Europe have established customer service operations on the island, and a number of garment manufacturers have begun operations there as well. The trade representative tells George that managers from these companies frequently visit the island, and they need a more luxurious hotel in which to stay. The hotel would certainly be profitable, reasons the trade rep.

Financial analysts for the company have created a report indicating that, using the present financial model, a small hotel would be a good investment. Data included in the model can be seen below.

Wilson International – St. Charles Operation
Preliminary Financial Analysis

Yearly Expected Cash Flow from Operations: $750,000US
Expected Life of the Investment 25 years

Wilson International Cost of Capital 12%
Investment $5,000,000US

Basic Financial Model: (12% PVF of 7.84314)

(Present Value of Cash Flows – Investment) = NPV
(5,882,355 – 5,000,000) = $882,355

Some Wilson analysts argue, however, that a higher discounting factor than cost of capital should be used. It is proposed by some that a more appropriate discounting factor would be 15% (with a PVF of 6.46415), due to the higher risks associated with the investment environment.

George is uncertain about the proposed investment. While he sees the need for the company to find new markets, he is also troubled by reports he has read about increasing social unrest on the island. Although George and his associates do not consider St. Charles to be a high-risk country, they are concerned about recent increases in petty street crime and social unrest. It has been reported that citizens have resorted to violent street protest to express their displeasure with the increasing prices of some consumer goods. The currency of St. Charles, the Caribbean dollar, has been devalued against most hard currencies of the world and, as a result, imported goods have increased in price. On the other hand, St. Charles has no currency or foreign direct investment restrictions, and allows for full repatriation of company profits. In recent years, the government has been attempting to promote the island as an attractive location for foreign investment.

With declining opportunities in more stable environments, George must consider the feasibility of this opportunity, and the necessary change of strategic direction it would mean for Wilson International.

Discussion Questions:

1. What additional information might be useful to consider before making this investment decision?

2. Can an international company avoid all political risk? Explain.

3. Would you recommend that Wilson International build a hotel on St. Charles? Are there any alternatives to consider other than building the hotel or staying out of the country? Explain.

Case prepared by Charles A. Rarick.

CASE 43

"BAA"D PRICING POLICIES

Tara Grant looked out at the rugged landscape of the Australian Outback. The young controller took a sip of coffee and thought about how drastically the view differed from the green pastures of her native home in Boston. Even after spending four years in Australia, she was still amazed by the contrasts. The "change of pace" of the Australian Outback had influenced her decision to accept the accounting position with Outback Woolworks, a wholly owned subsidiary of the United States - based Celtic Sweaters, Inc., after completing college.

Outback Woolworks is a large sheep ranch that had been owned by the Young family until five years ago, when it was incorporated and subsequently sold to Celtic Sweaters for cash and Celtic common stock. Two brothers, Aron and Joe Young, still managed the flock of sheep and oversaw the shearing, combing, and spinning activities necessary for production of worsted wool. During the 1990s, the Australian wool industry faced a depressed market with limited demand. In mid-1999, the Wool International Privatisation Act was passed by the Australian Parliament to deregulate the wool industry, and the following year, wool growers were given the opportunity to vote on future industry practices in the historic Wool Poll 2000. Both brothers were instrumental in the sweeping statutory reform and remained actively involved in various adhoc groups formed to address issues such as ongoing demand building, trade access, risk management, self-regulation and industry leadership, and wool contamination.

As a U.S. company, Celtic Sweaters, Inc. was required to comply with the Wool Products Labeling Act, a 1939 U.S. law requiring that all fabric containing wool carry identification indicating the percentage of wool in the cloth, as well as the appropriate legal description for the fiber according to category (i.e., new, reprocessed, reused wool). Therefore, Celtic purchased only new (or virgin) wool, importing over 75% of the virgin wool produced on the ranch for the manufacture of hand-knit sweaters and tweed jackets. The remaining virgin wool, as well as reprocessed wool made from scrap fibers or mill ends, was sold locally.

Tara headed back to her desk to review some paperwork for an upcoming meeting with J.R. Wolf, the controller of Celtic Sweaters, Outback's parent company. He was interested in the details of Australia's sweeping new tax reform. The country's previously high corporate tax rate was gradually being reduced from 36% to 30%, and a Goods and Services Tax (GST) was being introduced. Fortunately, the GST would not apply to the wool being exported, so Outback's overall tax liability would decrease. This was probably what J.R. wanted to discuss; the extent of the change in tax expense. Tara recalled that J.R. was always concerned with budget preparation and "increasing the bottom line." This was especially true during the past two years, when Outback's lower earnings had mirrored those of the entire Australian wool industry, which is the world's largest producer of raw wool.

The next day, J.R. arrived at the small, administrative offices of Outback Woolworks dressed in a navy-blue suit and tie. Tara recalled her college seminars on "Dress for Success" and smiled. J.R. would be right at home at a high-level corporate meeting on Wall Street, but he looked out of place on the ranch, where all the employees dressed in jeans. She was well aware of the fact that the ranch workers called the business executives from corporate headquarters "the Suits."

After presenting an overview of the changes to the tax law, Tara asked if J.R. had any questions. He quickly turned the conversation to pricing issues. Given the new tax laws, corporate headquarters wanted to increase the price that Outback was charging Celtic for wool purchases. The executives were considering a 30% increase in the transfer price between the entities. At first Tara was puzzled. She had expected J.R. to ask her for an estimate of the effect of the tax legislation on the "bottom line." Changing Outback's sales price (and revenue) would only increase Celtic's costs - the net effect would be zero after the two companies' financial statements were consolidated.

Then the real reason for the price change request occurred to her, and she felt her cheeks turn red. J.R. wanted to change the transfer price of the wool to decrease taxes paid in the United States, where the corporate tax rate was 35%, by shifting income to Australia, where the rate would decrease to 30%. To put the facts in their proper perspective, Tara prepared the following projected numbers for the upcoming year, before the price change (amounts in millions of U.S. dollars):

__Outback (Sales to Celtic)__		__Celtic (Parent Before Consolidation)__	
Sales revenue	$100	Sales revenue	$320
Operating expenses	- 90	Operating expenses	-240
Income before taxes	10	Income before taxes	80
Tax expense (30%)	- 3	Tax expense (35%)	- 28
Net Income	$ 7	Net Income	$ 52

After the proposed 30% transfer price increase (amounts in millions of U.S. dollars):

__Outback (Sales to Celtic)__		__Celtic (Parent Before Consolidation)__	
Sales revenue	$130.00	Sales revenue	$320.00
Operating expenses	- 90.00	Operating expenses	-270.00
Income before taxes	40.00	Income before taxes	50.00
Tax expense (30%)	- 12.00	Tax expense (35%)	- 17.50
Net Income	$ 28.00	Net Income	$ 32.50

While the potential tax savings looked appealing, Tara's mind raced. She knew that the Australian Competition and Consumer Commission (ACCC) has been given special powers by the Australian government to oversee wool prices during the transition to the new tax law. She excused herself and located the relevant information. ACCC guidelines noted that wool prices were expected to fall as producers passed tax savings onto purchasers. In fact, the ACCC literature noted penalties for price exploitation of up to $10 million for corporations, and $500,000 for individuals.

Later that day, having produced the appropriate documents, Tara was sure that J.R. would agree that the price increases were out of the question. Instead, he appeared somewhat agitated and simply replied, "Well Tara, how you structure and explain the price increase is up to you, but we'll be looking for higher sales prices beginning next quarter. I guess you'll just have to be creative. Besides you are not the only one who feels pressured by this scenario. Can you imagine how the middle managers at Celtic are going to react when I have to inform them that their profit margins are going to be reduced due to higher product costs?" When Tara boldly asked him what the pricing scheme for domestic sales or wool sales to other customers would look like, he reluctantly agreed that a price increase similar to the one proposed for Celtic would not be warranted. Then he added with a sly grin, "See, Tara, you'll still be in compliance with the ACCC guidelines. Just reduce the sales prices to all other customers to a competitive level; this should bury the inflated transfer prices charged to Celtic. The Aussie regulators don't care about the international business; they'll be happy to get some extra tax revenue from an American company. Heck, they should be glad to have our business!"

As Tara tossed and turned that night, she remembered from her college cost accounting and tax classes that the U.S. Internal Revenue Service (IRS) had transfer-pricing guidelines. The next morning, she located some information on the Internet and learned that the IRS regulations were specifically targeted at reducing U.S. corporate tax evasion. Transfer prices between related organizations should be comparable to market price, if available, or an "arms-length" transaction between two unrelated organizations. She also learned that transfer-pricing regulation dated back to the 1920s, but had been updated frequently. In fact, Congressional hearings in 1990 addressed perceived inbound transfer-pricing abuses and further expanded the IRS regulations. Thus, it appeared as though transfer prices were regularly monitored. Under U.S. tax law, tax agents have the authority to redistribute income to reduce tax evasion or properly reflect income. Violation of the IRS regulations could result in a 20% penalty on the additional assessed tax amounts.

Given diminished retail demand, an emphasis on increasing demand for the Australian wool industry, and the upcoming tax rate cuts, the market prices of Australian wool would be declining.

Tara realized that any pricing test that compared the transfer price proposed by J.R. to market or "arms-length" Australian wool prices would clearly draw attention to the higher price charged to Celtic.

While she personally would not be in trouble with the IRS because that was a corporate headquarters issue, she did not want to be involved in this pricing "scheme." Also, if the pricing issue were discovered, the negative publicity could prove devastating to Aron and Joe, who were so involved in the Australian wool industry. Finally, the fact that her meeting with J.R. was private could leave her as the "fall guy," since there was no paper trail. With that thought, Tara headed out to the barn to confer with the Young brothers, who both owned millions of dollars of Celtic Sweaters, Inc. common stock from the ranch's sale.

Discussion Questions:

1. How would a 30% increase in the transfer price affect the net income figures for Outback Woolworks and Celtic Sweaters? How would it affect the overall consolidated net income?

2. Generally, what are the pros and cons of increasing the transfer price for both companies' stakeholders, that is, investors, creditors, employees, and citizens? In other words, who are the winners and who are the losers?

3. Evaluate the managerial style of J.R. Wolf by commenting on his overall objective, interpersonal skills (attire and attitude toward locals), and methods (directive to a subordinate employee and sensitivity to key employees).

4. How might the increased transfer prices affect the managers' morale at Celtic, if the managers are eligible for profit sharing based on income from domestic operations? What if the managers hold stock options?

5. What should Tara do?

Case prepared by Suzanne Lowensohn and Lawrence Hudak.

CASE 44

"Baa"st Transfer Price

[Note: This case is a follow-up to the previous *"Baa"d Pricing Policies* case. Here the primary character (Tara Grant) must be a problem-solver rather than a whistleblower. Environmental and economic changes enable transfer prices to be adjusted to permit overall tax savings within a consolidated corporate group. The challenge is by how much, at what "cost" to whom, and could the "cost" be minimized among stakeholders?]

Tara Grant looks out the rain-soaked window of her airplane as it landed at Logan International Airport on a dreary April morning. Exhausted after the long flight, and excited about the opportunity to visit family and friends after spending the past five years in the Australian Outback, she prepared to deplane. Tara had been summoned to corporate headquarters in Boston to confer with her new boss, Alec Young, about a very important issue. Alec is the baby brother of the Young family, the previous owners of Outback Woolworks, the large sheep ranch where Grant is employed as controller. Six years ago, when Outback was acquired as a wholly owned subsidiary of Celtic Sweaters, Alec agreed to join Celtic's management team. Alec had requested that Tara come to the States to help devise an optimum transfer price for the virgin wool produced by her subsidiary company (Outback) and sold to his parent company (Celtic) that would *legally* reduce the combined taxes paid to the Australian and American governments, and thereby maximize consolidated earnings.

Tara was very anxious to make a good first impression with her parent company's top executives, because it was just one year ago that she had "blown the whistle" on her former boss, J.R. Wolf, who subsequently was asked to resign due to his unethical practices. Then she felt a sudden calm come over her as she was greeted at the gate by a familiar face and a warm, "good day mate." Alec, the newly promoted controller of the United States - based Celtic Sweater, Inc., Outback's parent company, took time out of his busy schedule to personally meet Tara at the airport. After exchanging a warm hello, Tara quickly filled in Alec about what his two older brothers were up to back on the Australian sheep ranch.

As the conversation shifted to business, Tara's anxiety level began to increase. Before dropping her off at her hotel, Alec cautioned her that his predecessor, J.R. Wolf, still had numerous friends at corporate headquarters that were not too happy that he had been forced to resign. This potentially hostile environment could make the task at hand for Tara and Alec even more formidable. So they agreed to meet early the next morning to sort out the facts, prior to the afternoon meeting with Celtic's top management. Since Celtic's corporate culture can be best described as a participatory management, consensus building among key executives is crucial to obtaining the necessary approval for business decisions.

The next morning, Tara exited her hotel, beaming with confidence, as she was greeted with bright sunshine and a rainbow, to hail a cab for her meeting with Alec at Celtic headquarters. Despite the typical hustle and bustle of the city, she smiled as she spotted a robin sitting in a tree, thinking about her fond memories of springtime in the Northeast. While riding in the cab, she double-checked her briefcase's contents to make sure she had the critical data about the projected prices of virgin wool and her watch to make sure she would arrive on time.

Upon entering Alec's office, Tara is introduced to Kaylee Ann Wright, a CPA tax consultant, who specializes in related party transactions within consolidated groups. After exchanging pleasantries, Alec informs Tara that Kaylee was hired to provide technical assistance to make sure their transfer price strategy is in compliance with the U.S. Internal Revenue Code and related Treasury regulations. "What a pleasure to meet you, Kaylee!" exclaims Tara. "I feel so much better about the whole transfer-pricing issue knowing you will review the intercompany transactions. In my opinion, transfer pricing is a complex issue that requires an expert opinion."

Kaylee smiles and replies, "Well, thank you for your vote of confidence, Tara. I tend to agree that these issues are important. In fact, Celtic's 100% ownership of Outback (a foreign subsidiary) requires us to file the IRS Form 5472. This form includes information about all intercompany transactions, such as Outback's sale of wool to Celtic Sweaters. Hence, information about transfer pricing between related parties is red flagged.

"Furthermore, the Internal Revenue Code Section 482 and the related Treasury Regulation 1.482 offer specific guidance about 'appropriate transfer prices' for related parties. The most appropriate transfer-price is a comparable uncontrolled sales price, if available; for example, the price Outback charges unrelated customers for virgin wool. If a comparable uncontrolled sales price is not readily available, then the next best transfer price is cost-plus when the parent performs substantial processing; for example, converting raw virgin wool into clothing. This method examines the selling price of Celtic's finished goods (wool clothes) and allows for a 'reasonable' gross profit (industry average) in determining an 'acceptable' cost of goods sold. Since cost of goods sold consists of direct labor and overhead costs incurred by Celtic, plus the 'unknown' cost of raw materials (virgin wool), the transfer price for wool is a plug number to arrive at an 'acceptable' cost of goods sold amount. Finally, any attempts to evade U.S. corporate income taxes through extremely high transfer prices may result in severe penalties ranging from 20-40% on the additional tax assessments."

Given the relevant tax rules, Tara proposes two transfer-price options, as approved by key executives from Outback. Under the first scenario, the selling price of wool would be increased to reflect market changes, and this cost increase would not be absorbed in the selling price of wool clothing (i.e., consumers would not pay a higher price for a Celtic sweater). According to Aron Young (Alec's oldest brother and vice president of production at Outback), environmental conditions, specifically a devastating "mad sheep" disease in Europe and the Americas, have drastically reduced the world's supply of virgin wool. The limited supply is projected to cause Australian wool prices to rise by up to 50% without any objections from the Australian Competition and Consumer Commission (ACCC). Furthermore, Outback plans to increase its prices for virgin wool across the board by 40% to all its unrelated customers, if there is any excess product not purchased by its parent company. [However, due to the worldwide shortage, it is doubtful that there will be any excess.] Tara demonstrate the impact of a 40% increase with the following projected numbers, presented before and after the change (amounts in millions of U.S, dollars):

Outback (Sales to Celtic)		**Celtic (before consolidation)**	
Sales revenue	$ 100	Sales revenue	$ 320
Operating expenses	- 90	Operating expenses (incl. wool)	- 240
Income before taxes	10	Income before taxes	80
Tax expense (30%)	- 3	Tax expense (35%)	- 28
Net Income	$ 7	Net Income	$ 52

After the proposed 40% transfer price increase (amounts in millions of U.S. dollars):

Outback (Sales to Celtic)		**Celtic (before Consolidation)**	
Sales revenue	$ 140	Sales revenue	$ 320
Operating expenses	- 90	Operating expenses (incl. wool)	- 280
Income before taxes	50	Income before taxes	40
Tax expense (30%)	- 15	Tax expense (35%)	- 14
Net Income	$ 35	Net Income	$ 26

Under the second scenario, the selling price of wool would be increased to reflect market changes, and this cost increase would be absorbed in the selling price of wool clothing (i.e., consumers would pay a higher price for a Celtic sweater). According to Joe Young (the middle brother and vice president of marketing at Outback), a combination of environmental and economic conditions should justify higher prices for wool products. Unseasonably cold weather around the world for the past few years and major fashion designer preferences create a very strong demand for wool products despite cost increases in raw materials. Unlike the first scenario, Joe's analysis (based on a thorough market research study) assumes that consumers will accept price increases equal to 31% for fine wool clothing. Hence, clothing manufacturers such as Celtic may be able to preserve gross profit margins, while absorbing significantly higher costs for raw material (virgin wool). Under this second scenario, the projected numbers for the upcoming year before the price increase are (amounts in millions of U.S. dollars):

Outback (Sales to Celtic)		**Celtic (before consolidation)**	
Sales revenue	$ 100	Sales revenue	$ 320
Cost of goods sold	- 50	Cost of goods sold*	- 160
Gross profit	50	Gross profit	160
Other expenses	- 40	Other expenses	- 80
Income before taxes	10	Income before taxes	80
Tax expense (30%)	- 3	Tax expense (35%)	- 28
Net Income	$ 7	Net Income	$ 52

* Where Celtic's cost of goods sold = $100 raw materials + $60 direct labor and overhead.

Furthermore, the industry average is very similar to Celtic's gross profit margin of 50%. After the proposed 31% price increase for wool clothing, Outback will be able to increase its transfer price to Celtic by 50% (amounts in millions of U.S. dollars):

Outback (Sales to Celtic)		**Celtic (before consolidation)**	
Sales revenue	$ 150	Sales revenue	$ 420.0
Cost of goods sold	- 50	Cost of goods sold**	- 210.0
Gross Profit	100	Gross Profit	210.0
Other expenses	- 40	Other expenses	- 80.0
Income before taxes	60	Income before taxes	130.0
Tax expense (30%)	- 18	Tax expense (35%)	- 45.5
Net Income	$ 42	Net Income	$ 84.5

** Where Celtic's cost of goods sold = (100 + 50) for wool + 60 for direct labor & overhead.

Alec noted, "Either of these *legal* options seems reasonable to me." Both women nodded in agreement. "However, before claiming victory we had better consider how the rest of the Celtic key executives might interpret the proposed price change." He was referring to the "old boy network" that is prevalent among Celtic's top executives, especially since his predecessor, J.R. Wolf, has two influential friends on the executive board: Sylvester (Sly) Fox, vice president of marketing, and Sam Coyote, vice president of operations. The two labored long and hard over the dismissal of their long-time friend, but finally agreed it was best that J.R. be "offered an early retirement." The real reason Sly and Sam did not support their friend was because they were fearful that his proposed scheme to increase the transfer-price of wool from Outback to Celtic by 30% (to illegally evade U.S. income taxes one year before) would hurt their profit-sharing bonus. "Can you image how these two will react when a 40-50% increase is proposed one year later?" added Alec.

After careful consideration, the team agreed that for the new transfer prices to be accepted by Celtic's executives, the "self-interest factor" had to be addressed. In addition to making a rational presentation about the legitimate price increase, something must be done to offset the price increase's effect on profit sharing. Hence, Tara suggested replacing the executives' profit sharing bonus (based on Celtic's domestic income) with a stock-option plan. Her logic was that the overall income tax savings should be reflected in higher stock prices in the future. Since the option would provide executives with the opportunity to purchase stock at a fixed lower price, they should be pleased with the new arrangement. Both Alec and Kaylee agreed. Alec congratulated Tara on her stock-option suggestion, especially considering that Celtic has plenty of authorized, but un-issued shares of common stock to cover the stock-option plan. They all left the office feeling adequately prepared for the upcoming big meeting.

Charles A. Rarick

Discussion Questions:

1. How would each of the proposed options regarding the transfer price for wool affect the net income figures for (a) Outback, (b) Celtic, and (c) the consolidated group?

2. Generally, what are the costs or benefits of increasing the transfer price for the following stakeholders under each scenario: (a) Outback's creditors, (b) Celtic's production employees, (c) Australian citizens, (d) Celtic's investors, (e) Celtic's executives, (f) Celtic's customers, and (g) American citizens? Be sure to identify which option each group would prefer.

3. What transfer-price increase for virgin wool would raise the least amount of controversy with respect to the two countries' government regulators, i.e., (a) the ACCC and (b) the IRS? Why?

4. In the spirit of consensus building, if scenarios # 1 and # 2 were to be combined, complete the following analysis by calculating (a) the appropriate sales revenue and (b) the increase in wool clothing prices. [Hint: Assume the 40% increase in virgin wool would be passed onto Celtic customers in order to preserve Celtic's gross profit margin of 50%. The gross margin is equal to gross profit divided by sales revenue.]

Outback (Sales to Celtic)

Sales revenue	$ 140
Cost of goods sold	- 50
Gross profit	90
Other expenses	- 40
Income before taxes	50
Tax expense (30%)	- 15
Net Income	$ 35

Celtic (before consolidation)

Sales revenue	$ (a)
Cost of goods sold ***	- 200
Gross profit	200
Other expenses	- 80
Income before taxes	120
Tax expense (35%)	- 42
Net Income	$ 78

*** Where Celtic's cost of goods sold = (100 + 40) for wool + 60 for direct labor and overhead.

(b) The increase in wool clothing prices = [(a) less $ 320] divided by $320 = ____% .

5. What is a "whistleblower"? If Tara did the appropriate thing by exposing J.R. Wolf's unethical scheme, why does the decision still affect her a year later?

6. While discussing the anticipated reactions of top management to the price changes, Alec, Kaylee, and Tara touched on the "self-interest factor." What were they referring to, and how does it affect business decision making?

Case prepared by Lawrence Hudack, and Suzanne Lowensohn.

CASE 45

DIVING INTO A TAX HAVEN: SHOULD WESTERN CALIFORNIA LIFE MOVE TO BERMUDA?

Dan Richardson, CEO of Western California Life Insurance, is an avid SCUBA diver. He often dives in the waters off his home state of California, and he frequently travels to the Florida Keys to engage in his favorite sport. Dan is now in Bermuda, diving a number of famous shipwrecks. While in Bermuda he has discovered that many insurance companies have established operations on this island off the East Coast of the United States. Bermuda, the Bahamas, the Cayman Islands, Belize, San Marino, and other countries are often referred to as tax havens, since they do not tax income or profits. Technically, the IRS considers any country with a lower tax rate than the U.S. a tax haven; however, certain countries (many in the Caribbean) are specifically known for their lack of taxation. Tax-haven countries earn revenue for their treasuries by assessing licensing fees. Although tax havens have existed for many years, they have recently become a more popular means of avoiding personal and corporate taxation.

Approximately 1,500 insurance companies operate on this tiny island of 57,000 residents. Bermuda is a self-governing British colony with an above-average GDP of over $26,000US per capita. The residents of Bermuda speak English, and the political environment is considered stable. The Bermuda dollar is pegged at parity to the U.S. dollar (1 Bermuda dollar = 1 U.S. dollar) and is freely convertible. One can reach the island quickly and easily from many cities along the East Coast, including New York City. Dan has been told that he can establish a corporate presence in Bermuda in 24 hours for only a few thousand dollars. Insurance companies frequently channel investment income to their subsidiaries in Bermuda, in the form of premiums paid for reinsurance in order to avoid taxation.

Dan reasons that if his small California insurance company relocates, or establishes a subsidiary in Bermuda, he would have a greater opportunity to further enjoy his diving hobby. The fact that the company would be able to avoid taxation is also appealing. As Dan boards his flight back to California, he is excited about the prospect of establishing an operation in Bermuda, but he wonders if he should consider other tax-haven countries. While on board, Dan reads in the newspaper that the Organization for Economic Cooperation and Development (OECD) has recently listed 35 countries as possessing unfair tax practices. The Paris-based organization accuses the 35 tax-haven countries of "poaching" tax revenue from other countries, and has asked for world pressure to be brought on these countries to end their policies. The tax-haven countries respond that they, as sovereign nations, have the right to make their countries attractive to foreign investment, much the same as other countries have done through other incentives.

Dan feels worried; however, he is somewhat reassured as he reads that Bermuda has not been placed on the list because government officials in Bermuda have agreed to share financial information with the OECD. As Dan heads back to California, he begins to plan for a Western California Life subsidiary in Bermuda, although he is not completely certain that it is the right thing to do.

Discussion Questions:

1. Do you feel that it is ethical for a company to channel income to a tax haven in order to reduce or eliminate taxation? Explain.

2. Are there any disadvantages to Western California Life in establishing a subsidiary in Bermuda? Explain.

3. What should Dan Richardson do?

Sources: D. Perry, "Lax on Tax Bermuda Causing Uproar in U.S." Minneapolis Star Tribune, April 14, 2000; B. O'Keefe, J. Burgess, "35 Countries Named as Unfair Tax Havens." The Washington Post, June 27, 2000; D. Mitchell, "OECD War on Low-Tax Countries" The Washington Times, August 20, 2000; "Havens Can Wait." Fortune, October 30, 2000; A. Pascual, "Taxing Times for Tax Havens." Business Week, October 30, 2000; "Organization for Economic Cooperation and Development (OECD) Web site (www.oecd.org); U.S. State Department Web site (www.state.gov).

Case prepared by Charles A. Rarick.

EXERCISE 13

EXERCISE IN INTERNATIONAL ACCOUNTING: CONSOLIDATED FINANCIAL STATEMENTS

Purpose: To better understand how the financial operations of a foreign subsidiary affect the financial condition of the parent company.

The following are selected amounts from the separate financial statements of a parent company (unconsolidated) and one of its foreign subsidiaries:

	Parent	Subsidiary
Cash	$180,000	$ 80,000
Receivables	380,000	200,000
Accounts payable	245,000	110,000
Retained earnings	790,000	680,000
Revenues	4,980,000	3,250,000
Rental income	0	200,000
Dividend income	250,000	0
Expenses	4,160,000	2,960,000

Parent owes subsidiary $70,000
Parent owns 100 percent of subsidiary.
Subsidiary paid the parent $250,000 dividend during the year.
Subsidiary owns the building that parent rents for $200,000.
During the year parent sold inventory to subsidiary for $2.2million.
The inventory had cost the parent $1.5 million.
The subsidiary sold the inventory for $3.2 million to a third party.

Procedure: Using the financial information above, determine the following:

1. The parent's (unconsolidated) net income.
2. The subsidiary's net income.
3. The consolidated profit on the inventory that the parent originally sold to the subsidiary.
4. The amounts of consolidated cash and receivables.

Exercise prepared by Charles W. L. Hill. Used with the permission of the author.

EXERCISE 14

WEB-BASED EXERCISE:
ORGANIZATION FOR ECONOMIC
CO-OPERATION AND DEVELOPMENT
(OECD)

Purpose: To gain an understanding of the basic objectives and functioning of the Organization for Economic Co-operation and Development (OECD) and the organization's position on international tax evasion.

Procedure: Visit the Web site of the OECD (www.oecd.org) and answer the questions listed below.

Questions:

1. What is the Organization for Economic Co-operation and Development and what does it seek to achieve?

2. How many member countries belong to the Organization and where is it headquartered?

3. Explain the position of the OECD on tax havens and transparency.

4. In your opinion, should countries be allowed to operate as tax havens? Explain your answer.

Part Nine

SOCIAL RESPONSIBILITY
IN INTERNATIONAL BUSINESS

Cases:
Sewing for Millionaires
Stew's Nigerian Business Troubles
Regal Cruise Lines
Gethal Amazonas
Fair Trade Coffee

Exercise
The Child Labor Question

CASE 46

SEWING FOR MILLIONAIRES MAJOR LEAGUE BASEBALL PRODUCTION

A two-hour drive from the capital of San José, Costa Rica, sits the small community of Turrialba where mostly young workers sit and sew baseballs destined for Major League Baseball teams. Rawlings Sporting Goods Company moved its baseball manufacturing operations from Haiti in 1986 when the political landscape of the country began to change.

Rawlings selected the town of Turrialba due to the incentives offered the company by the Costa Rican government. Rawlings was awarded a free-trade zone in which the company would be allowed to operate duty-free in the country. Rawlings pays no import tariffs on the goods it imports to manufacture its baseballs, and the finished product can be shipped duty-free into the United States under the Caribbean Basin Imitative. The Turrialba region was hard hit economically in the 1980s when a major highway from the capital bypassed the town. Since travelers no longer stopped in Turrialba, the Costa Rican government wanted to develop the local area through foreign investment. Rawlings found the potential workforce better educated, and more disciplined than its workers in Haiti. The country was also well known for being very politically stable. With few employment opportunities in the area, Rawlings had no difficulty in securing dedicated and motivated employees. Although Costa Rica is the wealthiest country in Central America, per capita income is still only about $4,200 a year. Costa Rica has an unemployment rate of 6.7% nationwide, however, the rate can vary from region to region. With the completion of the new highway and declining employment opportunities in the coffee and sugarcane industries, many local residents of Turrialba were eager to find stable employment.

Most Rawlings employees in Costa Rica are engaged in sewing operations. In the plant, 300 employees sit in rows of high back chairs and sew baseballs. Many employees break the boredom of the work by listening to music on their headphones. The plant employs a total of 575 workers. At one time Rawlings employed approximately 1,900 workers at the Costa Rican plant, however, employment fell when the Company shifted production of its lower quality baseballs to China. The Rawlings plant takes a baseball core and wraps it in yarn. The product is then covered with cowhide and sewn by hand. Baseballs must be sewn by hand in order to achieve the quality level demanded by the Major Leagues. Each worker sews 108 perfect stitches using a long needle and thread. The balls are then inspected, cleaned, and stamped with the MLB logo and the signature of the commissioner of baseball. The balls are then packed and shipped to the port city of Limón where they are loaded onto a ship bound for Port Everglades, Florida. The baseballs are then trucked to Rawlings' Springfield, Missouri facility, and then onto Major League teams or retail stores. Rawlings has been the exclusive supplier of baseballs to the Major Leagues since 1977. The Costa Rican facility produces approximately 2.2 million baseballs a year, with 1.8 million of those going to Major League Baseball. The remaining balls are sold to minor league and college baseball teams, or sold to the public through retail stores or the websites of MLB and Rawlings. While Rawlings refuses to disclose the price of the baseballs paid by MLB, the baseballs retail on the Company's website for $12.99 per unit.

Employees are paid $1.21 per hour and receive the value of 67 cents an hour in benefits, or about thirty cents per ball produced. Workers can go home early in the week if they complete their production quotas. Rawlings workers earn about 14% above the Costa Rican minimum wage. In addition to their wages, Rawlings employees in Costa Rica must be paid for eleven holidays, receive two weeks of paid vacation a year, and receive a Christmas bonus equal to one month's pay. The Company must also pay into a retirement and medical plan and provide four months of maternity leave when needed.

A 2004 *New York Times* article questioned the pay and working conditions of the Rawlings plant in Costa Rica. The article accused

Rawlings and MLB of running a sweatshop in Costa Rica where workers were underpaid and worked in an unhealthy environment. Consumer advocate Ralph Nader joined in the criticism by writing a letter to Bud Selig, MLB Commissioner and the Executive Director of the MLB Player Association. In the letter Nader condemned the two men for allowing baseballs to be manufactured in what he considered to be poor conditions. Portions of the letter follow:

> *"Your respective organizations must not ignore their roles in this exploitation and abuse of worker rights committed under Major League Baseball and Player Association product sourcing and licensing agreements."*

> *"American consumers and baseball fans currently have no guarantee that any licensed Major League Baseball products are not being made under sweatshop conditions that violate basic human and worker rights standards."*

Major League Baseball consumer products vice president, Howard Smith, responded to the rising complaints by stating: *"I can assure you that there is no company we do business with that knowingly goes into a factory with sub-par working conditions."* Not everyone agrees with Mr. Smith.

Maribel Alezondo Brenes worked at the Rawlings plant for seven years before her doctor told her to stop working there for health reasons. Carpal tunnel syndrome has been noticed in the Rawlings employees due to the repetitive nature of the work. Dr. Carlos Guerrero who worked at the Rawlings plant as company physician says that up to 90 percent of Rawlings employees may have experienced pain from the work, from minor cuts to disabling injuries. Others feel that the plant has been a good addition to the region, including Warny Gomez, who worked at the Rawlings facility for four years and made enough money to attend college and to become a teacher. With average pay for Major League Baseball players close to $2.3 million a year, some Rawlings employees feel that their compensation is unjust. Many, however, feel like Alan Cascante, an eight-year employee of the baseball factory: "We can live on that

(Rawlings wages). We never made that working in the fields." Plant manager, Ken West agrees with Cascante, by saying "The best thing's the pay. We're a good place to work."

The debate over pay and working conditions of employees who supply MLB with its products appears to be growing in some quarters. People like Kenneth Miller; a self-appointed champion of sweatshop workers takes his message to the fans by camping outside ballparks. He tells potential consumers of MLB products that the baseball player bobble head doll they are about to purchase was made by a Chinese worker who works 20 hour shifts for very little pay. Miller states that he often finds indifference among consumers. Some tell him: "Why are you trying to interrupt our nice day at the ballpark?" Miller and a handful of others are pressuring MLB to take greater control over the working conditions of its suppliers, such as Rawlings.

As the debate continues in the United States over the working conditions and pay of the Costa Rican employees and others, baseballs are sewn in Turrialba with pictures of Alex Rodriquez, Mike Piazza, and other baseball players hanging on the walls of the factory. Rawlings' employees, however, are too busy sewing baseballs for the millionaire players, to even notice the pictures hanging above them.

Charles A. Rarick

Discussion Questions:

1. In your opinion, is Rawlings exploiting its Costa Rican employees? Explain your answer.

2. Is it fair to compare the salary of Major League Baseball players to that of employees who sew baseballs?

3. If you were the CEO of Rawlings Sporting Goods' parent company (K2, Inc.) what action would you take, if any, given the present situation?

Sources: Hersh, P. (2003). *The sport of baseball has little popularity in Costa Rica, but big-league baseballs are produced here.* Chicago Tribune, July 15; Jones, D. (2004). *Baseball assailed for using sweatshops.* Pittsburgh Post-Gazette, October 16; Moore, C. (2004). *Baseball striking out in human rights league.* Western Catholic Reporter, March 1; Sloane, G. (2003). *Babe Ruth organizers eye world series try.* AM Costa Rica, February 17; Weiner, T. (2004). *Costa Rica: Low wage workers make baseballs for millionaires.* New York Times, January 25; www.state.gov. Country background notes – Costa Rica. Accessed on May 13, 2005.

Case prepared by Charles A. Rarick.

CASE 47

STEW'S NIGERIAN BUSINESS TROUBLES

Sitting at the desk in his office in Atlanta, Stew Morrison was elated by the contents of an envelope that had recently arrived from Africa. The envelope contained a letter and supporting documentation from a contact Stew had established in Nigeria and was promising to provide many new customers for Stew's company. Stew Morrison was the CEO of a company called, e-Future; a company that specialized in the sale of education vouchers for the developing world. The letter from Nigeria indicated that a number of businesses, and the government of Nigeria were very interested in purchasing the education vouchers. The letter invited Stew to come to Nigeria and meet with these important prospective customers. Stew was confident that the business was finally beginning to turn around and he was excited about the prospects awaiting him in Nigeria.

E-FUTURE

Begun with limited capital from a few wealthy investors in 2002, e-Future was a company with a dream. That dream was to bring education to the developing world. Stew Morrison, a former professor of education, had developed the idea of offering a simple means for potential students to pay for higher education and technical training through the use of electronic vouchers. Individuals could purchase the vouchers themselves, or the vouchers could be purchased by governments for their citizens. It was also assumed that businesses may offer them as incentives to their employees. The vouchers could be used in a number of universities and technical schools in Africa, Asia, and in Latin America. In addition, an on-line university created by e-Future offered a number of courses and would accept the voucher as payment. The voucher concept reduced the cost of a course significantly, as universities and schools deeply discounted their tuition under the program. The business concept, first developed by Morrison found its way to Jay Nettlehouse, who in turn convinced other private investors to fund startup of the organization. Nettlehouse became Chairman of e-Future and continued to provide financial support for the company. While the private investors hoped to profit from the business, they also hoped that their money would be used to help develop the poorer countries of the world. Unfortunately, sales of the vouchers proved to be more difficult than anticipated. The company had yet to make a profit and the private investors had to make additional contributions to keep the business operational.

NIGERIA

While Stew had never to been on the African continent, he had no concerns with the upcoming trip to Nigeria. Doing some research Stew learned that Nigeria had gained its independent from Britain in 1960 and that political instability had ensued up until 1999 when a democratic government was established. He discovered that Nigeria is a diverse country with over 250 ethnic groups. The country is divided by religious identity with the north being mostly Muslim and the south being mostly Christian. The political boundaries of present day Nigeria came into being when the British gained control of the area in the late 1800's and established the area as a colony. During World War II, Nigerians fought with the British and shortly thereafter gained some autonomy, and a constitution. Stew learned from his investigations that democracy has not been the norm during Nigeria's short existence. Due to differing religious and ethnic identities, a series of coups and dictators had exercised power during most of Nigeria's history. With democracy once again in place, Stew felt that perhaps e-Future could help Nigeria in its nation building effort. Stew was encouraged by the fact that Nigeria is a leading supplier of crude oil to the world and is the most populated country in Africa with over 90 million inhabitants. Stew also was happy to learn that English was the official language of Nigeria. While Stew felt that Nigeria offered great promise to e-Future, he also had some concerns about the level of corruption found in the country. He had read that corruption was a problem, and that some foreigners had been victims of various scams.

BIMBOLA

When Stew arrived at the Lagos airport he was overwhelmed by the sights and sounds he was experiencing. The airport was very noisy and crowded and being tired from his long journey, he felt as if he was too confused to find his way past immigration and get his luggage. As he wandered towards the immigration area he saw a sign being held up by a rather small, middle-aged man. The sign read "Welcome Mr. Stew Morrison". When he approached the man with the sign he realized that it was his contact in Nigeria, Bimbola Ogunk. The two men exchanged greetings and Bimbola took Stew's handbag and escorted him towards immigration. When Stew asked Bimbola if he would have any trouble passing through immigration Bimbola told him not to worry. He reminded Stew that he had connections and asked if he had acquired a Nigerian visa. Stew replied that he had not, as previously instructed by Bimbola, and Bimbola said "no problem." The two men proceeded to a separate line at the immigration stop and Bimbola told the official "this is my special friend." The official looked at Stew and waved the two through immigration. To Stew, it did appear that Bimbola had connections. Stew retrieved his luggage and the two men headed for the exit. Bimbola had arranged for Stew to stay at a hotel where he had further connections. Stew at that point just wanted to get to the hotel as quickly as possible and sleep. Unfortunately the traffic of Lagos would keep Stew from his room for another two hours. The two men chatted on the way to the hotel with Bimbola constantly reassuring Stew that he had connection in the government, and connections with education officials, and industry leaders. Stew would be meeting some of those officials later in the week, he was told. Bimbola also told Stew that he wanted to take him on a trip first; a trip he would "surely enjoy." Stew checked into his hotel to get some sleep.

Early the next morning the telephone in the hotel room rang and it was Bimbola. He told Stew that he was in the hotel lobby and ready to take him on a special tour. Stew arranged for a quick breakfast before leaving with Bimbola for a trip to Benin. The long trip, over 200 miles, allowed Stew the opportunity to get to know Bimbola better. The two men discussed many things, however, Bimbola seemed

255

unable or unwilling to provide any details as to how he was going to arrange for the sale of large quantities of e-Future vouchers. He frequently told Stew not to worry and that he, Bimbola, would handle everything. When pressed, Bimbola told Stew that he had arranged for a meeting with Dr. Kema Agaguelu, Minister of Education and that she was very interested in the educational voucher system offered by Stew's company. While not much business was discussed on the trip to Benin, Stew did learn much about the ancient walled city and about the once great kingdom. He was grateful to Bimbola for taking him to see the impressive sights.

MEET DR. AGAGUELA

The entire day, and much of the night was taken up by the trip to Benin. Stew was feeling weary and anxious to return to his room for a good night's rest. Although exhausted, he hardly slept due to the differences in time zones. The following morning he awoke to the sound of the telephone ringing. It was Bimbola greeting him good morning. The two ate breakfast in the hotel restaurant and Bimbola explained to Stew that the meeting with Dr. Agaguela was going to take place that day, later in the afternoon. He told Stew that he should get his presentation material together to show the education minister. Bimbola explained that while the government offices were in the capital, Abuja, the Education Minister had an office in Lagos and that it would not be necessary to travel to the capital to meet her.

The traffic in Lagos was horrendous and it took hours to reach the government building. Bimbola escorted Stew up the flights of stairs in the rather stark building to meet the minister. They arrived on the fifth floor and entered an office void of any marking to find a middle-aged woman sitting behind a desk looking at some papers. Bimbola introduced her as the Minister of Education and Stew began to make a presentation on what his company could offer Nigeria. He went into great detail explaining how the government could advance higher education through the e-Future program, all the time Dr. Agaguelu listened and smiled. While she never asked any questions, she seemed very interested in what Stew had told her, and she thanked him for visiting. Bimbola told Stew that he had made a very good impression on her and that she would certainly be recommending that the government purchase a very large quantity of vouchers. Stew felt a bit uneasy about the meeting but he was encouraged by what Bimbola was telling him. Stew began to press Bimbola for more details on other contacts but Bimbola told him not to worry. Bimbola stated that it was time for Stew to purchase some gifts for his family back in America.

Bimbola took Stew to a large market for shopping. While Stew had no interest in shopping at this time, he felt it best not to insult his host. The market was unlike anything Stew had ever seen. A mix of food and household items, along with crafts and animal skins and skulls. The variety and unique nature of the market was overwhelming to Stew. He managed to purchase some craft items and a special type of woven cloth recommended by Bimbola. It was approaching dinnertime and Bimbola told Stew that he had arranged for Stew to meet his family that evening. Bimbola took Stew to a restaurant where Bimbola's wife and many adults were waiting. The group represented Bimbola's immediate family as well as members of his extended family. Although the group was rather large, Stew enjoyed his meal and the company of this quite lively group of people. One of the dinner items Stew especially enjoyed was jollof rice, a Nigerian specialty. He was impressed when told by one of Bimbola's brothers that Bimbola's grandmother had invented the national dish. Some of the previous apprehensions Stew felt about Bimbola were beginning to be eased. When the waiter brought the restaurant bill to Stew, the moment was a bit uneasy. The bill was quite high and he wasn't sure who was expected to pay, but he reasoned that he would pay the bill since Bimbola had been so kind in taking him to Benin as a cultural side trip. The evening ended well and it appeared to Stew that Bimbola's family had enjoyed the meal. Bimbola took Stew back to the hotel and told him to "expect great things tomorrow."

GREAT EXPECTATIONS

Once again it was a night without much sleep for Stew. He was dragging during the day and awake most of the night. He hoped that he would be able to soon adjust to the time difference and get a good night's sleep. He was also uneasy because he still was not able to call home and speak to his wife, as the hotel's international telephone line was not working. As the telephone rang in his room, Stew knew that it Bimbola and he was looking forward to those great expectations promised by Bimbola. Bimbola told Stew that he had very good news for him and to come down to the hotel restaurant and they would discuss it. Over breakfast Bimbola had a hard time containing his happiness. He finally told Stew that he had heard from the Minister of Education and that she was arranging for the government of Nigeria to make an initial purchase of $500,000US e-Future education vouchers. Stew was excited about the news and thanked Bimbola for helping to arrange the meeting that produced these results. Bimbola told Stew that all that was needed now were three things. First, Bimbola would need the bank account number of e-Future in order to wire the funds, secondly, Stew would need to make a small payment of $10,000US to the education minister for her help, and lastly, e-Future would need to pay Bimbola a $50,000US finder's fee. Stew was taken aback by these requests. He asked Bimbola to explain more but all that Bimbola would tell him was that this is the way business was conducted in Nigeria. Bimbola told Stew that unless he wanted to lose this large contract, he would need to meet those three conditions. Stew told Bimbola that he was not sure if he would be able to do what was requested and that he would have to check with someone back in Atlanta. Bimbola told Stew that time was critical and that if he waited, he would certainly lose the contact.

Without the matter being resolved, Bimbola proceeded to tell Stew that he was going to meet with very high-level industry officials who were interested in hearing about the education vouchers for use with their companies. They were going to meet for lunch and so Stew needed once again to gather his presentation material and come along for a ride across town. On the drive across town Bimbola explained how many Americans are surprised by the way business is done in Nigeria but that "once they realize this they are able to acquire very good contracts and earn much money." Bimbola told Stew that "Nigeria is a good place to do business."

A LONG LUNCH

At lunch, Stew met with four men who were introduced by Bimbola as the leaders of Nigeria's business community. One gentleman, Segun Adelaja was introduced as Prince Segun, head of the Nigerian National Petroleum Corporation. Each man gave Stew a business card indicating their association with various business groups in Nigeria. In addition to the oil industry, the men represented textiles, agriculture, and manufacturing. The six men ate lunch and discussed many things including their love of "football" but not much attention was directed towards business, or e-Future's product. Stew felt very tired and his patience was getting thin. He asked to speak to Bimbola alone and expressed his concerns with the lack of business substance. Bimbola explained that in Nigeria it was customary for people to get to know each other first before they discussed business. Bimbola told Stew that he would provide the opportunity for Stew to present his business ideas before the group left. After many hours of entertaining Bimbola finally told the group "Mr. Morrison has a plan that is of great value to each of you." Acting on this cue, Stew proceeded to tell the men how e-Future could help their industries, and Nigeria in general. The men seemed very interested and asked a number of questions. Stew felt encouraged and continued to discuss product features at great length. After more than five hours of eating, drinking, and discussing, Bimbola told the group that Mr. Morrison had to get back to his hotel and that that they should contact him, Bimbola, if they were interested in having their companies buy the vouchers. He told the group that he strongly recommended that they take advantage of this opportunity. Once again Stew was presented with a rather large bill from the restaurant.

Bimbola drove Stew back to his hotel and explained that these men represented the best opportunity for Stew to sell thousands of vouchers. He told Stew that millions of dollars were at stake and that it was necessary that Stew completely trust Bimbola to make the deals. All that would be required was for Stew give Bimbola his normal ten percent fee, along with a retainer of "a few thousand dollars, today." Stew felt as if he was being played by Bimbola and told him that he needed to rest before making any decisions. Stew felt that it was time to make a call to Jay Nettlehouse back in Atlanta. At the hotel

Stew once again experienced difficulties making an international call. His frustration level was rising and he was unsure of what he should do. While he was worried that he might be taken advantage of by Bimbola, he didn't want to miss out on the opportunities that may emerge from the relationships Bimbola provided. Stew decided to try and find another way of calling America. Stew sat on his bed watching television, resting, worrying, and wondering what his next move should be.

AN OFFICIAL CONTRACT

When the telephone rang in his room Stew hoped that it would be someone from e-Future calling. It was Bimbola who told Stew that he was coming over to the hotel for dinner and that he was bringing Stew "something that would make him very happy." When pressed as to what the surprise was, Bimbola told him that it was a contract from the Nigerian government. Stew decided to rest a bit before dinner and was hopeful that perhaps something was finally developing.

Bimbola arrived for dinner with Stew and brought along Dr. Agaguelu who presented Stew with a three-page document. The document was a government contract for $500,000US and included many seals and official stamps. It had already been signed by the President of Nigeria and the Minister of Education. Dr. Agaguela explained that the government was receiving much oil revenue and that in an effort to develop support from the people of Nigeria, the President had decided to spend some of the money to expand the educational opportunities of its citizens. Bimbola explained that it was important that the contract be signed by Stew and that the necessary payments be made immediately. When Stew asked about how he could pay the necessary "fees" Bimbola told him that he could wire the funds into a bank account, or better yet, Stew "could get cash from his American Express card and be done with it." Bimbola stressed how important he and Dr. Agaguela were in getting this contract, and that many more could follow if Stew took care of them.

Sitting at the table, confused and totally exhausted, Stew wondered what he should do, as he looked at the smiling faces of Bimbola and Dr. Agaguela.

Discussion Questions:

1. What mistakes did Stew Morrison make in his Nigerian business trip?
2. Do you think Bimbola is trustworthy? Explain.
3. What should Stew do now?

Sources: Blauer, E. and J. Laure. (2001). Nigeria. New York: Scholastic; Nnoromele, S. (2002). Nigeria. San Diego: Lucent; www.countrywatch.com

Case was prepared by Charles A. Rarick

CASE 48

REGAL CRUISE LINES:
NO SOVEREIGNTY ON THESE SEAS

On a routine surveillance flight over the Caribbean Sea, a U.S. Coast Guard plane noticed an oil slick trailing a cruise ship bound for San Juan, Puerto Rico. The ship, which was owned by Regal Cruise Lines, sailed under a foreign flag. As is common in the cruise industry, ships are registered in countries such as Liberia, Panama, or the Bahamas, countries that provide "flags of convenience" to the cruise lines but exercise little regulation. Regal Cruise Lines was incorporated in Liberia but headquartered in Miami; thus, Regal did not consider itself a U.S. company.

The Coast Guard, using a tracking plane equipped with infrared cameras, determined that the oil slick was coming from the Regal ship. When the boat docked in San Juan, Coast Guard officials boarded the vessel and began an inspection. Captain John Smith made no attempt to interfere with the Coast Guard investigation; however, he told the inspectors that Regal was a foreign vessel and that they had no authority to board the ship. The Coast Guard officials disagreed and continued their inspection. The investigators informed the captain that his ship was producing an oil slick and he informed them that the ship's pollution treatment devices were operational and functioning properly. Captain Smith told the Coast Guard that all systems had been recently inspected and that they were found to be in perfect working order. Captain Smith summoned his engineer in charge of the ship's waste disposal system, Roberto Garcia.

While the Coast Guard conducted its inspection, the maintenance crew was one step ahead of the inspectors, attempting to cover up the alterations that had previously been made to the antipollution equipment and to dispose of incriminating evidence. The maintenance crew, supervised by Chief Engineer Garcia, had received word that the Coast Guard had boarded the ship. Garcia assured the inspectors that the system was in full compliance with regulations. Captain Smith telephoned the company's headquarters and requested advice. He was told that an attorney representing Regal in Puerto Rico would be sent to the ship immediately.

The Coast Guard inspection discovered suspicious drums of waste on board and other irregularities. For example, the inspectors found oil-soaked towels in bins that should have contained water. Although no direct evidence of systematic pollution could be found during the initial inspection, the Coast Guard inspectors suspected that the crew had hidden evidence. Regal's second officer on board in charge of the antipollution equipment showed the inspectors the Oil Record Book (a log of the ship's disposal of waste products) and assured them that the vessel was not producing any illegal discharge. Nevertheless, the Coast Guard refused to allow the ship to leave San Juan until it posted a bond and informed the captain that criminal charges might be brought in this case. Regal's attorney arrived on board and told the Coast Guard inspectors that they had conducted an illegal search of the ship.

Regal eventually posted the required bond and set sail for Miami. The company insisted that it was not in violation of any pollution laws and that it really didn't matter since the vessel was not a U.S. ship. The company pointed out that the United Nations Law of the Seas allows ships to be registered in foreign countries, and that those countries are responsible for their regulation. The company insisted that the United States had no authority to intervene in this case.

On the trip back to Miami, the maintenance officer instructed the crew to dismantle a pipe that was used to bypass the pollution control system. This device, which had been concealed from investigators by the crew members, was removed, cut into pieces and discarded in Miami. The officer also instructed the crew not to disclose any information to anyone who asked about the pollution control procedures on the ship.

The U.S. government continued its investigation and eventually charged Regal with lying to Coast Guard inspectors. The case received widespread media exposure and the Attorney General of the United States went on record saying, "Regal Cruise Lines gambled with the public trust and lost." The company continued to insist that it was not subject to American jurisdiction and that the U.S. had no sovereignty in this case.

Discussion Questions:

1. Is Regal correct in its position that the company is not liable due to a lack of jurisdiction?

2. Who is most responsible for the problem presented in this situation: Captain Smith, Chief Engineer Garcia, Regal's top management?

3. What responsibility does a company have when operating internationally with regard to the environment?

4. In your opinion, is it ethical for some cruise ships to register in countries known to provide little regulatory oversight?

Note: Although this situation is fictional, it is based on an actual case reported in the <u>Miami Herald</u> on September 26, 1999, and October 3, 1999.

Case prepared by Charles A. Rarick and Inge Nickerson.

CASE 49

GETHAL AMAZONAS:
SAVING THE RAIN FOREST
ONE YELLOW TREE AT A TIME

Gethal Amazonas is a Brazilian plywood producer. In the 1950s and 1960s, the company was responsible for destroying the Atlantic Forest of southern Brazil through excessive deforestation. When all the trees were removed from this forest, the company moved into the Amazon. Today Gethal Amazonas is considered one of the most socially responsible timber companies in Brazil. Its workers proudly paint the base of fallen trees a bright yellow, signifying that the timber is certified wood.

Gethal Amazonas has become the first plywood producer to be certified by the Forest Stewardship Council (FSC) as a company that promotes environmentally sound forest harvesting. The FSC is based in Mexico and its membership consists of environmental groups, timber companies, and lumber retailers. The organization seeks to make the timber industry more environmentally responsive. Environmental organizations such as Greenpeace and Friends of the Earth are members, as well as American retailer Home Depot, which gives preference in its purchasing to certified lumber companies.

FSC requires that companies wishing to be certified as practicing environmentally sound forest harvesting agree to abide by certain standards. Regulations are established for minimum tree circumference, limitations are placed on the harvesting of certain hardwoods, and companies are required to conduct an analysis and mapping of the environmental impact on soils, watersheds, and ecosystems.

During the 1980s, the Brazilian rain forests were being destroyed at an alarming rate. World attention became focused on the problem and a common refrain became "Save the Rain Forest." Politicians, actors/actresses, rock stars, and others joined environmental groups in calling for an end to the destruction. Madonna, the singer, organized a benefit concert called "Don't Bungle the Jungle." When then Tennessee Senator Al Gore visited Brazil, he called the destruction "one of the great tragedies of all history."

In the past 30 years, over 15% of Brazil's rain forests have been destroyed and the rain forests of Asia have been depleted at an even higher rate. Environmentalists fear that further destruction of the rain forests of the world will lead to dire climatic changes. Countless species of animals and plants will vanish from the earth and potential medical breakthroughs will be lost. The Brazilian rain forest has sometimes been called the world's greatest pharmaceutical factory. Many medicines, including some for cancer are derived from rain forest plants. Agronomists also worry about a potential loss of alternative food sources with further destruction.

Brazil has become more conscious of the environmental impact of harvesting the Amazon, and has begun to impose fines on companies that violate environmental laws. The Brazilian Institute for the Environment fined 26 timber companies in 2000 for crimes against the environment. Nevertheless, it is estimated that approximately 17,000 square kilometers of rain forest are destroyed each year.

Gethal and the FSC hope that consumers will demand timber products that carry environmental certification. Gethal had planned to price its products 30% above noncertified wood; however, certified wood at the present time only commands a premium of about 7.5%. While some consumers in the United States are requesting environmentally certified wood, most are unaware of the product. The concept is, however, more popular in Europe.

In the recent past, products have been sold that were considered Amazon friendly. Ben & Jerry's sells its Rainforest Crunch flavor ice cream, which contains nuts from the Amazon jungle. It was hoped that alternative sources of income could be generated for the people of the rain forest. Although this product is popular, it is unclear how many sales are based on the environmental appeal. Other products have not fared as well, including Amazon cereals, juices, and cookies, whose sales were intended to promote preservation of the rain forests.

While previous products promoting the rain forest may have had lackluster sales, Gethal is undaunted in its efforts to responsibly harvest Amazon timber and have consumers pay extra for its products. While not all timber companies are following the lead of Gethal, the company continues to paint its trees yellow and hopes for a bright future.

Discussion Questions:

1. Would you pay a premium to ensure that the wood you buy is harvested in an environmentally sound fashion? Explain.

2. Is green business good business in your opinion?

3. Will Gethal Amazonas survive in a price-sensitive global industry? What could Gethal do to increase demand for its product?

Sources: E. Linden, "Playing with Fire." Time, September 18, 1989; R. McMath, "Saving the Rain Forest One Nut at a Time." American Demographics, August 1, 1997; C. Kevin, "Its Not Easy Being Green." Geo Info Systems, July 30, 1998; "Hidden Rainforest Losses. "ScienceNow, April 7, 1999; J. Wheatley, "Saving the Forest for the Trees." Business Week, November 20, 2000; "Brazil Fines Crimes Against Environment." Xinhua News Agency, January 1, 2001.

Case prepared by Charles A. Rarick

CASE 50

FAIR-TRADE COFFEE

Most of the coffee production in the world takes place in elevations from sea level to 6,000 feet, in a 25-degree latitude belt on either side of the equator. Arabica grows best in higher elevations, while Robusta grows best in lower elevations. Moderate sunlight is desirable (tree shade or side of mountains that obscure the sun for part of the day), high humidity, and constant temperatures are most favorable. Major coffee-growing regions include countries in South America and the Caribbean, in Central America, in Africa, and in Asia. For many of these countries, coffee exports are a crucial source of employment for small farmers and farm workers and a vital means of procuring hard currencies. In 1997-1998, the largest producer was Brazil, followed by Colombia. Today, Brazil remains in first position with 35% of world production, but Vietnam has captured second place with 12% of world production through modernization and development of its coffee industry, in part due to international subsidies.

Since World War II, world coffee prices have been regulated by producer countries, organized under the auspices of the United Nations. They allocated export quotas among themselves to maintain a steady world supply and guarantee each producing country a certain share of the world market. The International Coffee Agreement was first signed in 1962 and renewed in 1968, 1976, and 1983. Member nations failed to agree on a new coffee agreement in 1989. Since then, the price of coffee has fluctuated on the world commodity market, according to climactic events that would favor or shrink world supply.

Untimely frosts in Brazil, the producer of over a third of world production, would drastically affect the market price. Brazil attempted to regulate the world price by building inventories of coffee beans in plentiful years to be depleted in leaner years. In the 1990s, Vietnam significantly increased the world supply through the fast development of its low-cost, modern coffee industry. In the past year alone, world coffee prices have plummeted 40% to about $60.00 per sack, while the cost of growing coffee is about $80.00 per sack. World coffee prices apply to "conventional" coffee, meaning coffee that is not "farm identified." Conventional coffee is bought and sold in bulk without regard to grower, or even to country of origin. The principal purveyors of such coffee are the three major coffee companies: Philip Morris (Kraft Foods' Maxwell House Coffee), Procter & Gamble (Folgers Coffee) and Nestle. Such coffee may retail from $3.00 to $5.00 per lb in the United States. Specialty coffee represents a very small share of world production; this refers to coffee that is "farm identified." The identification of the farm of origin may focus on the ownership of the "farm" (estate or cooperative), or on the harvesting practices (organic coffee and/or shade-grown coffee), or on the economic system under which the coffee is purchased (fair-trade coffee). Specialty coffee commands a price premium. It may retail at $9.00 to $15.00 or more per pound in the United States.

The fair trade movement focuses on commodities that constitute a large share of a developing nation's economy: coffee, tea, cocoa, bananas, sugar, lumber, and the like. Its goal is to organize farmers in fair trade cooperatives that eliminate the middlemen and to establish an economic system under which the product is produced and distributed. Certification agencies guarantee the integrity of the production/distribution chain and authorize a fair-trade label for products in compliance. The premise is that world trade is good for consumers and producers, depending wholly on how goods are made and sold. The activists feel they are using free-market economies to implement social change.

In the case of coffee, the roasters must purchase fair-trade coffee from fair-trade cooperatives at a guaranteed minimum base price that represents a "livable wage" for the farmer, regardless of world conditions. The cooperatives grant their members credit and advance payment to tide them over adverse economic conditions. Members are encouraged to adopt production methods that protect the environment and the health of consumers. Members are also encouraged to plow profits back into their community for daycare, medical care, schools, and the like. Certification agencies in Europe and in the U.S. inspect the cooperatives, the importers, and the roasters to guarantee the integrity of the fair trade coffee label. Social consciousness campaigns ensure that socially aware consumers pay a premium at the retail level for fair-trade label coffee with the intent of helping small farmers and their families attain a decent standard of living. The fair trade coffee movement was created in 1988 in the Netherlands. There are now 17 importing countries involved and 300 growers' cooperatives across 21 countries. In the U.S. (the world's largest coffee consumer), the movement is quite recent. The monitoring agency that certifies fair-trade coffee is Transfair USA, a not-for-profit organization established in 1996 under the auspices of the Ford Foundation.

Fair-trade coffee roasters are paying a price floor of $1.26/lb to fair-trade growers (the current market price is as low as $0.60/lb). They pay an additional premium of 0.15/lb for organically grown coffee. Roasters have the highest profit margin in the production chain, and they are encouraged to absorb a portion of the cost of fair trade; consumers absorb the other portion of the cost. Transfair USA has targeted specialty retailers and large grocery store chains to persuade them to sell fair-trade coffee. Under threat of boycott, chains such as Peet's Coffee and Starbucks offer whole bean fair-trade certified coffee on their shelves next to their own brands, but they haven't changed their own basic buying policies.

The demand for specialty coffee appears to be price insensitive. Starbucks' fair-trade coffee retails at $11.45/lb, while its own house blend retails at $9.95/lb. Peet's fair-trade brand retails at $10.95. Tully's fair- trade blend retails at $13.95. The typical U.S. consumer of fair-trade coffee lives on the West Coast or in the Northeast and is young, female, educated, urban, socially conscious, quality conscious, and able to pay a higher price to support fair-trade practices. Market studies in the United States reveal that 78% of adult consumers declare a willingness to buy a product associated with a cause they support, and 54% declare themselves willing to pay more for such a product.

Discussion Questions:

1. Do firms such as Starbucks and other roasters truly bear any cost for supporting the fair-trade label?

2. Is fair-trade fulfilling its objectives?

3. Do consumers in wealthy countries have a responsibility to the producers in poor countries?

Sources: F. Robles, "Ground Down by Debt - Low Prices Hurt Coffee Growers."
Miami Herald, April 7, 2001; "Coffee Falls More Than 3% as Growers Start Selling." Miami Herald, April 20, 2001; "Decline of the Coffee Republic." The Economist, April 21, 2001; www.transfairusa.org; www.globalexchange.org; www.virtualcoffee.com; www.realcoffee.co.uk; www.nationalgeographic.com; www.guardfoods.com/coffee.

Case prepared by Martine Duchatelet.

EXERCISE 15

THE CHILD LABOR QUESTION

Purpose: The purpose of this exercise is to explore the universalist argument for ethical standards, and to develop a better understanding of the ethical dilemmas faced by international managers.

Procedure: Read the background note that follows and then assemble into small groups. Your task to develop a reasoned argument which either attacks or defends child labor.

Background Note:
The International Labor Organization (ILO) estimates that over 250 million children are employed throughout the world, with ages ranging from four to fourteen. A large percentage of these children are employed full-time and do not attend school. Child laborers can be found in large numbers in Africa, Asia, and Latin America. One country known for its child labor is Pakistan. In Pakistan, carpet master, Sadique, recruits boys ages seven to ten to weave his carpets. Sadique states: "They make ideal employees. Boys at this stage of development are at the peak of their dexterity and endurance, and

they're wonderfully obedient." The carpet master can hire a child for about one-fourth the cost of an adult carpet weaver.

Critics of child labor, which includes many international organizations, argue that these children are exploited by their employers, forced to work long hours in poor and dangerous conditions, and are deprived of an opportunity for a better life. They argue that a universal standard should be agreed to by all nations that ensures that no child will be subjected to full-time employment before the age of fourteen.

Others argue that while child labor is never a country's first choice, it is necessary for the survival of some less developed countries. Critics of international standards argue that what is unethical in one country may not be unethical in another. This relativist perspective maintains that child labor standards cannot be applied globally because the economies of the world are not equal. While prosperous countries can afford to keep children in school for a long time, it is necessary that children work in poorer countries. They point out that rich countries today, such as the United States, had children working during their less prosperous times. It is further argued that without employment, many of these children would be homeless and subject to even greater exploitation on the streets. The families of the working children depend on them in many cases for money for food. The question is not education or work, but rather, work or starvation.

The carpet master in Pakistan quote is from J. Silvers, The Atlantic Monthly, February, 1996.

Exercise prepared by Charles A. Rarick

10893227R0

Made in the USA
Lexington, KY
31 August 2011